CREDIT
WHEN CREDIT IS DUE

By Paul Strassels

CREDIT WHEN CREDIT IS DUE

Published by Consumer Credit Counseling Service of the Black Hills
111 St. Joseph Street
Rapid City, SD 57701
1-605-348-3104

Printed and Bound in the United States of America

ISBN: 0-9661710-0-4

This book is dedicated to all those who, on their own and with-
out the benefit of guidance and help, have struggled mightily with
their personal finances. All hope that past mistakes will never be
repeated by future generations.

ACKNOWLEDGEMENTS

The acknowledgement page of a book provides the author an opportunity to say "Thank You" to all those people who have made the book possible. In this case, there are literally dozens of people and organizations who have my profound thanks and appreciation for the work they have performed. This book would not have been possible without the efforts of each and every one.

The fact is, projects such as this one rarely are completed, simply because they take vision and perserverance. There are two people who maintained the vision throughout and kept the project on course. To Bonnie Spain, Executive Director of Consumer Credit Counseling Service of the Black Hills, and Deborah Strassels, my wife, editor, cheerleader, and critic, I am grateful for all you have done and continue to do with this project.

Projects require financial support. To all those sponsoring organizations who contributed cash to make this possible, I want you to know that your commitment to this course will be appreciated by generations to come.

The financial sponsors of this project include: Associates Financial Services, BankWest, Black Hills Federal Credit Union, U.S. Bank, Wells Fargo Bank, Sentinel Federal Credit Union, and Telco Federal Credit Union.

For about a year, the Consumer Credit Counseling Service of the Black Hills office was turned a bit upside down. While everyone in the office continued to perform their work at the highest levels, there was the added pressure of dealing with a major book project, the author, reviews, and more. The extra effort put in by each of the people in the office cannot be ignored. For what you did to make this book possible, thank you Carey Albers, Patricia A. Allen, R. Donald Doney, Natalie Hatch, Judith Kinsella, LaVon Muzzy, Wallace Norum, Ruth O'Neill, and Julie Stone. I hope this course will make your job easier. I know that your work made mine a pleasure.

To the Board of Review, you have my sincere thanks. You contributed your time and efforts. You met with me every couple of weeks throughout the better part of a year. You read and re-read my drafts, you criticized, you provided great insight, you read some more. Without each and every one of you, this book would not be what it is.

To all of you, you have performed a service so valuable that I cannot begin to adequately express my appreciation. Fred Anderson, Customer Assistance Supervisor, Black Hills Power & Light; Qusi R. Al Haj, Owner, Micro Solutions; Keith Brugger, Teacher; Brett Distel, Msgt, Superintendent, 28th MMS, Family Support Center; Angie Einerwold, Past CCCS Graduate.

Joann Gaffaney, Retired; Barbara K. Garcia, Loan Officer, U.S. Bank.; Barbara A. Gill, Asst. VP, Commercial Lender, Rushmore Bank & Trust; Jennifer Isley, Educator; Patty Hogan, Asst. VP, U.S. Bank; Donna Hurley, Branch Director, Associates Financial Services; Jason Jares, Loan Officer, Real Estate Originator, BankWest; Samuel D. Kerr, Sr., Program Manager, Personal Finance, USAF.

Mary Kopco, Director-Curator, Adams Museum; Robert M. Nash, Attorney; Randy Silver, VP, Wells Fargo Bank; Amanda Paige Stanfield, Consumer; Shirley Stover, Business Manager, Rapid Motors; Chuck Wendling, VP, Black Hills Federal Credit Union; Dennis Whetzal, Attorney, Chapter 7 Bankruptcy Trustee; and Larry Kaiser, Credit Bureau of Rapid City.

And finally, there are those who do so well what I have absolutely no talent for. The author can write a book, but it takes those who understand design, layout and other stuff that is just too complicated to discuss to make the book magically appear.

To Joan S. Martin, your art and design are up to your usual exemplary standards. Fortunately, there are those of us who are not linear thinkers.

To the folks at Grelind Printing Center for your cover production, I know it wasn't easy.

To Ed Martley of Top Dog Publishing for your print management, I bet you never thought it would be a project of this magnitude.

INFORMATION FOR SELF-STUDY USERS

If you self-study any or all of the 12 lessons in the *Credit When Credit is Due* course, you will have your tests graded by the teaching organization that provided you with this book. When you have completed all 12 lessons and all twelve tests, remove them from the book. In addition, remove the *Credit When Credit is Due* Sign-Off Form, located on page 269 in front of the tests.

Fill in the **top portion** of the Sign-Off Form – your name, CWCID registration number, address and phone number. Be sure to **print legibly** – this is the information ACCE uses to return your graduation certificates and documentation. In addition to filling out the top portion of the Sign-Off Form, also print your name and CWCID registration number on the top of each completed test. Send the Sign-Off Form and the tests to the teaching organization that provided the book to you.

The organization will grade your tests and, assuming you have passed each of them, will forward your completion information to ACCE. If you have not passed any particular test, the teaching organization will send you a new test to take.

INFORMATION FOR CLASSROOM USERS

You may complete any of the *Credit When Credit is Due* lessons by attending class sessions presented by a teaching organization in your community. Ask the organization that provided your book for a *Credit When Credit is Due* class schedule.

You may attend classroom sessions in any order. However, you probably will benefit most if you study the lessons in order. To gain the most, you should read the material before attending class. In class, the teacher/facilitator and students will take about 45 minutes to discuss the lesson material. Immediately following the discussion, you will be asked to take the test, which is found at the back of the book.

When you pass the test, the teacher/facilitator will sign the Sign-Off Form, located in the back of your book on page 269 in front of the tests, indicating that you have successfully completed the lesson. When you have completed all 12 lessons and all 12 tests, remove them from the book. In addition, remove the *Credit When Credit is Due* Sign-Off Form. Fill in the **top portion** of the Sign-Off Form – your name, CWCID registration number, address and phone number. Be sure to **print legibly** – this is the information ACCE uses to return your graduation certificates and documentation. In addition to filling out the top portion of the Sign-Off Form, print your name and CWCID registration number on the top of each completed test. Give the Sign-Off Form and the 12 graded tests to the teaching organization.

Your CWCID registration number is found on the spine of your book. It is very important that you use this number on all your tests, your Sign-Off Form, and in any correspondence with your local teaching organization or with the American Center for Credit Education.

HOW TO USE THIS BOOK

GENERAL INFORMATION

Congratulations on taking the first step toward gaining a better understanding of credit in your life. The *Credit When Credit is Due* (CWCID) course is designed for the adult consumer who has used credit, or plans to use credit, and wants a better understanding of the terms, concepts and "rules" of credit use in the United States.

The *Credit When Credit is Due* course is available nationwide through local teaching organizations. These organizations, which have an interest in providing quality, standardized adult credit education for their clients and communities, obtain the course from the American Center for Credit Education (ACCE) and then deliver and administer the course in their local communities. Individuals enroll in the *Credit When Credit is Due* course through the local teaching organization. To find the one closest to you, you may contact ACCE at 605-348-3104.

Once you have enrolled, you have a choice of how you complete the course. You may complete the *Credit When Credit is Due* course by attending classroom sessions, by completing it through self-study, or by a combination of the two. The course includes 12 separate lessons. Each lesson is a self-contained unit, so you can read and study any lesson you want in any order you want. However, you probably will benefit the most if you study the lessons in order. Each lesson should take you about 45 minutes whether you read and self-study or if you complete by attending a classroom session. The total time to complete this course will vary with the individual and the method of completion. In addition, the teaching organization you are working with may set expected deadlines for your completion of the course.

Once you have completed a lesson, go to the back of the book and complete the test for that lesson. Tests should take about 10 minutes and are taken "open book." The idea is for you to learn the information, not to trick you in any way.

There is a number on the spine of your book. No one else has this number. It is important to remember that two people, even married couples, cannot be registered under the same number. When you successfully complete the *Credit When Credit is Due* course, your name and registration number will be listed in the ACCE national registry. ACCE will send you a letter stating you have finished the 12-lesson *Credit When Credit is Due* course. In addition, you will receive three consumer cards that you will send to the three credit reporting agencies. This is how your participation in this course may be added to your individual credit report – and why only one person can be registered as a graduate of CWCID. Finally, you will receive a card certifying that your name and accomplishment have been recorded in a national registry which lenders can contact if they should want confirmation of your achievement.

If you have questions about the *Credit When Credit is Due* course, contact the Teaching Organization that provided your book. If you have more questions, contact the American Center for Credit Education at 605-348-3104.

THE AMERICAN CENTER FOR CREDIT EDUCATION (ACCE)

This non-profit agency has been organized to establish a national standardized credit education program by encouraging individuals of all ages to take and complete the *Credit When Credit Is Due* course, either through classroom study or self-study in their homes. The course is designed to help individuals gain a basic understanding of money issues and their responsibilities revolving around the world of credit.

The concept it uses is similar to the well-known driver's education course. When teenagers take driver's education, they learn the rules of the road and necessary driving skills. As a result, they are considered to be better drivers than those who have not taken the course. Auto insurance companies recognize them as better driving risks and grant discounts on insurance premiums.

The same concept applies to consumers who successfully complete the *Credit When Credit Is Due* course. They should be better risks in the eyes of lenders, and should be better prepared to handle their personal finances in the future.

Among other activities, the American Center For Credit Education is actively encouraging lenders to acknowledge that graduates of the *Credit When Credit Is Due* course are better credit risks than those who have not completed the course by granting them interest rate discounts and other considerations on their loans.

To find lenders in your community that offer incentives to graduates of the Credit When Credit is Due program, please visit our Web site at www.creditwhencreditisdue.com.

ABOUT THE AUTHOR

One of America's premier analysts and commentators on the subjects of money, taxes, consumer credit issues and economic trends, Paul Strassels is a highly respected speaker and writer on a wide range of financial topics. His education, training and experience have earned him a well-deserved national reputation as an expert on taxes, banking, investments, credit and other aspects of personal and business financial planning. He was the honored recipient of the Louis M.Linxwiler Award, presented by the National Foundation for Consumer Credit "in recognition of his outstanding contribution to the field of consumer credit education."

Paul Strassels started his career in 1970 with the Internal Revenue Service at its national headquarters in Washington, D.C. He left in 1975 to become editor-in-chief of the Washington Tax and Business Report. He has gone on to direct his own firm, Money Matters, Inc. for more than 20 years.

His client list has included such well-known firms as the Associated Press, Boardroom Reports, Tax Hotline, American Express, Dow Jones, Family Circle, the U.S. Chamber of Commerce, National Taxpayers Union, and Financial News Network, among others.

His widely acclaimed series of televised tax and money tips have been broadcast throughout the country, and for 6 years, Mr. Strassels hosted his own daily local radio show. He has been featured on 60 Minutes, CBS Morning News, Good Morning America, Nightline, CNN, the Tonight Show, Donahue and Larry King. His opinions have been published by such prominent publications as *Money Magazine*, *U.S. News and World Report*, *Time*, *Newsweek*, *Forbes*, *The Wall Street Journal*, *The New York Times*, and *USA Today*.

Author of 13 books on money and taxes, Paul Strassels' first book, *All You Need To Know About The IRS* (Random House) was a runaway best-seller. *Money Matters* (Addison Wessley) is a guide to personal money management. Other books written by Mr. Strassels are: *The 1986 Tax Reform Act: Making It Work For You* (Dow Jones), *Strassels Quick And Easy Guide To Money Management* (Dow Jones), *Strassels Tax Savers* (Times Books), and *Money In Your Pocket* (Doubleday). His most recent book for Consumer Credit Counseling Service of the Black Hills, South Dakota, *Credit When Credit Is Due*, establishes a much-needed national standardized credit education program that is presently marketed by the American Center for Credit Education.

Mr. Strassels is working on his 14th book, *How Much Money Is Enough?*, conducts strategic planning sessions for small businesses, and ever the entrepreneur, oversees operations for his four companies.

TABLE OF CONTENTS

SIGN-OFF SHEET AND TESTS FOR LESSONS ONE THROUGH TWELVE

INTRODUCTION

There is a serious problem in the United States, one that seems to be getting worse year after year. The problem is, too many people spend more money than they make so they use ever larger amounts of credit to make up the difference between what they spend and what they need. The result is that their personal finances deteriorate over time to the point where they cannot take on any more debt. By then, it is often too late to dig themselves out of the financial hole in which they have put themselves.

How does this happen? It's usually unintentional. Typically, events conspire, and then, before they know it, they are head over heels in smothering debt.

Most people plan to pay their bills. They really do. But then the unexpected occurs. They lose a job, are unemployed for longer than they anticipated, suffer a medical emergency, experience an unplanned pregnancy, divorce, or similar event. Something happens either to their income or expenses and their life is thrown into turmoil.

So, what should a person do? In most cases, the answer is either take proper steps before the unexpected occurs or have sufficient savings to cover expenses during the hard times.

Consider these comments from people who work in the credit counseling field. When it comes to people in financial trouble, they have seen it all:

"Watching the struggles of the clients who come in to see us has given me a new perspective on life. I was taught the value of being financially responsible from a young age. Yet, in such a fast-paced, materialistic "me" society, lessons can easily be ignored. Working with and learning from our clients' mistakes has reaffirmed the lessons my parents taught me as a child."

"Although we cannot possibly control all the circumstances around us, we can be as prepared as possible for any surprise that life throws our way. Seeing some of the struggles clients have faced has caused me to resolve to do whatever is within my power not to be caught unprepared for an unexpected situation."

"I had a counseling session where only the husband came in to see me. He had created the problem of excessive debt (he was a compulsive buyer) and his wife wanted him to fix it. I set up a budget for them to follow and asked him to return with his wife. When they came in, you could cut the tension with a knife. After bringing everything out into the open, she broke down and cried. So did he. The good news was that with their debt management program, they found that they could be out of debt within 22 months. They left my office and made an appointment with a marriage counselor to help repair the damage that too much debt had caused. I think they'll make it."

"I have been counseling a couple for more than 3 years, and they still have another 2 years to go before they will be debt free. They called to let me know that they had managed to save enough extra money to travel out of state to visit their parents over the Christmas holiday and also to buy some presents. This was something they had not had the luxury of doing the last 3 years."

"I had a visit from a man who was out of work. He had spent his last few dollars on a motel room. He never called back for another appointment. We've just had some bitterly cold days. It makes me wonder — did he find a home or a job, or is he wandering the streets, or worse?"

These are not idle comments. Nor are they extraordinary. Not one of the people referred to planned on being in the situation in which they found themselves. It just goes to show you that if you don't plan your personal finances, if you overextend your credit, if you take on too much debt, or if you fail to save for that proverbial rainy day, then you too could be the subject of these credit counselors' comments.

How you live your life is, by and large, up to you. If you learn early in your adult life how to properly handle your personal finances and make good money decisions, you can be very comfortable no matter how much money you make. If you fail to learn these lessons, or you learn them but then ignore them, you face what may be insurmountable financial hurdles. Life's lessons can be easy to master or they can be tough to take. The choice is yours. This much is certain. Those who master their personal finances early in life tend to have an easier time of it than those who do not.

Listen to advice offered by one young woman. "My husband and I are in our early 30's. We've discovered that most of our friends are in the same boat we are. In our 20's, we wanted all that our parents had in their 50's, so we charged clothes, cars, and big ticket toys. We bought homes. We had children that we love but couldn't yet afford. Now we are paying all that off, and there still is no savings account, no nest egg. Are we doing it backwards? Probably. Are we a trend? Certainly. It's no wonder that credit card companies and car dealers love us. Will the next generation do better? I hope so, because digging out of debt is no fun."

Subjects like personal finance, credit and debt, budgets, retirement plans, investments, taxes and health insurance, among others, are not so difficult that you cannot understand them. It's not going to hurt your head. You're not going to feel stupid or inferior. Everybody needs to learn these lessons. Unfortunately, not everyone does.

There's no preaching or nagging going on here. These lessons are not "you must not do this and you cannot do that." It's more, "here's what you need to know in order to make informed decisions about this or that aspect of your financial life."

There are no guarantees in life. However, when you make good money decisions and plan for the unexpected, your life can be comfortable and secure. You will be able to afford those dreams. When you make poor choices and decisions and you fail to plan for the unexpected, your life can be difficult and strained.

Take it from those who deal every day with people who have severe money problems: There is a comfort in living within your budget, paying your bills on time, and watching your savings and investments grow. These money professionals will also tell you that there is worry, anger and often terrible stress when you do not have the money you need to pay the rent or to buy groceries.

You can learn about earning, saving, budgeting, and similar topics so you will be prepared to handle the financial decisions you will be called on to make all your adult life.

Please take these lessons to heart. Believe me. It is far more enjoyable to live life with money in your checking account than it is being chased by bill collectors.

Paul Strassels
October, 1997
Rapid City, South Dakota

THE FACTS OF LIFE

Welcome to the real world of personal finance and the responsibility that goes with it. Bundle up, because it can be cold and lonely out there when you are on your own.

This lesson provides an overview of credit and debt issues that all adults face. It points out many of the pitfalls and hazards that significantly affect people's lives, either temporarily or permanently.

When it comes to money, life's lessons can be harsh and unforgiving but they don't have to be. You have choices to make. How well you make those choices will determine whether you live the good life or you live a life of constant worry. You can have money in savings or you can have serious money problems.

The unfortunate reality is that too many people choose the difficult path. They spend more money than they make. They give in to the urge of impulse buying. They fail to plan for the inevitable emergency. The result is they often find themselves only a couple of paychecks away from the homeless shelter. Rarely does it have to be that way. Most financial problems can be avoided in the first place, or resolved when they do crop up.

Life doesn't have to be gray, like it is for those with constant money worries. Life can and should be bright, colorful and enjoyable.

To have a chance to live a life free of excessive money worries, there are at least 20 areas of personal money management that you need to master.

- Live within your means. Don't spend more than you make. Don't take on more debt than you can afford to repay even if someone is willing to lend you the money.

- Budget your money. Budgets are not only for older folks or the young. Budgets are for everyone. Period. If you don't use a budget, you're missing the single most important financial tool available to you.

- Anticipate your expenses. You have to know what bills are coming due this month and next, and you have to know how you are going to pay them.

- Save a little every payday and learn how to invest what you save. If you don't see the money, you won't miss it. With savings, you will be able to get through that inevitable emergency. If you don't invest your savings, you won't have much of a nest egg when you need it.

- Understand how credit and debt work, and determine how much debt you can comfortably repay. Credit is the amount of money that is available to you through lenders; debt is simply the amount of credit you are using at any given time. Credit and debt are like opposite ends of that childhood teeter-totter. Credit is on one end; debt is on the other. You can have high (large) amounts of credit and low (small) amounts of debt, or it can be the other way around. When you use all of your credit, your available credit is zero; your debt load is maxed out.

- Develop smart money habits. You don't have to be a tightwad and you don't have to squeeze every quarter until you get change. But you do need to keep track of what you spend and where you spend it so you can plug spending leaks.

- Buy smart. That means you have to learn to be a good consumer. Stop overpaying for things that you neither want nor need. Learn what is good value for everything from houses and cars to groceries and clothing.

- Learn to spot and then avoid budget-busters. That's money you spend which you didn't plan to spend. It's also spending where you don't have anything to show for the money. Don't make purchases that throw your budget out of balance. Guard against impulse buying, even when the amounts are small.

- Get an education, job skills and work experience.

- Learn how to interview for a job in the career field you want, and assess the job's potential.

- Become familiar with your job benefits, such as vacation time, flex time, sick leave and tuition assistance.

- Learn to be a good employee. You are going to be working for 4 or 5 decades, or more. There are things expected of employees, and if you hope to keep your job or advance in it, you're going to have to do these things, like show up on time, put in a full day's work, go the extra mile, and so on.

- Learn about retirement plans. Many companies have pension, profit sharing or 401(k) plans. You'll have to learn the ins and outs of what is available to you. If you don't have a work-provided retirement plan, you will have to start one of your own, such as an IRA.

- Learn about everyday financial services. This includes checking accounts, savings accounts, money market accounts, and other accounts available to you. There's automatic transfer, direct deposit, banking by computer. You have to learn about fees and charges, ATM cards, credit cards, debit cards, bad check fees, overdraft protection, joint versus separate accounts, safe deposit boxes, how to balance your checkbook, and so on. One banker says he feels that learning to balance your checkbook is one of the essential financial cornerstones on which all other money issues can be built.

- Learn how to borrow money and what is required of you when you do. That includes everything from applying for a loan to filling out a credit card application.

- Learn about health insurance and medical plans offered through work (if you are working) and through independent insurance agents (if you are not).

- Learn how to shop for auto, homeowners, renters, life and disability insurance.

- Learn about contracts, especially those which require you to pay money to others, and those which require others to pay money to you.

- Learn what is needed to qualify for a mortgage before it is time for you to buy a house.

- Learn about federal, state and local taxes, how they affect you, how you can legally reduce the amount you have to pay, increase your deductions, and even fill out your tax forms.

Then and only then can you get along as a financially responsible adult.

Those are 20 things you need to learn and do, and this is a minimum. There's a lot more about money matters that you can and should learn, and you probably will over time.

It would be nice if people learned at least these 20 essentials in high school or college but they don't. In most schools, these courses simply are not available. And when they are available, students usually are not financially independent adults so the lessons tend to be lost. It's not until people are on their own that these lessons make sense.

Most people gain at least some of the necessary education and experience through the school of hard knocks. It's on-the-job-training. People tend to learn from their mistakes because all too often the mistakes wind up costing a pile of money that they can ill afford to lose.

It Can Be Tough When You Are on Your Own

You may not like to hear this but it is hard being a financially independent adult every day of your life. Those who have been on their own know they have to pay their bills and make financial decisions every day. They worry about their next paycheck and if they will have a job next week. They worry about the VISA or MasterCard bill when they have exceeded their spending limit. They try to save on electricity by turning off a light or the television when leaving a room. They worry about paying the doctor.

It doesn't matter what your position in life is. It doesn't matter if you are male or female, single or married, divorced or widowed. It doesn't matter if you come from a rich family or a poor one. It doesn't matter if you come from a family of bankers and stockbrokers or hairdressers and bricklayers. It doesn't matter what your race, political affiliation, or religious beliefs are.

Everyone is subject to the same set of rules. **Money plays no favorites. There is only one rule. Pay your bills on time, in full, with checks that do not bounce no matter what is happening in your life.**

The Good Old Days

Remember the good old days when you didn't have a financial care in the world? You lived at home and your parents took care of everything. Think back to when you lived under your parents' roof. Oh sure, you probably complained about their rules, and how they required approval of the clothes you bought with their money, your boyfriend or girlfriend, your curfew, and all those other things that teens complain about when it comes to their parents. At the time, you probably didn't appreciate how good you had it. You worried about teen stuff, but you didn't worry about paying the rent, buying food, or covering telephone bills. Now you do.

As an independent adult, you pay your own way in life, and because you do, no one has the right to approve or disapprove of the way you live.

To be *Truly* Independent, You Have to Acknowledge One Important Fact, and Perform One Particular Duty

The fact you have to acknowledge is that it is your responsibility, and yours alone, to see to it that you pay all of your bills, on time, in full, with checks that don't bounce. You've heard that before, but it is worth repeating. Paying your own way is difficult because it is relentless. You have to do it, every day, every week, every month, of your adult life. It is a task that never ceases, once you become independent.

Most bills show up in the mail, once each month, like the utilities and telephone. Some, like the rent, you just have to remember; there's no reminder. Still others you find in the drawer where you keep your financial papers, because your creditors have sent you a coupon booklet; one coupon each month (along with your check) goes to cover the car loan, or the bank loan, or any other similar loan.When you miss a payment, it's on your head. Parents and teachers may have accepted excuses, but landlords, lenders and utility companies do not.

The duty you have to perform is that you have to generate enough money and keep a sufficiently large savings account to cover your lifestyle, your bills, and emergencies. The money you need to pay the landlord has to come from somewhere. The same is true for groceries. It usually comes from your paycheck, but not always. It may come from a loan, your savings, or even a gift. It doesn't matter. The money simply has to come from somewhere because the bills you have taken on have to be paid. That's the deal.

Decisions, Decisions, Decisions

All your adult life, you will be asked to make decisions about your money matters. Perhaps the most difficult is

that you must decide what you can and cannot afford. You will probably base your decisions on the amount of money you currently earn, whether or not you think you will be able to keep your job and the salary which goes with it, if you are likely to get a raise, and the amount of money you have set aside for that proverbial rainy day.

You decide first what you need, then what you want, and finally what you must forego until a later date because you cannot afford it at the present time. You prioritize. You determine what is a requirement in your life and what is not. You exhibit self-discipline when spending your money. You find that you deny yourself things you want because you cannot afford to pay for them.

There are stories upon stories of couples who fight over money, or more likely the lack of money. He wants a new fishing rod; she wants new curtains. He wants to save; she wants new carpeting. He wants a trip; she wants to save. There are no stereotypes here. **Money shows no favorites**.

Money requires decisions. Do you buy that new car, lease it, or repair the old one and run it until the wheels fall off? The decision is yours. The result of the decision will determine how well or how poorly you live over the next couple of years. Perhaps even longer.

Do you take that long overdue vacation that you feel you so badly need but can't afford? Do you finance a $2,500 trip that's over in a week, or do you pay cash for a camping trip close to home that is a fraction of the cost?

Why Didn't Someone Tell Me?

Credit counselors, bankruptcy attorneys, loan officers, car dealers, and others tell story after story of individuals who are drowning in debt. These people complain bitterly that they would have never, ever found themselves in the mess they are in if only someone had bothered to warn them of the potential problems and educate them in the ways of proper financial management.

The fact is, most people have had this help offered to them at one time or another, usually by a concerned parent. If you listen to parents of young adults, they too complain that their youngsters are headed for financial trouble but won't listen.

One sums it up when she says, "I have a graduating senior who has no idea what financial trouble is. His spending habits will cause him trouble on his own, and he won't listen to me when I talk to him about money."

No One Will Lend Me Any Money

Don't blame credit card companies, banks, credit unions, finance companies and others when they don't want to lend you money. Most individuals are turned down for credit because they either have no credit experience or they have a bad credit history.

If you have a good credit history, lenders are usually anxious to extend still more credit to you. Nothing is quite as important as a good credit history; a history that shows that others have lent you money and that you have paid it back on time and as agreed. Without that history and experience behind you, most potential creditors won't want to take a chance on you.

You can't blame them. Just look at the statistics. Over the past couple of years, more than 1.5 million personal bankruptcies were filed. These are men and women who have given up on their debts. The cost runs into billions of dollars every year, dollars these lenders counted on to pay their own bills and meet their payrolls.

Granted, some of these bankruptcies are filed for legitimate reasons beyond the control of the individuals involved. However, there are too many cases where others have simply taken advantage of the system.

Of the existing credit card debt outstanding, more than 3 percent are delinquent more than 30 days; many more are far more delinquent than that. Some of that money will never be collected.

If you want credit, you need to demonstrate to a prospective lender that you are a good credit risk. It can be tough to do when you have never had credit before. It may be difficult, but you will probably be able to find a lender willing to take a chance on the first-time borrower, especially if you show them that you have completed a course such as this one.

Worse than having no credit experience is trying to get new credit when you already have a history of not repaying what you already owe. That problem is much more difficult to solve. However, it can be accomplished by using secured debt and offering collateral.

There are ways to establish credit when you have no previous credit history and there are legitimate ways to repair a damaged credit history. Both take time and effort, but the tasks can be accomplished. There will be more on how to accomplish these goals in later lessons.

No One Cares What You Do for a Living; Just Do Something

Prior to your financial independence, parents, teachers, counselors, friends and neighbors all wanted to know, "What do you want to do when you grow up? What career fields interest you? What are you studying at school?"

As an independent adult, you no longer have the luxury of searching for a fulfilling career. No one cares anymore what you do for a living, just as long as you do something that brings in enough money to pay your bills.

Want to be a doctor? Fine. A mechanic? Okay. A teacher? Terrific. Join the military? No problem. Go into business for yourself? Good choice. Be whatever you want. Take the job that interests you. Change jobs that do not work out. Just get a job, earn a salary and pay your bills. You are responsible for earning a living and making enough money to pay your own way. How you do it is your own business, as long as it's legal of course. Remember, excuses rarely work.

In Good Times, and in Bad

Much of a person's financial life goes on without a great deal of thought. You go to work, get paid every other week or so, pay your bills and live your life. Think for a minute about what happens to your paycheck. For most people, it goes into the checking account, and every so often, probably twice a month, on the 1st and the 15th, you sit down with the bills and write out the checks.

In a perfect world, you budget upcoming expenses, set aside some savings, take a look at how your actual expenses compare to what you anticipated, and take care of the emergencies. That's what you do during the good times when you are working and getting that steady paycheck.

It's not a perfect world. It is during the bad times that money troubles can become overwhelming. It is for the bad times that you have to plan. What do you do when that paycheck gets cut off? The bills still have to be paid. But where's the money to come from?

On the first of the month, you have to pay your rent or you stand to be evicted. That's what you agreed to do when you signed the lease. There was no discussion about skipping the rent during those times that you were out of work, or when you needed the money for other bills, or you decided to take a vacation and spend the money on a ski trip or a cruise.

When the car payment is due, you have to send a check to whoever financed the loan. If you don't, they will send someone to repossess the car.

When you get the phone and utility bills, you have to pay or you will lose phone service and have your utilities turned off. You can feel awfully isolated without a telephone. It can get awfully uncomfortable without power or heat.

Hungry? Go to the grocery store and buy what you need. Just remember the cashier expects to be paid.

Sick? Go to the doctor. You'll quickly find out that doctors expect to be paid for their services, as do hospitals, pharmacies and everyone else connected with health care.

Hot water heater blow up? Need new brakes or a new engine for the car? You may not expect these emergencies, but they happen, and when they do, you will be glad you have a savings account to fall back on.

Life Can be Awfully Fragile

One fact you must understand is that life is unpredictable. You can count on the unexpected because it happens all the time. Through no fault of your own, life may throw you a curve, or a bean ball, and you have to deal with it. It's not fair, it's not easy, but it's the truth.

Jim was a corporate executive who got caught in company downsizing. He lost his job of 12 years. His 3 months severance pay didn't go far. His wife, Joanie, used to work, but when she was pregnant with their second child, she quit to stay at home with the kids. Joanie could have gone back to work after the baby was born, but there was a heart problem with their new son. The hospital stay was 6 months, out-of-state.

What more could go wrong? There are costly medical problems. They stand to lose their house. Their two cars are financed. They owe $15,000 on credit cards. They have no savings to fall back on. He doesn't have great prospects for a new, high-paying job, and while she's staying at the hospital with the baby, he is at home caring for the older child while he should be out looking for a new job.

None of what has happened is their fault. Nevertheless, events have conspired to utterly disrupt their lives.

They can probably work their way out of the financial mess they are in, but it's going to be difficult and it will probably take some time, at least a couple of years if not longer. However, if they are not careful, they could find their lives more than temporarily disrupted. The quicker he can find gainful employment, the better. All of his efforts should be spent locating work.

Then there is the story of the young couple who got married some 8 years ago. Both had just reached their 30th birthdays and were making a decent living when he came down with leukemia. Fortunately, the disease was treatable medically. Financially, it was not.

Neither spouse had health insurance, not because they felt the cost of the insurance was too high but because they were unwilling to spend $150 a month for a catastrophic health plan with a $2,500 deductible. They gambled they could get by without a major illness and they lost. Now they are suffering the consequences.

These people were uninsured by choice. According to government statistics, at least 35 percent of Americans have no health insurance. Some are uninsured by choice like this couple. Others are simply uninsurable; to them cost is irrelevant because no company will insure them at any price.

Leukemia is treatable today but this victim doesn't have the money to pay for the medical care he needs. Chances are he will survive medically despite the cost because people receive treatment in this country whether they can pay for it or not. But if he is to survive financially, he will have to rely on the generosity of his friends and neighbors to cover his bills.

Either that, or he will have to declare bankruptcy, a black mark that will restrict his access to credit for as long as 10 years. There's nothing he could have done to avoid the medical problem, but there was a way to avoid the financial one, if he would have only been a bit more financially responsible by purchasing low cost catastrophic health coverage.

Bad Luck Can Happen to Anyone

Almost everyone gets a pink slip sometime during his or her working career. Statistics show that you stand a very real risk of losing your job at least once or twice during your work life span, maybe even more often than that.

You can get downsized, laid off or even merged out of a job.

When it happens, you may not be given much warning or severance pay. Tough luck. There is no such thing as job security anymore. Unless you work for yourself, there is a strong possibility that sometime during your working life, you will be invited into your boss's office and told to clean out your desk or locker.

Let's be honest. The problem is not the loss of the job but rather the loss of that regular paycheck. If money were of no concern, you wouldn't worry about losing a job. You would just go out and take whatever time you needed to find another, perhaps a more personally satisfying position. The truth is, job loss is about money. Without your salary, you are going to have a very tough time paying your bills. The only solution to the crisis you face when you lose a job is to have enough money saved to get you through until you can find another job and another paycheck.

Kathy's story is typical. She always worked hard, putting in a full 8 hours a day, 5 days a week. She didn't complain when asked to work overtime. She had been a good employee for 7 years. Then one day, she was given 2 weeks notice and 2 weeks severance pay, and a "Sorry, but business isn't what it used to be. Someone had to go, and it was you. Good luck."

Or Ted, who was working at his company, and wasn't even thinking about changing jobs. Then, one day, out of the blue, he got a job offer with another employer. It was a better position, more money and terrific benefits. He took it. Then, 3 months later, the owner told him that he didn't think Ted was working out. He was fired on the spot.

Kathy is a single mother with 2 youngsters in elementary school. Ted has a wife and teenage son to support. Each has bills to pay. Each is without a job. Neither saw it coming. Could it happen to you? Certainly, and it may at some point in time. Plan on it by having enough cash reserve in savings so you will be able to survive financially while you are between jobs. **When you lose a job, those around you will feel badly, and they will offer their sympathy. Rarely will they offer you money.** They have their own bills to pay.

Even when you are between jobs, your creditors expect you to pay your bills, despite the fact that you have little or no income. After all, when you bought that appliance, car, or house, you agreed to make your payments on time. It may not be your fault that you are out of work, in fact in many instances it is not. Nevertheless, it is not the creditors' fault either that you are not working and cannot make your payments.

A word of advice. If and when you find yourself between jobs and no money coming in, contact your creditors and tell them what's going on. You may be surprised to find that some may be willing to give you an extension of time to make up payments that you miss. In any case, it will be to your advantage to face the problem head on rather than ignore it.

Wouldn't it be nice if when you are most in need of money you could approach a lender to help you out? Don't count on it. Lenders don't want to lend to people who are not working. Would you?

Should you lose your job, you may have to accept another job at less pay, work nights, take two part-time jobs, cash in savings accounts, and ask parents and others to loan you what you need until you can get back on your feet. You will have to do whatever it takes.

Marital Problems

When you marry, you intend to live the rest of your life, happy and content, with the mate of your dreams. Unfortunately, it doesn't always work out that way. There is a very real risk that you will get divorced. In fact, one of every two couples splits up.

Don and Caroline had been married for 15 years when they decided to divorce. Predictably, it got messy. They argued about everything — the house, bills, credit cards, savings accounts, investments, retirement accounts.

Their creditors didn't want to take sides. The mortgage company still expected to be paid. So did the telephone company, VISA and MasterCard, Sears, Penney's, the appliance store, local department store, furniture store, the bank that financed their two cars, and everybody else they did business with around town who had extended credit to them. The fact is, your marital problems are yours, not your creditors. Lenders are not bad guys just because they want their money repaid. Talk to a financial professional immediately if you are contemplating a divorce. There are many issues to resolve, and most people will need help.

Accidents Happen

Chances are pretty high that sometime in your life, you or a family member will face a medical emergency. The cost of a hospital visit can devastate your finances unless you are adequately covered by medical insurance. Even then, your share of the bill after the insurance company has paid may be more than you can afford. The fact is, no one cares how costly your medical care is just as long as you cover it.

Peter was driving home from work, around 5 in the afternoon. He stopped at the red light, and when it turned green, he started through the intersection. That's when another car ran the intersection, slamming into Peter's car. That driver was driving illegally, without insurance. Despite his seat belt, Peter was tossed around, hitting his head, drawing blood, cracking three ribs, and breaking an ankle. The price tag for the ambulance ride to the hospital, emergency room care, surgery on the ankle and two months of rehab, stitches in the head, doctors, nurses, medication, and two days in the hospital came to $35,000. That's in addition to the damage to his car.

Fortunately, Peter had his own car insurance, but it wasn't nearly enough. His insurance paid $4,000, which was the value of the car. It wasn't enough to pay for a replacement vehicle. The insurance paid $10,000 toward his medical bills. That still left him $25,000 short.

If you drive a car, chances are you will be involved in an accident, and whether it is your fault or not, you will have to meet your financial obligations.

Bad Decisions

You make financial decisions all your adult life. If you make bad decisions, they can come back to haunt you.

Tom was one who didn't learn much about money, and made bad choices about what to do with what he made. He didn't save much. He didn't budget. He wasn't a smart shopper.

Tom struggled with money all his life. Then, at age 60, he filed for bankruptcy protection from his creditors. Imagine being 60 years old, bankrupt, with a wife and three teenagers depending on you for support.

Tom didn't owe an extraordinary amount of money; he listed debts of $48,000 the day he filed. He earned about $20,000 a year. His wife worked, too, making another $16,000, but her hours had just been cut back, further reducing their monthly income. Tom and his family were making $2,400 a month (take home pay) and spending $3,000. It was just a matter of time before they could no longer juggle their finances.

He had honestly tried to work things out. He had been to a very good financial counseling service. He had tried a debt management program. But it had become evident very quickly that he just had too much month for the money. Those he owed wanted their money, and they had grown impatient waiting for it. Tom simply didn't have it and didn't have any way to get it. So, he declared bankruptcy, and all those creditors had to write off their loans.

One point needs to be mentioned here. Tom and his family were not living a lavish lifestyle. Nevertheless, they could have made sacrifices that would have saved some money. Now that he has declared bankruptcy, they have no choice but to make those serious lifestyle changes.

At age 60, he has to regroup. He acknowledges that he is going to have to live without access to credit and credit cards. He realizes that retirement is a term that simply doesn't apply to him, and probably never will, because he has no retirement nest egg set aside and no prospect to acquire one. He knows he is going to have to rely on social security and Medicare to support him in his later years, either that or he is going to have to depend on family, children, friends, and neighbors for his financial security. If they fall through, he is going to have to rely on charity. All this because he made bad money choices.

He hadn't saved and invested his money like he should have. He had bet too much money on the success of some of his business decisions that didn't work out as well as he had hoped and planned. He had invested what money he had in the riskiest of investments and he had lost.

Then there's Jimmy. He had just joined the Air Force and was on his own for the first time in his life. Jimmy wanted that sports car, but before he signed on the dotted line, he knew enough to ask about auto insurance. The agent quoted a price. Jimmy thought he could swing the monthly car payment, including the insurance. What he didn't know is that he had to tell the insurance agent about his 3 speeding tickets. When they came to light, the insurance went up to the point that Jimmy couldn't afford the car. The dealership didn't want the car back, and neither did the bank which financed the loan. What a mess. All because Jimmy didn't know everything he should have known about shopping for car insurance.

Addictive Behavior

There are all sorts of addictive behaviors that affect people and their family finances.

There's the gambling addiction. Henry didn't have a problem, at least he didn't admit it. He gambled a little. He rationalized that it was just entertainment. The fact is, Henry has more than $250,000 in debts he can't pay, because he is addicted to gambling. His paycheck never makes it home. There isn't enough for groceries, the car payment, rent, or anything else. But Henry doesn't see a problem.

Maybe it's Ellen who has the problem. She's Henry's wife, and she's leaving. She can't take it anymore. Henry needs help. And Ellen has to get on with her life. It's going to take a while, but she'll make it. But she will, at age 40, have to establish an independent life, establish a work career, establish credit, and take on the role of single mother.

Jane was a closet gambler. She held a 9-5 job. It was during her lunch break that she went gambling. She used her charge cards to finance her addictive behavior. She explained to the bank officer that she had lost as much as $2,000 in one hour. Finally, after getting treatment through Gamblers Anonymous, she was able to consolidate her debt, reduce her monthly payments, and get control of her life. After a year, she was doing so well that her husband, Jim, bought her a diamond ring to celebrate.

More Addictive Behavior

There's the spending addiction. There are people who are so addicted to buying that they program their speed-dial on their telephone to QVC and Home Shopping Network.

There are folks who are actually addicted to buying on credit. For whatever reason, they impulse buy. They don't have the money to pay cash, but that doesn't stop them. Instead they buy on credit, until the addiction becomes so severe that they have no more credit to use. Credit counselors have been told "people in debt often go out and buy things on credit, things they often don't even want or need, just to make themselves feel better. But it only adds to their problem of excessive debt."

Life is Full of Pitfalls

Pitfalls come in all sizes and shapes. Some are bigger than others. Some you can face alone. Others can be overwhelming.

One of your parents goes into a nursing home and the other parent needs financial support.

You lose your job two months after buying that new car.

The hot water heater blows up and most of your stuff in the basement is ruined.

You're sued because someone slips and falls on your sidewalk.

Your dog bites someone.

The wind rips the roof off your house.

You get sick, very sick, and miss three months work, without pay.

Your son falls off a horse and punctures a lung.

You get the idea. What you do with your life and how you live it is entirely your business, as long as you pay your own way. When you don't, people begin to care. They care about their money and worry about when they can expect to receive it.

When you miss your rent payment, your landlord cares.

When you miss the car payment, the lender cares.

When you miss the credit card payment, the card issuer cares.

When you miss the telephone bill, the telephone company cares.

When you have no money and are hungry and you decide to steal some food, then not only does the store care, but so do the police.

When you write a check but do not have money to cover it, the person or business to whom you wrote the check cares, and once again, so do the police.

When a judgment is filed against you, and you don't pay it, your employer cares because he has to honor the garnishment of your wages.

You see, lots of people care about you and your money. But they only care when you're in trouble.

Actually, most people understand what you are going

through. They've probably been there at some time during their lives or are close to someone who has. They sympathize but they are not going to bail you out. They care, but not that much.

The Facts of Life Can be Tough to Accept

Carol had always been a good, upright, responsible person. She couldn't understand what was happening to her. She had just graduated from school, and was looking for a job. She needed transportation, so she went car shopping, settling on a new $20,000 model. Then she found out that no one would lend her the money to pay for it.

She tried to finance it through the dealership but because she had no job and no credit history, they wouldn't finance it for her.

She applied for a loan at her credit union where she had maintainted an account since she was a freshman in high school, but same story. No job, no credit history, and no co-signer means no loan.

"You would get the car as collateral," she said.

"We don't want the car, we want you to repay what we lend, and without a job, we don't see how you will be able to make the loan payments," they said. "We're here to help you buy the car. We are not here to buy it for you."

She tried to get her father to finance it. "Dad," she said, "You buy the car and I'll pay you back." Again, she was turned down.

"I don't have that kind of money just sitting around. You're out of school. Get a job and then take out a car loan like everyone else."

"Will you at least co-sign on the loan?"

"No, I can't do that either. Every time I co-sign, it ties up my credit. You will be okay once you start working. Then you won't need my guarantee.

"I don't want to commit myself to paying your bills if you hit tough times and don't have the money to pay the car loan. I can't afford the extra financial burden it would place on me."

Carol fussed and fumed. She couldn't understand why no one would loan her the money. She promised she would repay the money. "Why won't they lend me the money?

I'm good for it. Why won't they give me a chance? It's not my fault that I don't have a job yet."

Here the potential lenders, Dad included, know better than to lend money to someone they feel is ready and willing but completely unable to repay what they want to borrow. Without a solid job history and good prospects of getting their money back on time as agreed, lenders don't want any part of this kind of deal. Can you blame them?

Once Carol finds that job, starts working and earning some money, traditional lenders like banks, credit unions and car dealers will fall all over themselves to take the loan. And she won't have to go to Dad.

Getting Good Value for Your Money

There is an important relationship that exists between what you earn and what you spend.

Chris is a teacher. She earns $30,000 a year. Of that, $7,500 goes to pay her federal and state income taxes, social security and Medicare taxes, her health insurance (which she gets through work) and her contribution to her retirement account (also a company benefit).

That leaves her $22,500 a year, or $1,875 a month on which to live. She pays her rent, car payment, utilities, auto insurance, the vet bills, food, and so on. On a good month, she has an extra $300 to do with as she pleases. Of course, she could save and invest some or all of it, or she could spend it. That's her choice to make.

If she has no unexpected emergencies, she will have a discretionary $3,600 to spend for the year.

Chris sees a new set of skis and outfit in her future. The price tag is $600. She is also eyeing a week-long ski trip that sounds too good to be true. Price tag $2,000.

The question is, should Chris spend $2,600 of her "extra" $3,600 this way?

Now, it's Chris' money. She's earned it, and she has the right to spend it any way she pleases. That's not the issue. The issue is, do purchases such as these have the value that they should?

If she decides to use her old skis and stay closer to home rather than blowing $2,000 on a fancy vacation, what will she do with the money she saves?

Still More Decisions

Let's look at the question another way. At $30,000 a year, Chris makes $14.42 an hour. (Employees typically work 2,080 hours in a year, so divide 2,080 hours into $30,000 to get the hourly wage.)

When you consider take home pay, that $14.42 becomes $11 an hour. (Take approximately 25 percent off your gross pay to get your net pay. That 25 percent goes to cover taxes and all the other stuff.)

At $11 an hour, Chris will have to work 236 hours to pay for the new skis and the vacation. That's 29.5 workdays, or almost a month and a half. Is that worth the price? Perhaps. Perhaps not.

That's how you determine, in your own mind, if something is worth the price to you.

There was a concert in town. Tickets were $40 each. For two, that's $80. If your take home pay is $10 an hour, you have to work a full day for you and your (spouse, friend, date) to attend. Are you willing to give up a full day's pay for a 3-hour concert? You decide if it represents good value.

You have your eye on that fishing boat, motor and trailer — price tag $6,500. At $10 an hour, you will have to work 650 hours to pay for it. Now, do you really want that boat so badly that you are willing to spend every dollar you bring home for 4 months to pay for it? The price tag for a new hot tub is just about the same.

Ask yourself if you are willing to work a given number of hours, or days, or weeks, or months, for that "thing" you have identified. If so, fine. If, after determining the hours you need to put in to pay for it, you decide it is not a good value, that's fine, too. It's just a process you need to go through before you can make an informed decision.

Pay Now or Pay Later

You may say that you don't need to pay all at once for that boat, hot tub, ski trip, furniture, washer and dryer, or new clothes. If you can find someone who is willing to lend you the money, you can finance your purchases. Then you can repay your debts every month until they are paid off.

Once you find that person (bank, credit card company, finance company, store, parent, friend, employer, other) to lend you the money, you have established credit for yourself. Just because you have access to the money (credit) does not mean you have to use it. If and when you do decide to use the money, it does not mean you have to use every last dollar available to you.

Sally works for a company that has always paid a holiday bonus. For the past 4 years, she received $1,000 on the Friday before Christmas. This past year, in November. Sally went out and spent (charged) some pretty substantial amounts. She planned to use her Christmas bonus to pay everything off. You guessed it. The boss announced that there would be no bonus this year because business was not what it should have been. Now Sally has to scramble. Sally spent money she didn't have.

There's an old cliché. "Don't spend it until you have it in your hand."

Go back to the example of the $2,000 ski trip. Chris is making $11 an hour take home pay. Just the ski trip is going to cost her 181 hours of work if she pays for it all at once.

Well, Chris doesn't have that extra $2,000 sitting in her checking account. And she doesn't want to tap her savings account for it.

So, she decides to finance the trip by taking out a loan. She has decided to take the trip and pay for it over time.

If she puts the $2,000 on her credit card, she will pay interest at an 18 percent annual rate unless she can find a credit card issuer that charges a lower rate. That's $100 a month for two years, for a total of $2,400. Suddenly, the trip has become more expensive. Not only is Chris going to pay an extra $100 out of her discretionary money every month, but she is also going to increase the cost of the trip by $400.

If she goes to her bank or credit union, she will probably be able to get better terms. Still, a 12 percent loan that takes two years to pay off, comes to $94 a month, or $2,256 for the trip, including finance charge.

Consider that Chris has been contributing to her retirement plan since she started working, so she has some savings. And Chris is due to get a raise of $1,500 a year in just a few months because of extra education courses she has taken. Does taking the vacation now and financing it seem more reasonable? As an adult, Chris will decide. It's her money so it's her choice.

Fringe Banking

Not all banking services are available to everyone. Most people consider access to banking services to be a right. The reality is, checking and savings accounts, credit cards, and loans are a privilege. Those who abuse the privilege will find it withdrawn. Those who have no income and bad credit will find that they simply are not desirable customers at mainstream banks and credit unions.

Bill had a history of bad checks, and as a result, his bank closed his checking account. He tried and tried but no other bank or credit union would open an account for him.

Phyllis had no fixed address. Again, no one wanted to establish a bank account for her.

Those who do not have access to banking privileges must resort to "fringe banking." Fringe banking is very expensive. Only resort to fringe banking when you have absolutely no other choice.

What is fringe banking? Having to pay your expenses with money orders, taking your paycheck to a nearby payday check-cashing place and paying the fees they charge — instead of using an ATM at the bank to access your savings or checking, writing post-dated checks or using a pawn shop as you local lender.

Predatory Lending Practices

A trap that too many people fall into is the one set by lenders who resort to predatory lending practices. Don't confuse these bad guys and what they do with traditional lenders who play such an important role in your finances. Traditional lenders charge reasonable interest rates and fees to their customers. They base those rates and fees on your credit standing. Their's is an honest and respectable business.

And then there are predators who charge excessively high interest rates and fees. They get away with it because too many people don't care enough about their finances to bother reading the terms and conditions of loans they take out. These predators often write their loan contracts in such a way as to confuse people as much as possible.

How can you tell the good guys from the bad guys? When someone is trying to charge you 400 percent interest and make you pay 10 percent or more of the loan in fees, flee from their midst. Unfortunately, there are precious few laws protecting consumers from these predatory practices. Your only defense is to learn how to handle your personal finances, something that you will learn as you complete the *Credit When Credit is Due* course.

Summing Up

Reflect on how you have handled your money up to this point in your life. Be honest. Identify those areas that you handle well, those that require immediate change, those that will need attention but are not critical, and those that require only a bit more self-discipline on your part.

Rest assured that you can accomplish your financial goals, that the task is not overwhelming. When you gain control of your finances, credit and debt, and all those other areas of personal money management, you can live your life without money worries. It's a nice way to live.

Of course, you need to live within your means, and you need to budget for unforeseen problems. While you cannot predict with great certainty, you certainly can plan. By budgeting and living within your means, you can ease the everyday problems we all face as we go through life.

Completing all the lessons in this course will help, too. Not only will you gain the knowledge that will help you understand personal finances and to make informed decisions, you will also benefit by qualifying for better interest rates and lower fees on loans you take out later on. Look at the growing list of lenders who are courting graduates of the *Credit When Credit is Due* course. Go to the www.creditwhencreditisdue.com Web site for a listing.

By completing the course, you can add a positive statement to your credit report, free of charge.

If you put into practice the advice offered in *Credit When Credit is Due*, like the tens of thousands who have completed it before you, it is very likely that you will learn to pay your bills on time, take out no more credit than you need, learn to save, learn to budget and learn all those other basics of personal finance. Your reward is that your credit rating will improve, and your access to credit will improve substantially.

LIVING ON THE EDGE

The cold, hard fact is too many people have too much debt and not enough income; consider your own household. A household is defined as an address with somebody living there. It may be a single individual or it could be a family with lots of kids and up to three generations living together. The government says that the average household income is somewhere around $40,000 a year, and that is before taxes are taken out. Can you cover all your bills on what you make? Or do you need more income?

Whatever you earn and whatever your lifestyle, you need enough income to cover your bills. When you have enough money, life is good. When you don't, you worry.

The fact is, too many people don't make enough money to pay their bills, or they make just enough to squeak by, and often that takes two incomes. They are living on the edge, worried about how they will pay their bills. They may wake up in the middle of the night worrying about their jobs, unexpected medical expenses, an upcoming divorce, or just worrying about all sorts of money matters.

They should be concerned. They don't bring home enough money. They have too many expenses. At best they live paycheck to paycheck. They do not plan their money matters, because, they say, what's to plan? They feel they don't make enough money to do more than get by day to day. When a financial emergency strikes, and eventually it always does, they are overwhelmed. They do not have sufficient savings to see them through a financial crisis. They have nowhere to turn. They need help from a reputable non-profit credit counseling agency.

When they lose a job, have their work hours cut, the plant closes for two months, there's a strike, someone in the family gets seriously ill, interest rates go up, gasoline prices soar, the car breaks down, the water heater bursts, there's a divorce, one of the kids needs braces, or any of a dozen other common problems, they have precious few options. They are out of money with a mountain of bills and they fail to seek help until they are too deep in debt.

Carol Lost Her Job, and She Never Saw it Coming

Consider what happened to Carol. She had just graduated from college and landed a job paying $28,000 a year to start, plus a nice package of benefits. It was a business which had been in the community for more than 50 years. Within a week she found herself at the new car lot, anxious to trade in her "red hunk of junk" which had seen her through the last 4 years of school. The price tag for the new car was $28,000. "What the heck," she thought. "I can afford the $489 a month payment over the next 5 years. I'm working now. I don't have to wait."

She was right about one thing. She could afford the car payment, as long **as she kept her job.** She didn't. She didn't do anything wrong. In fact, she was getting along quite well. She thought everything was terrific. Then, 4 months after she began, the owners brought in a new management team. Carol found herself out of work.

Worse than out of work, she found herself without a paycheck. You know what that meant. All of a sudden, Carol had no way to make her car payment. She was too afraid and embarrassed to call and try to work out a solution, something almost every lender will discuss. It was more than a month later when the lender repossessed the car. Carol was on foot.

Carol wasn't a bad person. She meant well but she couldn't pay the bill, and the car was gone. She suffered in other ways too. She found herself without any transportation. (The old car, which was paid for, would have been a godsend but that was gone too. She only got $1,000 for it on the trade in.) She has a "repossession" on her credit report; a black mark almost as bad as a bankruptcy. It's going to be there for years.

She still owes a sizable amount of money on the repossessed car. That's right. She must pay the difference between what the bank eventually sold the car for and what she owed on the loan.

She may have trouble finding another job because of her debt-repayment problem. It is becoming almost standard operating procedure for a prospective employer to run a credit check (with your permission of course) before offering a job to a prospective employee. A bad report will often lead to an immediate rejection of candidates, no matter how well qualified they may be.

Terry Violated the Most Basic Concept of Responsible Money Management

She failed to save for an emergency. Terry thought she had the ideal job. She had a knack for sales. Everyone always told her that she could sell ice cubes in Alaska. The problem was, Terry was paid a commission. Some months were very good and when they were, there was a lot of money. Eight thousand dollars a month covered a lot of bills and left enough extra for a very good time.

But not all months were good. Some were only okay. Those months there was enough money to cover the basics but not much more. Then there were the bad months.

During the very good months Terry spent her money on the things she needed and wanted. That's fine. After all, it was her money. She earned it.

What Terry didn't do was save some of the money she earned during the good times to see her through the bad. Terry hit a string of 5 bad months in a row. She made next to nothing, and she still had bills to pay.

So Terry used her credit cards to take cash advances. She used the money just like a commission check. She justified her actions saying, "I'll pay the credit cards back when business gets better. This happens to everybody sometime. I know lots of people who do this."

Business did get better and Terry did make payments on the credit cards. But she didn't make full payments.

And she still didn't save for the next slow period.

It was inevitable. When the next slow time hit, Terry did not have enough income to meet her regular monthly bills and she had no more room to borrow on her credit cards. Unless Terry learns how to save during the good months and also cut back on some spending, she is headed for the bankruptcy court. It is only a matter of time.

Tim Always Wanted to be a Teacher, but the Pay Doesn't Allow Him to Achieve the Lifestyle He Wants

Ever since Tim could remember, he wanted to be a teacher. In college, he majored in Elementary Education. He graduated, got his teaching certificate, and within a couple of months landed a job teaching 5th grade.

Then reality set in. Tim was told the starting salary was $23,000 a year plus benefits. He realized that at $23,000 a year he would not be able to live without a roommate, buy a new car, and afford some of the things he was looking forward to, like traveling and eating out. Tim realized he was going to have to get a second job and also work during the summer months just to make ends meet. To add insult to injury, Tim graduated with $40,000 in student loans he needs to repay.

Tim should have asked how much he could earn as a teacher before investing time and money becoming one. If you are thinking of any profession, you should look into how well or poorly it pays. While Tim's teaching salary was enough to cover most necessities, it was not nearly enough to cover things that he felt he wanted.

Tim has to make some tough choices. He can take part-time work to supplement his income so he can afford those things he wants. He can switch to a career that offers more pay. Or he can stay in a job that he truly enjoys but cut back on his expectations.

There are a lot of occupations and professions that are personally rewarding and fulfilling. The harsh reality is many of them do not pay as much as they should. The bottom line is this — you should know what a career is likely to pay before you pursue it.

Some people keep score based on how much money they make. Others use a different measure. Today's corporate executive earns well over $100,000 a year but spends at least 52 hours a week on the job and will have to move the family at least 3 times during his or her career. If that's for you, so be it. Others are very happy earning $23,000 a year to start teaching the 5th grade.

You Will Face Hard Times Sometime During Your Life

Everyone does. How well you weather the storm of a job loss, or other interruption of your income will be determined by how well or how poorly you plan.

Carol got excited. She had worked hard in school. She landed the job she had wanted. The pay was good. Her prospects were bright. Why not buy that car? She soon learned why she should have waited.

What should she have done besides contact the lender and try to work out an arrangement so she wouldn't have lost her car? How about waiting until she had saved some money to help her through an emergency? By having an emergency fund, also called a savings account, Carol could have kept her car and weathered her emergency.

Terry needed $4,000 a month to cover her basic living expenses. When she was earning $8,000 during a great month, she didn't save a dime. Instead she spent it, and was left high and dry when she really needed the money.

Tim chose a personally rewarding occupation that doesn't pay very well. Either someone should have told Tim what teachers earn or he should have taken it upon himself to find out before he invested so much time, effort and money into becoming one. It's not that teaching is a bad deal; it's a fine and honorable profession. It just doesn't pay very well. If luxuries are important, then find an occupation that pays enough so you can afford them.

More Fallout During Hard Times

When hard times hit, people fall behind on their payments. As you might expect, late and missed payments are reported by many creditors to the credit bureau. This information becomes available not only to existing creditors (who may want to tighten up on the amount of credit they make available) but also to future creditors.

The black mark of late payments and non-payments can stay on your credit record for years, making your future access to reasonably priced credit all that more difficult.

A credit report that carries with it a high score (this is explained in some detail in lesson 12) is something of great value. It can take you years to get to the point that your credit report is a source of pride.

By paying your bills on time, month after month, year after year, you build a positive credit report. And then, just like that, you can destroy what has taken years to build. A job loss with the corresponding interruption in pay can mean late payments and a devastating impact on your credit report. Years of making your payments on time will be lost. Just a few months of late payments can mean years of trying (often in vain) to reestablish credit.

Even in the worst of financial times, do not even consider writing bad checks. In some states, you can be sent to jail for years for passing bad checks. Yes, it is that serious an offense.

The fees, fines and penalties associated with bad checks are prohibitively expensive. Write a check for $35 that bounces and you could face hundreds of dollars in bank and other fees.

Perhaps most important from a long-range point of view, those who demonstrate that they are unable to handle the responsibilities of a checking account will find that the privilege of a checking account will be denied to them. That's right. Banks and credit unions have access to a national registry of those who have abused their checking accounts in the past. Show up in a lobby and ask to open a new account, and the clerk will check to see if your name (and social security number) appear on this "do not open a new account for these people" list. If it does, you will be told (perhaps not so politely) to take your business elsewhere.

Functioning in today's financial world without access to a checking account is truly living on the edge.

Saving for that proverbial rainy day is not just an old cliche. It's a necessary fact of financial life, unless you enjoy living on the edge.

The Real Reason You Must Keep a Budget

You know that you need to work within a budget. You also know you probably won't do it. There are so many things that you would like to do that are much more enjoyable. Budgets are boring and restrictive; budgets tell you that you can't spend money on this and you have to save money for that. It doesn't have to be that way.

The reason you budget is so you can get the things you want. Of course, you have to actually have some goals. What are your dreams, goals, priorities? Do you want to go on a cruise? Maybe you want to buy a house. Maybe your dream is as simple as getting a new set of golf clubs. Maybe it's as big as getting and staying out of debt. Maybe you want to quit work and raise a family.

Whatever your goals, write them down on a piece of paper and carry it with you wherever you go. It will serve to remind you of your priorities when you are tempted to buy something that may seem important at the moment but will delay the achievement of your dreams.

Debbie wants to go to Scotland. She figures it will cost $5,000 for her and her husband to go for 3 weeks. She has checked with a travel agent and has figured out where they will stay. She has everything but the money. So, Debbie wrote her dream down on paper and posted copies in various places. She has cut back on Christmas presents. She canceled her magazine subscriptions. Instead she now goes to the library. She gave up sodas and is putting $1.50 into her Scotland fund every day. Within one year, Debbie was half-way there. She is so confident that she will have her money that she has gone ahead and made reservations for next year.

There are immediate goals and there are long-term goals. You may want that new television. You may want to buy a house. What are your immediate goals as compared with your 5-year goals?

Most people can, and will live within the constraints of a budget if they can see the result. People don't like to make sacrifices simply because they know they should. They will, however, make sacrifices when they see that the sacrifices will get them what they want.

How Much Money Do You Make, and How Much Money Do You Spend?

The sad truth is that many people don't have any idea how much money comes in, how much goes out, and where it goes. If you don't know (and chances are you don't), you need to find out, because the answers to these three basic questions determine whether or not you will succeed in handling your personal finances.

Start at the beginning. How much money do you bring in from all sources? Consider the following:

- Salary from your job. There may be overtime, or a year-end bonus.

- Alimony or child support in case of a divorce.

- Money from a parent or someone else.

- Interest from a savings account.

- Investments. That means dividends and capital gains income.

- Income from a trust thanks to a far-sighted parent or grandparent.

- A small business that generates extra income.

- Pension income if you are retired.

If you have a checking account, **go through your checkbook register for a year and note the source of each deposit.** You may be pleasantly surprised at the various sources of income you have.

Whatever your monthly income, and whatever source it comes from, you need to know the amount. You need to know the various sources and at what time during the month the cash comes in.

You don't need to shout aloud the amount of money you make, but just so you become familiar with "the number," write it down. You don't have to show it to anyone. Writing down your monthly income will help you keep track of how much money you have.

When asked what they make, most people immediately think of what is known as **gross income. Gross income is the amount you make before any deductions are taken out to pay for taxes and benefits.**

Say you were hired at $22,880 a year. If asked what you make, the answer is $22,880 a year. It is not the amount you take home and spend on your bills.

What you earn is not what you receive in your paycheck. That's because of withholding for federal income tax (about 15 percent of your pay), state income tax (in those states which have an income tax), social security (6.20 percent of pay), Medicare (1.45 percent), employee's share of health insurance (which may be a hundred dollars a month or more), employee's share of retirement plan contributions (say 5 percent), and so on. The amount that is left over is your **net income**, or take-home pay.

What you earn is not the amount which you can apply to your bills, unless, of course, you consider social security, Medicare, and other taxes, along with other expenses to be part of your monthly expenses. After all is said and done, **you probably take home somewhere between 70 and 80 percent of your gross income.**

Take a look at your latest pay stub. Review each item. It will tell you the amount of your gross income. Then look at all that money withheld from your pay for various reasons — social security tax, Medicare tax, health Insurance, and retirement. Finally, see what is actually paid to you. Don't get angry and don't let it get you down when you see how much is withheld.

Withholding is just a fact of life and so is the fact that you don't get to spend everything you earn. You can only spend what you get in your check.

You've already written down the amount you make. Now write down the amount you deposit into your checking and savings accounts each month. These are the numbers you have to keep in mind.

What are you spending? As vague as most people are about what they make and bring home, they have even less of an idea of how much they spend.

Try this. What do you think you spend on a monthly basis? Don't check. Don't go through any papers. Don't search your memory for the amount of the rent and other bills. Just, off the cuff, estimate what you think you pay out each month and write it down on that same piece of paper that you've been using.

Now that you have estimated your spending, check it out. You may be shocked at what you find. Get out your checkbook and from the first day through the last day of a month total the amount of the checks you have written. Try it for three or four months and take an average.

Finally, compare what you've been spending each month against your take-home income. Also, compare the amount you actually spend to what you thought you were spending. How do you come out?

YOUR MONTHLY BUDGET

INCOME:
  Salary #1   _____
  Salary #2   _____
  Child support/alimony   _____
  Other income   _____

TOTAL INCOME   _____

EXPENSES:
  Fixed expenses
       Savings   _____
       Rent or mortgage   _____
       Car payment   _____
       Insurance payment   _____
       Child support/alimony   _____
       Child care   _____
       Student loans   _____
       Cable TV   _____
       Health club   _____
       Other   _____

  Flexible expenses
       Food   _____
       Utilities   _____
       Telephone   _____
       Clothing   _____
       Gasoline   _____
       Car maintenance   _____
       Doctor/dentist   _____
       Medicine   _____
       Home maintenance   _____
       Contributions   _____
       Hobbies   _____
       Laundry/dry cleaning   _____
       Pet care   _____
       Hair care   _____
       Vacations   _____
       Other flexible expenses   _____

TOTAL EXPENSES   _____

NET PROFIT OR LOSS FOR THE MONTH   _____

Step 1: Budgeting Made Easy

You are going to set up a budget for you and your household, so you will know what you are making, what you are spending, and what you are likely to make and spend next month and the month after that. Remember that you are doing this so you can get closer to your dreams. You are going to do the same thing that all businesses do every year.

You'll need a couple of things. Get a loose-leaf notebook and some paper, a pen or pencil and a hand-held calculator. You will need your checkbook register for the past six months and your credit card statements.

In this age of computers, you may want to do your budgeting work with a computer program. However, paper and pencil will do just fine.

At the top of the page, write down the month you are going to check.

Let's start with your income. Make a heading marked "**INCOME**." Under it, write "**Salary**" and then list each additional source of income you regularly receive. Then, go through your checkbook register and write down the date and amount of each deposit. When you come to the end of the month, strike a total. That was easy enough.

Next come your "**EXPENSES**."

Make two headings. One is "**FIXED EXPENSES**." The other is "**FLEXIBLE EXPENSES**." Before you write anything else, take a glance through your checkbook register for the month and see what you wrote checks for. Then write down your categories under the appropriate **FIXED** or **FLEXIBLE EXPENSE** headings. You'll have listings for **FIXED EXPENSES** for the rent or mortgage, car payment, and insurance premiums. A listing for savings should be under **FIXED EXPENSES**. Under **FLEXIBLE EXPENSES**, you will have your utilities (electric, gas, water, trash, telephone), food, cleaning, clothing, gasoline, and the like.

Then, starting at the first of the month, write down the amount of each check you spent in each category.

There's a wrinkle you should keep in mind. Most people these days have a credit card or two, or more. When it comes to listing your monthly expenses, don't list items such as Texaco. Instead, list what the purchases went for. In this case, write down gasoline. Don't say Penney's, Walmart or Dayton's. Say clothing, household, gifts, or whatever a particular purchase was for.

Never use headings like VISA or MasterCard. Instead, go through the monthly itemized statement and break down each expense. You'll have items like clothing, finance charges, medical expenses (prescriptions), household expenses, and the like.

If you use the name of the credit card as the expense, you are hiding where the money is actually going. The charges that appear on your VISA card will be for a wide variety of expenses. The same is true for charges to your Sears card. Even gasoline cards may be for more than fuel as people purchase all sorts of convenience items.

If you don't pay off a charge card in full, categorize your purchases and include them in your expenses for the month. Don't forget to include the finance charge. After all, that's what you spent. When you're done reviewing all your checks and credit card purchases, strike a total for each category. Then total your spending.

Finally compare your spending to your income. Hopefully, your income exceeds your expenses. If not, don't despair. There are ways to resolve the problem and still keep you on track to achieving your dreams, but you will have to change the way you spend your money.

Step 2: The Real Budgeting Process Begins

After you have become familiar with your spending habits and patterns, you should have a pretty good idea of what money you have to spend and where it goes. By going through the past 6 months of your checkbook register and credit card statements, you probably know more about yourself than you have for some time. If you are married and your spouse has been the one handling the checking account, you probably have had a real eye-opening experience. All that was history.

Budgeting is about the future. You think you know what will be coming in, and you probably have a pretty good idea of what will be going out. Thinking you know isn't good enough. You have to put it on paper.

Get out your budget book and a fresh sheet of paper.

At the top, put the name of the upcoming month. Under "**INCOME**," write down what you anticipate receiving. Under "**EXPENSES**," write down each of your expense categories, and beside each one, what you think you will be spending. Again, add up your totals.

If you will be making more than you will be spending, great. On the other hand, if you will be spending more than you make, you will have to find some savings somewhere, so you won't be living on the edge.

The Budget Process is Continuous and Ongoing

Budgeting needs to become a habit. You probably pay your bills twice a month. As the month progresses, you need to compare income and expense projections with actual income and expenses and see how they stack up. It's better to know than to be surprised. It gives you time to find solutions to problems before they get out of hand.

The reality is, there are always surprises, and those surprises can destroy a budget, such as an unexpected visit to the doctor or a mishap with the car. You name it.

Budgeting is more than simply recording your income and expenses on paper. For the budgeting process to work, you need to refer to and adjust your budget on a regular basis. You need to know how much you have budgeted for certain expenses, and you need to know how much more you can spend on a budget item if needed.

Make Savings a Part of Your Budget

Experts are unanimous when they say that the first check you write every month should be to your savings account. While it may not be the first check (the rent and car payments usually take priority), a check to your savings account should be written each and every payday.

Even when money is tight (and money is always tight), you can probably find $10 to salt away. It may mean that you deny yourself a pack of cigarettes, a soft drink, magazine, or something that by itself doesn't cost much, but over the course of a month it can mean the difference between having something to save and having absolutely nothing to show for the month.

For example, at 50 cents for a bottle of soda, you could save over $182 a year. If you don't believe it, multiply it for yourself. Take 50 cents a bottle and multiply it by 365 days in a year and it comes to $182.50.

Think what you could save on magazine subscriptions. A magazine subscription may come to $35 a year, a magazine that you may not even read, and certainly one that is available free at the library. Forego a pack of cigarettes every day and you will save more than $1,000 a year.

There's a wonderful little book called *The Richest Man In Babylon*. Most libraries have a copy. In it, the author tells wonderful stories that show people how to save and how savings can mount up over time.

He points out that if you save 10 percent of your (take-home) pay each year for 10 years, you will have accumulated an entire year's income; considerably more if you count the interest you will collect over that time. That may seem obvious, but just think what you might do with a full year's salary to do with as you please.

Save early and save often. Even $10 a month is something. When calamities like those that befell Carol and Terry strike, you will have savings to fall back on.

Also remember that it is your savings that will help you reach your financial goals. Again the experts have found that once you have some money in savings, you will probably guard your nest egg. You will do without in order to keep it. You will like the peace of mind that a savings account brings.

There are all sorts of savings accounts. The most basic is the good old-fashioned savings account. It doesn't pay much interest but it's available at a moment's notice.

There's the more modern day money market account. All the financial institutions have them. The interest rates are often higher than a regular savings account. If that's more your style, fine. It's still a savings account. The money is still available to you at a moment's notice.

How Much Should You Have in Savings

Years ago, the standard advice was you should have enough money in your savings account to cover 6 months worth of your expenses. With incomes and expenses reaching higher and higher levels, that amount became too high for most people to reach. If you're making $40,000 a year, for example, and spending the same, you would need $20,000 in savings. For most people, that was just unobtainable. So, conventional wisdom was revised downward to say you should have 3 months worth of savings to cover your expenses.

Today, some say even that standard is too high. They say that all you need to do is be able to borrow three months' living expenses; that way, you don't have to actually put anything away. That is terrible advice. How can you expect to borrow money when you are out of work?

Can you imagine being out of a job, no savings to fall back on, no income on the horizon, and borrowing money, probably on high interest credit cards to make ends meet? No, it's better to have that nest egg set aside, available to you at a moment's notice, just in case. How much should you save? Two month's worth of expenses is probably not quite enough, but it's a goal. And if and when needed, it will be of immeasurable help. Three months is better.

Not All Savings Accounts Are Alike

In this day of 401(k)s, IRA's and the rest of the alphabet soup of retirement plans, most workers have started a retirement savings account, and that's good. The longer you work, the more likely you will have some company-sponsored savings/retirement plan. This is not the kind of savings account used to cover emergencies like unemployment, medical emergencies, and so on. That's separate. These work-related accounts are not easily accessed.

In addition to your retirement savings, you need to have access to your personal emergency fund. If you don't have one, start one just as soon as you can.

Keeping Up With the Joneses

Want to know how your neighbors spend their money? There are ratios financial people look at when they consider loan applications. For example, if you want to buy a house, chances are you're going to need a mortgage loan. A potential lender is going to look at your monthly income, and is not going to want you to spend more than

28 to 31 percent of your income on your housing expenses. They check how much you make and see if you can afford the mortgage, using that 28 to 31 percent figure as the rule of thumb.

So, the Joneses and your neighbors, according to the statistics people, are spending about:

- 30 percent of their income on housing;

- 20 percent on transportation;

- 7 percent on entertainment;

- 15 percent on food (at home and out);

- 6 percent on clothing;

- 6 percent on health care;

- 16 percent on all the other stuff that comes up. 16 percent to cover cable, haircuts, dry cleaning, and all the other stuff. No wonder people are stretched.

There are 2 more points here. When looking at that mortgage loan, they don't want your monthly payment to be more than 30 percent or so of your income. In addition, they don't want your housing expenses and your other monthly debt repayment to exceed 40 percent. That's important when you have a car payment, bills for appliances and credit card balances.

When you look at all these expenses, you'll see they add up to 100 percent. The Joneses aren't saving. Since you know everyone should save and should contribute to savings on a regular basis, the money is going to have to come from among these categories. Perhaps the Joneses don't have any savings. Perhaps they spend everything they make. Perhaps the Joneses are living on the edge.

Fine-Tuning and Plugging Spending Leaks

Very few people are disciplined enough to follow their budgets down to the last penny. When they try, they become discouraged and sooner or later they quit. In fact, budgets shouldn't be that restrictive, and they are not when you are budgeting so you can achieve your goals. You may want to round your income and expenses to the nearest $10 just to make your budget more manageable. On the other hand, when you have a $30,000 a year income, you can lose a lot of $10's.

Now that you have seen how much money is coming in and where it's going, you are going to have to do some fine-tuning. Then you're going to have to plug some leaks.

First, **fine-tuning**. It's not terribly difficult to remember you have to pay the rent or mortgage each month. Same for your utility bills, telephone, student loan, and other regular expenses you have. These are needs and must be covered before you think about anything else.

What is more difficult to remember is that it's likely that you will have a few bills to pay that show up infrequently, perhaps only once or twice a year.

For example some people pay their car insurance every month while others choose to pay every 3 or 6 months. For homeowners insurance, you can pay annually and save on the charge, or pay more frequently.

Three of the biggest off-budget expenses families have show up once a year. One is the Christmas holiday. The second is birthdays and anniversaries. The third is the family vacation.

All too often, spending on Christmas can get out of hand. When you add everything that you spend on presents, travel, mailing, the tree, decorations, extra food and drink, cards and postage, you may set yourself back many thousands of dollars. No one is saying that you shouldn't celebrate the holiday. Just be aware of what it is setting you back, and budget for it.

Birthdays, anniversaries, weddings and other special days require presents, visits, long distance calls. Plan for those, and include the cost of postage, gift-wrap, etc.

The final sizable, one-time annual event can be the family or personal vacation. While it can be enjoyable to travel, it can also be very expensive. Just budget for it.

That's the fine tuning you need to make to your monthly budgeted income and expenses.

After checking your monthly income and your budgeted expenses, chances are all too high that you are not going to have the money to meet all your bills. Now what?

Step 3: Plug Your Spending Leaks

What do you mean we can't afford it? You get everything you want. Why can't I get a few of the things I want? I deserve it. I certainly work hard enough.

Sound familiar? It should. It's not what you may or may not deserve, rather, it is simply a matter of what you can afford.

Jim and Kim had been married for 4 years. Both were in their 20s. Both worked, earning a combined family income over $60,000. They didn't have any children, yet, but they planned to in a couple of years. They bought their first home a year ago. After moving from the apartment to the house, they spent a lot of money on fixing up the place, buying new furniture, paint, lawn mower, and more. They joked that the great big sucking sound they heard was the house taking their money.

If they think a house takes a lot of unbudgeted money, just wait until they have a family. There's no question that kids are expensive. Added to the cost of the house and the children is the fact that they may lose one of the incomes when they start a family.

They joked about their spending and what it was costing them to live, but it really wasn't funny.

Before they purchased the house, they didn't give much thought to how they spent their money. They ate out a lot. When they wanted new clothes, they bought them. They were generous with their presents to others.

After moving into the house, money got tight and they started to fight about money. She got her hair done. He played golf and bought new clubs. She went on a shopping trip with some girl friends. He sent a gift to his sister for her birthday.

They kept the same spending patterns that they had when they lived in the apartment. But now, because of the cost of maintaining the house, they didn't have as much discretionary income as they did before. Still they continued to spend.

To help maintain their old apartment-living lifestyle, they turned to their credit cards. Over a 2-year period they went from almost no credit card debt to over $15,000. Then the fighting started about who was being irresponsible about money. The answer is, they both were.

But arguing wasn't the answer. Budgeting was. They needed to learn to adapt their spending to their income.

When you laid out the expenses you have every month as well as those which show up every once in a while, you probably didn't give much thought to the necessity of each of those expense categories. You just wrote them down.

Go back to your list of what you spend each month and mark each item as either a "need" or a "want".

A "need" is an absolute necessity. It's something you cannot do without. It's something that if you didn't have, you couldn't make it in this world of ours. Include here things like your rent or mortgage, food, utilities, telephone, car insurance, car and home maintenance. You get the idea.

A "want" is something that is nice to have but is not a necessity of life. A "want" may look like a "need," but you will be able to tell the difference. A new golf club is a "want." So is going to the hairdresser. Membership in a health club is a "want."

Now, recalculate your monthly budget. First, compare your income to your "needs." Then, compare what's left over to your "wants." The line between a "want" and a "need" can blur.

Take the young working couple who go to buy their first car. They want something sleek and sporty. Invariably they buy a 2-door model. A year or so later, they are back at the same dealership, trading that car for a more practical 4-door model now that they are having their first child. Did they anticipate having a family? Probably. Should they have opted for the more practical car in the first place and saved themselves a lot of money? Certainly.

Mark and Cathy used to have money problems and it took them a long time and a great deal of effort to resolve them. They have an agreement. They promise each other that before they will purchase anything that costs $100 or more, they will give themselves 3 days to think about it before they actually make the purchase. They promise that they will discuss the purchase, whether they need it or simply want it, and whether it is worth the price. Then, in 3 days, if they both still agree to buy it, they go ahead. If they don't agree, they don't buy it. They both have developed a healthy money habit.

Your needs come first. If there's enough money left over after contributing to your savings so you can have your dreams, then you can spend your money on your wants.

Review your "wants" and your "needs" list at least once every 6 months just to make sure that those "wants" don't sneak into the "needs" column.

Earlier there were examples of spending leaks. You can save a few bucks here and there by giving up a pack of cigarettes, a bottle of soda or a magazine.

There are other ways to save, too. The list is almost endless. But if you are having trouble making ends meet, if you have too many needs for your income, if there are some things that you want but can't afford, cheer up. There are always ways to cut expenses so you can afford other things.

All you have to do is be creative.

John Took Coupon-Clipping to a New Level

John had retired early. He didn't have terribly high money needs. He had a government pension and that was enough for him, his wife, and young daughter. Once retired, John discovered a passion. He made it his personal goal to feed the household on less than $25 a week.

How? Easy, according to John. He became an expert at clipping coupons. He found double and triple coupons. He found sales. He found money-back coupons. John actually was able to go to some grocery stores and walk out with a basket full of food, having paid as little as $5. It became a game, a money-saving game, to be sure. It also allowed John and his family to spend their money on other things. It was money they would not have had if they had spent it at the grocery store.

There are lots of creative ways to reduce your spending. Coupon clipping is only one.

You can save money by conserving energy. Turn off that light when you leave a room. The bulb will last longer and you'll pay less for electricity.

Insulate your home.

Tune your car. Keep your tires properly inflated. You'll use less gas.

Drive that car until the wheels fall off. Remember, cars last longer these days, and whether you believe it or not, it is usually much less costly to repair an old one than it is to make monthly payments for the next 5 years.

Barb is still driving her 1990 Toyota van with 152,000 miles on it and a rebuilt engine. Recently she took it in for $575 worth of brakes and other work. Her co-workers wanted to know why she was pouring money into a vehicle that old and with that many miles instead of buying a new one. "You're just pouring money down the drain," they said. She replied, "One bill for $575 is a whole lot better than $400 for 60 months." People wrongly assume that everyone always has a car payment.

Tim has been paying on his truck for 3 years, 8 months. In 4 more months, it's going to be paid off. Tim is already checking out new trucks. When asked why he was looking for a new truck, he said that when the old one was paid off it was time to get a new one. He didn't understand that it was okay to pay off the truck and then drive it for a few more years. If he did that and saved what he was paying on the truck every month, he could buy the new one for cash and avoid all those interest charges.

Select a car that gives you good fuel economy as well as one that is relatively inexpensive to insure. When it comes to car insurance, select higher deductibles for collision and comprehensive coverage; you'll pay less.

If you pay for your own health insurance, select a high deductible, so you can save on your premium. Of course you have to be able to afford the high deductible, so put the amount you save on the premium in your own savings.

Stay healthy. Adopt good health practices. Avoid smoking and excessive drinking. Medical costs will bust almost any budget so avoiding unnecessary health care expenses will certainly help. Get a flu shot. It's better than missing work.

Avoid costly vacations. You would be surprised at what you can do for family recreation that is really inexpensive. A fancy cruise or a week's skiing in the Rockies is nice but there are enjoyable things to do closer to home and at a fraction of the price. Day trips, hikes, special days at home, short visits are all enjoyable and much less expensive than that cruise.

Do your own ironing. Eat in. Drop cable TV. Read a book from the library. Buy quality, basic clothing; avoid trendy fashions. Eliminate the cell phone. Write letters rather than making long distance telephone calls. Buy phone cards. Cut out long distance calls.

How many more money-saving ideas can you come up with? By adopting some of these ideas and finding others, you will be plugging spending leaks so that you can balance your monthly budget and at the same time treat yourself to some of those things you want but are having trouble finding the money to pay for.

Buy Now and Pay Later or Save Now and Buy Later

That's the decision you are required to make almost every day of your adult life.

You don't have to deny yourself much of anything these days especially if you have a job, because, if you're working, you're probably a good credit risk. Credit card companies will overstuff your mailbox with offers of easy credit.

Want those new clothes? Charge them. Feel a need for a long-overdue vacation? Enjoy yourself. Just put it on your credit card. Don't feel like cooking or grocery shopping? Go out on the town. Charge your meals. Tired of that old furniture? Use the convenient store financing where you buy now and pay no interest for a year. Need money to pay your taxes? Take out a loan.

Notice the "buy now, pay later" theme. It is really "buy now and you will pay more later!"

It seems it is all too easy for you to have most anything

you want. All you have to do is whip out that old credit card, and charge it. Some credit card issuers have made credit so easy that people are charging automobiles to their cards. Credit limits of over $25,000 are not the least bit uncommon. Of course, when you use credit, you have an obligation to repay what you borrow.

When you finance furniture or appliances or a car, or something else that is tangible, at least you have something to show for it. When you finance meals, entertainment, vacations and the like, the good times are gone, and all you have left is the bill.

One father gave his adult children the following advice about the proper use of credit cards. He said, "If you can eat it, drink it, or smoke it, don't charge it." Makes sense.

Now, there's nothing wrong with the intelligent use of credit and credit cards. Credit cards provide you with valuable protections that are not available to consumers who pay cash for their purchases, especially when it comes to catalog purchases. The fact is, of the millions of credit card users in America today, fully 1 out of 3 pay their balances in full each and every month. And millions more carry small balances for only a month or so. Good for them.

It is the other two-thirds who carry those balances forward month after month after month who have a heavy debt burden to repay. And, of course, they have to pay a price for the debt they have taken on. It's called interest or finance charges. So, they not only have to repay the debt, but they have to pay interest, too.

Lori Had a Choice to Make

She had her eye on a washer and dryer and a refrigerator/freezer. She and her husband, Dennis, had talked about it but $2,000 seemed more than they could comfortably afford. Then the new credit card offer arrived in the mail. Just sign up, it said, and we'll send you our credit card with a credit limit of $2,500. All of a sudden those appliances seemed much more affordable. Lori made her choice. She felt she could afford the appliances because all she had to do was put them on the card, and then make minimum payments of $40 a month (that's 2 percent) until they could afford to pay more.

When you make a minimum 2 percent monthly pay-

ment on a credit card that is charging you 18 percent annual interest, it is going to take you more than 30 years to pay what you owe. Looking at it that way, it doesn't seem like all that good an idea.

In reality, Lori has at least 4 choices.

1. She can purchase the appliances now and pay for them over a period of years, and pay the interest charged on the credit card.

2. She can save some money to use as a down payment and finance the rest, paying less interest.

3. She can save until she can purchase the appliances for cash and avoid all finance charges.

4. She can buy a used or scratched model at a substantial savings.

What would you advise her to do? What would you do? Are these appliances Lori's dream?

Summing Up

When you develop healthy money habits, you will no longer be living on the edge. No one cares how you spend your money, just as long as you pay your bills. No one cares if you spend your money on frivolous fashions, glitzy vacations, jewelry, or a membership in an exclusive wine-tasting club, just as long as you pay your own way.

You know you have developed healthy money habits when you know how much money you make, how much money you bring home, how much money you must earn every month to cover your "needs," and how much money you need every month to cover your "wants."

You know you have developed healthy money habits when you save each month, when you make a budget projection for the current and next month and stick to it.

You know you have developed healthy money habits when you refuse to spend money on something that you didn't budget for.

You know you have developed healthy money habits when you will forego purchasing something right now on credit, deciding instead to save the money.

(Rev. September 2002)

TO BORROW OR NOT TO BORROW

That is the question. It is a far, far nobler thing you do when you ask yourself before you make a purchase if you really want or need to borrow money to pay for it.

There is an essential lesson to learn in this chapter. **Before you make a purchase, any purchase, large or small, you need to ask yourself if you will pay for it with cash from your wallet, checkbook or savings account, or if you will charge or finance your purchase and pay for it over the next few months or years.** The problem is, too many people fail to consciously ask and then answer the question of "cash or charge." You need to make it second nature to ask yourself this question before each and every purchase you make, whether it's chewing gum at the grocery store, a can of soda at work, or a new car at the local dealership.

There Are Two Types of Purchases — the Everyday Checkbook Variety and The Big Stuff That Doesn't Come Along Very Often

Let's get the big stuff out of the way first.

Certainly, there are at least 2 items, perhaps 3, that you will probably purchase during your lifetime where you have no choice but to take out loans. They include buying a house, buying a car, and if you choose, attending college. The costs of these items are simply too high for most people to cover with their savings.

Even modest housing can cost upwards of $100,000 or more, and in some areas of the country (like San Francisco and Hawaii) that starter home will set you back over $200,000. Almost no one has enough money in savings to be able to pay cash for their house. No one expects you to. You will, most likely, visit with a mortgage lender and arrange for a loan that can take up to 30 years to repay, assuming of course that you have good credit references, a favorable job outlook, and modest bills in relation to your income. (You will find more on mortgages in a later lesson.)

Cars are a different story, but not by much. Some people, but not many, save enough money to pay for their cars. There are fewer and fewer people every year who can manage it now that the average price of a new vehicle exceeds $22,000. If you're buying a new car, it's typical for you to take out a 3 to 5 year loan. Some lenders are even going to 6- or 7-year loans in an effort to keep monthly payments affordable. If you take out a loan for that length of time, make sure you are confident that the vehicle will last as long as your payments. Otherwise, you could be paying for a car that is sitting in the junk yard.

Of course, there's the option of leasing a car instead of buying it. But the reality is, you're still making those monthly payments and you better be able to afford them.

Used vehicles are usually less expensive than new. Still, they can cost tens of thousands of dollars. For used cars, loans will run for a shorter period of time, but you still have to be able to afford the monthly payments.

The cost of a college education can cost almost as much as a house. It is not the least bit unusual for a student to graduate with a degree that costs well over $50,000. Only the wealthy can afford to attend college without some sort of financial assistance. These days, that assistance is usually in the form of student loans which will eventually have to be repaid over the 10 years after you leave school.

The cost of attending a state supported college or university is significantly less than what the Ivy League schools charge. Harvard and Yale will set you back over $30,000 a year. Even a state-run school will cost at least $10,000 when you include tuition, room, board and all the other expenses associated with attending.

You take out house, car and college loans out of necessity, not out of choice. It's just that simple.

As for your everyday purchases, you might refer to them as your checkbook items. You buy food, clothes, prescriptions, gasoline, the health club membership, soft drinks. The list is almost endless. For your everyday purchases, you have two ways of paying. You can pay cash (or check), or with a credit card, assuming you have access to one.

There are a lot of purchases where you pay cash and don't even think about charging them. The standard method of paying the telephone bill, utilities, and similar everyday bills is with cash or check, not credit card. However, more and more of these purchases will be made with a credit card in the future. Grocery stores accept credit cards. Utilities are also starting to accept credit card payments.

The question of cash or charge applies to almost everything you purchase.

When you use a credit card, remember that you are taking out a loan. It is just like approaching a loan officer at a financial organization and asking for money so you can eat out at that restaurant, or attend a concert, or buy those clothes.

Of course you wouldn't do something like that. But that's the way you need to think.

If you wouldn't go to a lender and ask for money to make a purchase, don't put it on your credit card. Pay cash instead.

When you charge a purchase, it does not mean you do not have to pay. Everybody knows that.

Charging simply means you do not have to pay immediately. You are only putting off the inevitable. Charging your purchase also means that you will have to pay interest, sometimes a sizable amount, to a lender for the privilege of using the lender's money.

Charging Purchases Can Lead to Impulse Buying

Charging is easy, and because it's easy you can be lulled into impulse buying. There's no other way to put it. It can happen to anyone. Advertising and marketing experts are good at getting people to buy things they probably don't need and sometimes don't even want. Remember the pet rock? Are you tempted to buy one of those sensational newspapers at the check out stand?

Later in this lesson, you will meet Jennifer and Steve, a young couple who have charged themselves into a financial hole. They have accumulated more than $20,000 in credit card debt over a period of 5 years and they are having a problem paying it off. When asked what they bought, they confessed that they didn't know. "It was this and that. We charged meals, and tickets to shows, and shoes, and clothes and all the regular stuff." The point is, after their 5 year buying spree they have next to nothing to show for the money, and they have a long road to travel before it will be repaid.

Charging a purchase that you need with a credit card is one thing. Charging impulse items is something else. No one says you have to deny yourself those things in life that you want and enjoy. Just pay for them in full with cash or when the credit card bill arrives. Avoid financing purchases that you should pay for with cash.

Charging "Needs" Can Lead to Trouble, Too

There are those people who have vowed to use their credit cards only in case of emergencies. The hot water heater goes out. The car has to have new brakes and tires. You take an emergency flight home to visit a dying relative. These are just three examples that credit counselors hear repeatedly. So, people pull out that credit card and charge a new water heater, the car repair bill, or the airline ticket. And then the bill comes in. They end up paying on that bill for the next 5 years.

The point is that access to that emergency credit account can lead to problems. Years ago, if the water heater went out and the person did not have access to credit, he or she went out and got a part-time, second job to generate enough cash to cover the emergency. Now, it goes on the credit card.

The Benefits of Charging Your Purchases

There can be definite advantages and protections when you charge your purchases. This is especially true when you purchase through mail order and use a credit card for payment. When you pay with cash and there is a problem with the merchandise, you have precious few options available to you to resolve your dispute other than the good will of the merchant. If you use a credit card, you have the right to return your purchase within a given amount of time. You can lodge a complaint which will, in most instances, be honored by the credit card company.

An alternative to the credit card would be the debit card. When you use a debit card, the amount of your purchase comes directly out of your checkbook. Nevertheless, you retain the same safeguards and consumer protections that you have when you use a credit card.

A Good Example to Follow

Bill and Carol had always made it a practice to pay their credit card balance in full every month. Every once in a while, it was more than they could comfortably afford, but when that happened, they always were able to bring the balance down to zero within 2 months. One month, Bill casually asked Carol how much she had charged during the month. Carol went to her purse, pulled out a little note pad, and read off the total of her credit card purchases that she had made since the last bill. She knew exactly how much she had charged because she had made it a habit of recording each purchase. Unfortunately, there are few who are quite so disciplined. It's a good idea to keep a little notebook with you so when you make a credit card purchase, you can write down the amount you spent. Do that and you won't be surprised when the bill comes in at the end of the month.

You also have the ability to charge your purchase, receive it, examine it, even use it, while you wait for the bill to arrive in the mail. Then, depending on the terms associated with your account, you can pay off the balance that you owe and not be charged any interest. If you time it right, and you pay off your credit card purchases in full, you may be able to get as many as 45 days free use of the money.

Cash and Charge Can Mean the Same Thing

Of the tens of millions of individuals in this country who use hundreds of millions of credit cards in their everyday lives, fully 1 out of 3 has developed the self-discipline of paying their credit card balances in full each and every month. They simply use their credit cards like cash. They have found that their cards can be a convenient way to pay for their purchases. They get a record of what they buy. They have the consumer protections afforded those who use credit cards. They get additional benefits when they use cards such as those which offer airline mileage perks.

John, an astute businessman, has been using his GM VISA card exclusively for years now, charging everything and anything he buys on it. The reason is, the GM card gives him credit for these purchases when he buys a new GM vehicle. The result is that he has been able to cut thousands of dollars off the purchase price of his car. In the time he has been doing this, he has always paid his balance in full, avoiding all finance charges.

Use your credit card for even the most ordinary of purchases if you are going to treat that credit card just like cash and pay the bill in full at the end of the month.

(Remember, this requires discipline and good record keeping.) Otherwise, be careful when and what you charge, because the bill will arrive in the mail.

Actually, for many people, this is not a wise option. You may have every intention of paying your credit card in full, and then one of life's little events takes place. The car breaks down. The water heater blows. The result is you will fall behind with your credit card payment, and interest will start to mount.

There is Another Way to Pay

Up to this point, the only 2 options for paying for your purchases have been either to write a check or borrow the money. There is a third option. You can take the money you need out of your savings. If you want something, or at least think you want something, but don't have the money in your checkbook to pay for it, would you be willing to take money out of your savings account to pay for it? Or put another way, if you don't have the money in your savings right now, would you be willing to save until you do?

In a few pages, you will meet Cathy. She really wants to buy furniture for her apartment. One of the options available to Cathy is to save until she has put enough money away so she can afford the purchase.

Ours is a society where we seek instant gratification. If we want something, often on the spur of the moment, we buy it. We give little thought to how we will pay for it. If there is not enough money in the checkbook, we pay with a credit card. Rarely do we save until we can afford those things we want. We don't save all year so we can afford to buy Christmas presents for everyone in the family. We don't save all year so we can afford that special vacation. In fact, we probably don't save nearly as much as we should.

Perhaps if we saved more we would spend less, especially on impulse items. Studies indicate that when people save and invest they are reluctant to tap into that nest egg except in the most extreme circumstances. It would seem that just by establishing a savings account and contributing to it regularly, people would be more aware of what they spend and what they charge. Try it and see if it works for you.

Of course you will have your regular savings. You can also have special savings accounts. People have used

Christmas Club Accounts for years, putting away $25 or $50 a month so that at the end of the year they will have enough money to afford the Christmas holidays.

Cathy wants her furniture; the price tag is $12,000. Paul has always wanted a Corvette; the cost is $45,000. Nick, 14, wants a snowboard and a season pass to the ski slopes; it will put him back $800. No one should tell any of these people that they cannot have what they want. They can. Each of them has a goal. It is just a matter of working out exactly how they are going to pay for what they want. Once they do, they can work toward realizing their goals.

Cathy should save at least half of the purchase price before she buys her furniture even though the furniture may be a bit more expensive when she has saved enough to get what she wants.

Paul will have to save all of the purchase price. His wife insists. He's been saving in a special Corvette account for 6 years and already has more than $25,000. He knows that the price of the car keeps going up, but that's the price he has to pay.

Nick will have to deliver a lot of papers, cut a lot of lawns, and shovel a lot of snow to get what he wants. It's just that simple. He can't charge it and he can't write a check because he doesn't have nearly enough in his account.

How Much Debt Can You Afford?

Recall the lesson on budgeting. You have your fixed expenses and you have your flexible or variable expenses. You know how much you pay every month for the rent or mortgage, the car loan, insurance premiums, and savings. You know, approximately, how much you pay for groceries, gasoline, utilities, and all the other things that gobble up your paycheck.

It's time to go back to your budget and check it for debt.

Here's the rule of thumb:

Your monthly payments on your installment debt, which includes your car, appliances, furniture, credit cards, bank and credit union loans, and student loans, should amount to no more than 20 percent of your income.

There you have it. If you make $3,000 a month, the experts say you should be able to afford installment payments of no more than $600 a month.

Now, that's the rule of thumb. There are always exceptions. Just use this percentage as a guideline.

Chuck and Diane were doing all right for themselves. Between the two of them they were making $5,000 a month. That means they should be able to buy what they want on credit as long as their monthly payments do not exceed $1,000. But that's only half the story. They have been married for 3 years, and they wanted to start a family, which means that Diane's $2,500 a month income was going to be reduced, if not eliminated entirely. What's more, if Diane went back to work after the baby, they would have an extra significant expense for child care. So, even though the rule says they can afford $1,000 in installment payments, they feel they cannot. They are right because of their changing financial circumstance.

Then there's Billy and Wendy. They, too, are good, solid people making their way. They aren't doing as well as Chuck and Diane, but they have great prospects. Billy is finishing graduate school and Wendy is working as an elementary school teacher. When he finishes school, she plans on getting her Masters Degree, too. They are living on $2,800 a month. They want a big screen television in the worst way. But because they are already paying $350 on their two cars, another $200 on the credit cards, and $100 on her student loan, they are over their limit. They will put off the jumbo-TV until one of the car loans is paid off. That's the responsible thing to do.

Now, if Billy gets the job he is hoping for, and the money that goes with it, he will get that television in a heart beat. He'll be able to afford it.

Take time to work through the worksheet found on the next page. It helps you to find out exactly how much income is left over at the end of the month to pay your living expenses and for your discretionary spending.

Refer to your budget. You should find that from your gross income, you only receive about 80 percent of what you earn after federal income and payroll taxes are taken out.

INSTALLMENT DEBT WORKSHEET

Percentages

Gross income   100

Withholding   <u>-20</u>
                      80% of your income remains

Housing   <u>-33</u>
                      47% of your income remains

Installment payments   <u>-20</u>
                      27% of your income remains

Savings   <u>-10</u>
                      17% of your income remains

Your Actual Income, Withholding, and Expenses

Gross income   _____

Withholding   _____

Housing   _____

Installment payments   _____

Savings   _____

Remaining income   _____

Of that 80 percent, about 33 percent goes to cover your housing. That leaves 47 percent to cover your food, clothing, utilities, and all those other necessities of life. If you have installment debt which must be repaid, and the payments come to 20 percent of your income, that will leave you with a mere 27 percent of your income to cover the everyday cost of living for you and your family. It may be that 27 percent is simply not enough to make ends meet. And don't forget that you're supposed to pay 10 percent of your income into your savings account each month.

So, start with your income, then subtract what it costs you for housing and the essentials (including savings). The remainder is what is available for installment debt, and it should never exceed 20 percent of your income.

Cathy Wants Her Furniture and She Wants it Now

Sometimes people simply want things. It doesn't make any difference what those things are. They may be extravagant to some. They may even be wasteful. That's not the point. What's important is answering the question of how you are going to pay for a purchase.

Here is the decision that Cathy and her husband are facing. Put yourself in their place. What would you do?

Cathy and her husband had moved into their apartment about 3 months earlier. She wanted new furniture then, and she hasn't gotten it. She is not happy about their beat-up hand-me-down furniture. (He doesn't much care, except he doesn't like to see Cathy so upset.) Cathy says she is embarrassed. She refers to their furniture as "ancient-attic" and "old orange crate" junk. She scans the newspaper and almost every weekend goes to area furniture stores and yard sales. She wants to furnish her living room, dining room, and bedroom with nice stuff. Finally, she has found what she wants. The store's price tag comes to $12,000.

Furniture is definitely high on Cathy's priority list. She wants this furniture, she wants it as soon as she can get it, and she has made her wishes known in no uncertain terms to her husband. The only question is, how is she going to pay for it? You see, as much as the furniture store wants to please its customers, it won't give the merchandise away. It needs to see some cash from those customers.

Cathy has at least 4 options.

Option A: Cathy has 3 or 4 credit cards with enough unused credit on them to cover the purchase. The interest rate is a whopping 21.9 percent.

Option B: Cathy may be able to get a loan at her bank or credit union. She hasn't filled out a loan application, but when she called on the telephone, she found out that the going rate was a far more reasonable 12 percent interest rate.

Option C: Cathy can use the furniture store's financing. It's easy. It's convenient. The only problem is, this lender wants 36 percent annual interest. (There's no law where she lives against charging high interest rates. They get it because people are willing to pay it.)

There is a later chapter on looking at all the various terms offered by lenders. In this case, it is quite common for furniture and appliance stores to entice customers with offers of "no money down, and no interest for 12 months." Watch those terms because typically if you do not pay the balance off in full when your year is up, you will have to pay interest back to the date of purchase and suffer an above market interest rate to boot.

Option D: Cathy can wait a year or 2, save what she would have had to pay in monthly installments, and then make her purchase for cash.

Take this one step further. If Cathy continues making the same $360 monthly payment for 52 months, just like under Option A, only this time put the money in her savings account rather than sending it to the lender, she will accumulate a tidy little nest egg.

The one option that Cathy does not have with this furniture is "rent-to-own." It's just not available with this new furniture. But it is a choice for some people depending on the circumstances.

Compare the results of Cathy's actions.

If she whips out her credit cards (*Option A*), she will get her furniture and the $12,000 debt at 21.9 percent annual interest that goes along with it. Assume that she will pay $360 a month on this debt, each and every month until the balance is paid off. The balance of the $12,000 loan will be reduced as follows:

After 1 year, she will have paid $4,320, while the balance will have gone down only $1,900. She will still owe $10,100.

After 2 years, she will have paid another $4,320 (total of $8,640), while the balance will have gone down $4,200. She will still owe $7,800.

After 3 years, she will have paid yet another $4,320 (total of $12,960), while the balance will have gone down $7,680. She will still owe $4,320.

After 4 years, she will have paid another $4,320 (total of $17,280), and the balance will still be $1,310.

It will take still another 4 payments (for a total of 52 payments) to pay off the loan for the furniture if Cathy finances it through her credit cards. The original price of the furniture was $12,000. After you include all the interest she will have to pay on the loan, the total cost of the furniture will come to a whopping $18,650.

Option B is a bit better, if her loan application is approved at her credit union or bank. It's the same loan amount ($12,000), only the terms are quite a bit better. Assume the same $360 for a monthly payment, only this time the interest charge is 12 percent annually rather than 21.9 percent. The balance of the $12,000 loan will be reduced as follows:

After 1 year, she will have paid $4,320, and the balance will be $8,950.

After 2 years, she will have paid $8,640, and the balance will be $5,520.

After 3 years, she will have paid $12,960, and the balance will be $1,660.

She will have to make another 5 payments (for a total of 41 payments) to pay off the furniture. That's a far cry from 52 payments. She pays it off almost a full year sooner.

The original price of the furniture was $12,000. After you include all the interest paid on the 12 percent loan, the total cost of the furniture comes to a much more reasonable $14,670.

Option C is really no option at all. Still, for some people it is their only option if they want to get the furniture. Either pay exorbitant interest rates or walk away from the furniture. If Cathy's credit is tarnished and she has no other way to finance her purchase, she may be tempted to agree to the lender's terms. At 36 percent interest charged by the finance company and with Cathy paying $360 a month, Cathy will pay and pay and pay, and she will never reduce the amount that she owes. $12,000 at 36 percent annually comes to $360 a month.

If you think 36 percent interest is bad, think again. There are lenders who charge and get even more than that. Believe it or not, you could actually make monthly payments and the amount you owe could be increasing.

Don't ever think that the terms offered by this particular lender are the same that you will find at all stores. They vary all over the place. Some terms are better than others. We'll get into comparing terms in later lessons.

Option D is probably Cathy's best bet from a money standpoint, although she's not crazy about it. While $12,000 worth of furniture is not what you would call an impulse purchase, it is not a necessity of life. There already is furniture in the apartment, and while it is not new or even shiny, it isn't costing Cathy and her husband anything. If they could afford to pay cash or put a substantial down payment on the furniture, that would be one thing. But they can't.

Here's what happens if Cathy waits.

She makes her $360 a month payment to her savings account, even earning a small amount of interest. Cathy then learns whether or not if she can really afford to put aside $360 a month and still pay the rent, put food on the table, pay her utilities and other essentials.

After the first year, she has accumulated $4,320 in savings.

During the second year, she waits for a sale. (There are always furniture sales). She finds that she is able to buy half the furniture she wants for $5,000, paying cash. She continues to put away the same $360 into her savings. At the end of the second year, she has half her furniture in the apartment, it's paid for, and she has $3,640 in savings.

In the third year she buys the other half of the furniture she wants, again for $5,000, and still puts away her monthly savings. At the end of the third year Cathy has all her furniture, no debt, and $2,960 in savings. And you may note that the furniture is that much newer.

Cathy continues to save for the same 52 months that she would have had to pay under Option A. If she does this, she will have purchased the furniture for $10,000 rather than $12,000. The total cost would be $10,000, rather than $18,650 under Option A or $14,670 under Option B, and she will have $7,280 in savings. Wow!

That's how you make a decision.

Cathy is not a bad person because she wants to buy new furniture. She can afford the $360 a month. It falls within the 20 percent guideline. Here, it's just a matter of deciding the best way to pay for it.

There are all sorts of so-called "special" expenses that need to be considered when you charge your purchases. Special expenses are those that people try to justify somehow when they know that they shouldn't. Two that come up every year are the annual family vacation and Christmas.

When it comes to a personal or family vacation, there are expensive ones and there are inexpensive ones. Vacations can rejuvenate, no question about that. But no matter how much you think you need one, a vacation is still a luxury. If taking a vacation is your goal, work toward that goal. Save what you need to save in order to afford it. Sure, take some time off and relax. Go wherever you want. Just pay cash. Or charge your trip and expenses and pay those charges off in full upon your return. Financing a vacation is just a poor personal financial planning decision, no matter how badly you think you need that week in Maui, and no matter how enticing Madison Avenue advertising executives make it sound.

Christmas is a similar story. No one wants to be thought of as cheap, cheap, cheap. Open up the family checkbook if that's what you want to do, but don't end up with a credit card headache for the New Year. It makes no sense at all. Set a holiday spending budget and stick to it. Buy what you can afford, without charging. Or charge what you need to charge, especially mail order stuff, and have the cash available in January to pay for the Christmas holiday in full.

How You Borrow Can Make a World of Difference

Not all loans are created equal. Say you are spending $400, or 10 percent of your income, on installment debt each month. $250 of that is a car loan at 9 percent annual interest over 4 years with 2-1/2 years remaining on the loan. The remaining $150 is what you are paying on your 2 credit cards. One is a VISA which charges 18 percent. The other is the department store which sets you back 21 percent.

There are plenty of ways to restructure these loans so that your monthly payments will be lower, the time it will take to pay them off with be unchanged, and you will have an extra $50 to $100 a month to save or spend as you see fit.

The point is, the less interest you have to pay over the life of a loan, the more money you will have to spend on yourself.

John got himself into trouble by making minimum payments. He always thought that his credit card payment was the same as the car payment and his student loan payment. With those all he had to pay was what they put on the bill. So, that's exactly what he did for his credit card payment, too.

The balance on his car loan kept going down. So did his student loan.

But when it came to his credit card balance, it hardly went down at all. No one had ever explained to John that he had better pay more than the absolute minimum on his credit card if he ever hoped to pay off the balance of his debt.

John didn't mind that the balance didn't decline until one day he wanted to buy something and pay for it with his credit card. The clerk told him that the credit card was declined. He found out later that the reason for the turn-down was that the purchase would have put him over his credit limit.

John was fortunate. Often, the charge will be approved, the limit will be exceeded, and the cardholder will be charged a stiff fine for violating this ceiling.

Not All Credit Cards Are Alike

In a later lesson you will learn about the various terms and conditions that can be imposed on a borrower and the decisions you will have to make on whether or not to accept these conditions. At this point, it is probably sufficient to point out that you can apply for a credit card that charges anywhere from 0 percent annually to one that will charge you over 36 percent. The choice is yours. Just remember the higher the interest rate, the more money you will have to pay in interest to the lender. The lower the rate, the less interest you will be charged.

Just Because You Have Access to Credit Does Not Mean You Have to Use All of it at Once

You should spend some time with people who are living on the edge and listen to their stories. These are people who make just enough money to cover their housing, essential living expenses, and installment and revolving debt. There is a common theme voiced by almost everyone who finds themselves living from paycheck to paycheck.

"We would have more money than we would know what to do with **if only we didn't have all that credit card and installment debt** taking every last nickel."

Typically they are right. They would be just fine. They would have more than enough cash to cover their living expenses, put money into savings, or pay for their vacations, Christmas presents, and other incidentals.

But because they charged purchases in years past, because they took out loans for things they probably didn't need and no longer use, they are saddled with debt which has them living from hand to mouth. Professional credit counselors say that it is more than likely that they will find themselves in the same bind years from now unless they seek some help and follow a debt repayment plan.

Once saddled with a substantial amount of debt, it is next to impossible to get it paid off. Credit counselors say that unless you take immediate steps to break bad spending habits and stick to a debt repayment plan that will eventually get you out of debt, you will stay trapped in the same vicious cycle of living from paycheck to paycheck.

Jennifer and Steve got married about 5 years ago. They both work, making a very nice living, earning over $60,000 a year between them. They have quite a bit of debt, probably too much debt. You would think that they could get by on $5,000 a month. After all, that's a pretty substantial income, and they don't have any kids. Even after taxes are taken out, they clear $4,000 a month. They live in a nice house; the mortgage, including taxes and insurance only comes to $1,000 a month. That leaves $3,000 for food, etc. Family living expenses come to $2,000, so there is $1,000 left over for installment debt. That's fine. In fact, it is right in line with the 20 percent rule.

The problem is, they have run up over $20,000 on installment loans and their credit cards. While $20,000 is a pretty good chunk of money, it's not extraordinary, not by any means. Still, they have to make $2,400 in monthly payments to cover their debt obligations and they only have $1,000 to do it with. So they are juggling their payments. They are sending in the minimum on their credit cards. They are taking on new credit cards and using the cash advance feature to pay on their existing credit cards.

How did they find themselves in this mess? That's easily explained. When they wanted something, they bought it with credit cards, giving little thought to how or when they would repay the credit card issuer (lender). They didn't worry because they made a substantial income. And because of their incomes, they didn't have any problem qualifying for additional credit cards with substantial limits. At Christmas time every year, they were generous. When people came to visit, they treated their guests well, paying for meals and other expenses.

This debt didn't just materialize all at once. It just sort of grew over time. When asked about it by a credit counselor, they both shrugged their shoulders and said that they didn't think there was a serious problem because lenders seemed only too willing to give them still more credit cards.

They were asked to review their credit card statements over the past 3 years to see where all the money had gone. They were shocked to find that they had precious little to show for their spending. They also vowed to never repeat this mistake.

Jennifer and Steve will be able to work their way through their financial problems by substantially cutting their spending, restructuring their debt, and perhaps getting a bill consolidation loan, although an unsecured bill consolidation loan is one of the most difficult loans to get. They have already sold their more expensive cars for cheaper models, saving themselves over $250 a month.

They have agreed to follow a highly structured debt management program and they are sticking to it. They have put away their credit cards. They pay cash for everything. If there is not enough money in the checkbook, they simply do without. They have more money in savings than ever before, and they are paying down their debt. They have determined that they will demand value for their money, and are unwilling to spend unless they agree that the purchase is of value to them. Jennifer is up for a raise in another couple of weeks. They have already decided what they are going to do with the money. They are going to save half and use the other half to pay down their debts even faster.

They have also said that they don't care if lenders tell them they can afford to buy this or that. If they don't want it and they don't need it, they are no longer in the market.

They have determined that they are more impressed by being out of debt and having money in the bank.

Credit and Debt Management

A fancy name for your budget is an income and expense management program. With your budget (or program), you determine (at least once or twice a month) where your income is coming from and how much you are likely to get. Then you use your budget to determine where the money goes.

A credit and debt management program works much the same way that a budget does, and it should be included in your regular budget planning process.

On the credit side of the program, you should list everyone who has agreed to extend credit to you. That includes your bank and/or credit union, mortgage lender, the car financing, and of course each and every credit card, and how much you can borrow from each. It may also include parents who will lend you something in an emergency.

On the debt side, you should list each and every creditor you owe, the outstanding balance, the minimum monthly payment, the monthly payment you make, and when appropriate, what you add to your balance during the month, including any finance charge.

You should recall that at the beginning of this book in Lesson One, the relationship between credit and debt was defined. Credit and debt are at the opposite ends of the same line. Credit is the amount of money you can borrow (but have not yet borrowed) to pay for things you want to buy. Debt is credit that you have used.

CREDIT & DEBT MANAGEMENT WORKSHEET

CREDIT & LIMIT		DEBT		
		Name	Balance	Payment
Bank	————	1.		
Bank	————	2.		
Credit union	————	3.		
Credit union	————	4.		
Finance company	————	5.		
Credit card	————	6.		
Credit card	————	7.		
Credit card	————	8.		
Credit card	————	9.		
Parents	————			
Other	————			
Other	————			

A Credit and Debt Management Program comes into play any time that you have any credit or any debt, even small amounts. Working within your personal program becomes absolutely essential when you find that you have too much debt and that you cannot repay your debt with your present income and still take care of your essential living expenses. When you have too many debts for your income, you have a serious problem. The earlier you discover and admit to the problem and take steps to resolve it, the better off everyone will be.

The Warning Signs

- Are you taking cash advances on your credit cards to pay your everyday living expenses?

- Are you taking cash advances to pay on your other credit cards?

- Are you spending over 20 percent of your income on installment credit?

- Are you charging purchases that you used to pay for with cash?

- Are you making only minimum payments on your credit cards?

- Is your overall debt increasing every month?

- Do you owe more now than you did at this time last year?

- Are you using more than 3 credit cards?

- Are you suffering late fees and high interest charges?

- Are you paying your bills later and later?

- Are you hearing from bill collectors, asking when they can expect their money?

Recognizing the warning signs of getting in over your head is only half the battle. Once you know you have a problem, you have to do something about it.

If you cannot bear the thought of facing your creditors, enlist the aid of a reputable, non-profit credit counseling service. They have counselors in offices throughout the country who are trained to help people manage their debt obligations. They will attempt to intercede with your creditors and put you on a formal debt repayment program. They will show you how to budget and they will counsel you through the tough times. But they will require that you stay with the program, give up your credit cards, and stop buying on credit. You get the idea.

Everyone should have a credit and debt management program of their own. If you find yourself in financial trouble, you may need the professional guidance and help that only trained credit counselors can provide. Don't hesitate to use them should your situation call for it.

Summing Up

We end this lesson the same way we began. When you go to purchase something, first determine if you really want to buy it, and second determine how you are going to pay for it (cash, loan, or out of savings.) Finally, get comfortable with the purchasing and financing method you have chosen.

No one should tell you what to buy and how much you should pay. However, you must tell yourself if you think it's a good deal or not, keeping in perspective your payment options.

(Rev. August 2003)

SO YOU HAVE DECIDED
TO BORROW SOME MONEY

What makes you think that anybody is willing to lend money to you? If the tables were turned and you were a lender, would you lend money to someone with your income, your job security, and your debts? Now be honest.

There is nothing wrong with borrowing money. People do it all the time. Lenders lend, and borrowers borrow. Borrowers use the money they borrow to pay for all sorts of things. Lenders want their borrowers to pay back what they borrowed plus interest. For the most part, borrowers do. That's the way of the world.

In the last lesson, you were asked the question, do you want to borrow some money so you can buy this or that, or would you rather pay for your purchases when you have the cash? You learned that you have lots of options when it comes to paying for the things you buy. You learned that saving until you can afford to pay for an item in full may be a better option than charging a purchase on a credit card. You learned to judge whether or not it is preferable to charge or to take money out of savings. You learned that you can delay paying for a purchase by finding someone who is willing to trust you to repay what you borrow. You learned that it is your decision as to whether or not you are going to pay cash or repay a lender over time.

This is not exactly the complete story. Certainly you and you alone decide when you are going to buy something and pay cash for it. The decision about buying on credit is a bit more complicated because in order to pay over time, someone has to be willing to extend credit to you. The real question becomes, who are you going to ask to trust you to repay a loan?

There are all sorts of lenders who are only too eager to lend money to creditworthy borrowers. After all that's their business. There are banks, credit unions, car dealers, finance companies and credit card issuers to name just a few. But notice that the key word here is "creditworthy." While all these lenders are in the business of lending money to people, they really are quite choosy. They only want certain people to ask them for loans. They only want to do business with those people who they are pretty confident will pay them back. They would rather not lend to those people who will not make timely and full payments. You can't blame them for that.

Deciding Who is Creditworthy and Who is Not

There are 2 approaches you can take to learn about lending practices. Both involve some role-playing. In the first case, put yourself in this position: one of your friends, neighbors, relatives or co-workers asks to borrow some money. In the second instance, put yourself in a lender's shoes and ask yourself if you would lend to someone like yourself.

Let's set the scene for the first case. You can be almost anywhere. You may be doing yard work, taking a walk through the neighborhood, sitting at home eating dinner or watching television. You could be at your desk at work or spending a few minutes in the break room. You might be at lunch or shopping.

Unexpectedly, your friend, neighbor, colleague, or relative stops by and strikes up a conversation. At first it seems harmless enough. He might remark about the weather, what the boss is wearing, or how some sports team is doing. The conversation is casual, like it always is. But this time it's different, because, eventually, the subject comes up. **He wants you to lend him some money.**

Let's assume the reason he wants the money is worthwhile and legal. Let's also assume that the amount he wants to borrow is substantial, certainly more than the $25 your roommate or brother used to borrow.

Would you do it? Or would you turn him down? Before you answer, take a few minutes to think about this loan request.

Would you demand knowing how the money was going to be used?

How much money would you be willing to lend? If he was asking for $2,500 and you felt it was too much, would you lend $1,000?

How long would you extend the loan before you wanted repayment?

Would you want your money back all at once or would

you ask for monthly payments?

Would you charge interest? At what rate?

Would you be willing to enforce the loan contract by taking him to court if the money was not repaid on time?

Would you demand collateral?

Would you require a written loan document or would a handshake be good enough?

Would you require that the person use some of his own money for a down payment, or would you be willing to finance 100 percent of it?

Do you really believe that the person will be able to pay you back?

These are the things a lender thinks about. Put yourself in the same position. Think of Uncle Bill stopping by and asking you to lend him $6,000 so he could take a vacation, invest in a business, pay the dentist for a new set of dentures, or for any of a dozen other reasons, some more palatable than others. Would you do it? Or would you tell him to find a local lender and leave you alone?

Would making the loan depend on what Uncle Bill wants the money for? Are you going to sit in judgment over how he wants to spend what he is borrowing or is any legitimate reason okay with you just as long as he repays what he is borrowing?

Let's change the situation. In this second role-playing situation, put yourself in the chair of a real lender. It may be a car dealer, a credit union, bank, or finance company. Maybe you are the person who decides whether or not to issue a credit card based on the application that arrives in the mail.

Picture yourself sitting behind the desk where it is your job to decide whether or not you lend money to applicant after applicant. Then someone who looks just like you, talks just like you, and dresses just like you walks in the door. This stranger sits down across from you, introduces himself, tells you the most personal details about his finances, and asks you to trust him. He wants to borrow $25,000 to buy a new truck, $10,000 so he can go to school for a year, $12,000 so he can buy furniture, or any one of a hundred other amounts and purposes.

He promises to pay you back under the terms and conditions of the loan contract. He promises to make each monthly payment on time. He promises to pay all the interest. He promises he will be a model borrower. Will you do it? Keep in mind that you are in the business of lending money only to creditworthy people.

This situation is quite similar to the previous one, except in this case, you are not loaning your own money. Here, you are loaning money that belongs to the company.

Again, you have to decide what specific information you want to know? In your opinion, how long should someone be working before you are confident that they have some job security?

How much should they make before you will tell them that they are trying to borrow too much? How much of their income do you think they can spend on debt?

Do you want to look into their past credit history? How deeply? Will you be willing to lend to someone who has a bad credit past, or no credit past for that matter? Are you willing to give people a second chance? What problems are you willing to forgive? What's unforgivable?

Typically, when you get into this kind of role-playing, you will find that you will be a tougher loan officer than the ones who actually make loans for a living even though it is not your money that you are being asked to lend. You will be less likely to grant that loan than someone whose job it is to assess the creditworthiness of people every day. Why? Perhaps it is human nature. Perhaps it is because you know how difficult it is for you to come up with the money that you need, month after month, to make those payments on time, and you are not confident that the person asking for the loan will really be able to make the payments.

The Loan Application

When it comes to borrowing money, the first step in the process is to fill out the loan application. You have to fill it out completely and honestly. Whether it is a bank, credit union, mortgage lender, or finance company, loan officers universally say that they want and need a complete picture of the person's finances before they will start processing the application.

Credit Application

Credit I Am Applying For

A Line of Credit ☐ Ready Reserve ☐ Preferred Line of Credit

A Consumer Loan

Purpose _____ Amount $ _____

☐ Installment loan ☐ Balloon loan ☐ Single payment loan Amount $ _____ Months to repay _____

I am applying ☐ Alone ☐ With a Co-applicant ☐ As a Co-signer for _____

My co-applicant is one ☐ Who will be liable to repay my loan (co-borrower) ☐ Whose income I am relying on to repay my loan (source of income)

Information About Me / About My Co-applicant Only if applying with co-applicant

Me				Co-applicant		
Full name	Social Security number	Date of birth		Full name	Social Security number	Date of birth
Street address				Street address		
City	State	Zip	Time at this address yrs. mos.	City	State	Zip / Time at this address yrs. mos.
Number of dependents (excluding self)	Home phone	Business phone		Number of dependents (excluding self)	Home phone	Business phone
☐ Own ☐ Rent ☐ Other	If own: purchase price	Current value		☐ Own ☐ Rent ☐ Other	If own: purchase price	Current value
Previous street address				Previous street address		
City	State	Zip	Time at this address yrs. mos.	City	State	Zip / Time at this address yrs. mos.
Current employer	Position or title	Monthly gross income $		Current employer	Position or title	Monthly gross income $
City	State	Zip	How long with employer yrs. mos.	City	State	Zip / How long with employer yrs. mos.
Previous employer (within last 5 years)	Position or Title	Monthly gross income $		Previous employer (within last 5 years)	Position or Title	Monthly gross income $
City	State	Zip	How long with previous employer yrs. mos.	City	State	Zip / How long with previous employer yrs. mos.

Additional income

I do not have to reveal alimony, child support, maintenance income, or food stamps unless I wish it to be considered as a basis for repayment.

Nature of additional income	Monthly amount $	How long income will continue

Bank References (mine or my co-applicant's)

Current checking account number	Name of financial institution and city	Current savings account number	Name of financial institution and city

Loan account number	Bank name or location	Loan account number	Bank name or location

–73–

Credit Obligations: *I will include those of my co-applicant if different from my own.*

Type	Creditor's name	Monthly payment	Balance outstanding	Type	Creditor's name	Monthly payment	Balance outstanding
Housing		$	$	Credit account		$	$
Auto loan		$	$	Credit account		$	$
Other loan		$	$	Credit account		$	$

Total other obligations including alimony, support payments, day care, etc.

	Monthly payments	Balance outstanding
Describe:	$	$

Remaining credit line limits (the maximum line less the outstanding balance shown above, *if any*)

	Bank	Visa	MasterCard	Other
	$	$	$	$

Collateral I Am Giving   ☐ New ☐ Used   *I will furnish you with proof of insurance.*

Description (make, property address, etc.)

	Year	Existing liens? ☐ No ☐ Yes	Serial/Identification number

A. Value or price	B. Down payment	C. Trade-in	D. Payoff on trade-in	Balance (A - B - C + D)		

Owner's or seller's name(s)	County	Phone number	Insurance agent/company	If yes, where?	Phone number

Additional Collateral *(if applicable)*   ☐ New ☐ Used   *I will furnish you with proof of insurance.*

Description (make, property address, etc.)

	Year	Existing liens? ☐ No ☐ Yes	Serial/Identification number

A. Value or price (includes trade-in)	B. Down payment	C. Trade-in	D. Payoff on trade-in	Balance (A - B - C + D)		

Owner's or seller's name(s)	County	Phone number	Insurance agent/company	If yes, where?	Phone number

Signatures

Applicant's driver's license or other I.D.	Co-applicant's driver's license or other I.D.	Application number	Transaction Data

Bank Use Only

My Income Replacement Options

1. Sick Pay ☐ Yes ☐ No Duration: _____ 2. Long Term Disability ☐ Yes ☐ No Percent of Income _____ %

Waiting Period: ☐ 90 Days ☐ 180 Days ☐ Other _____

3. Life Insurance: My own $ _____ ,000 My Employer $ _____ ,000 4. Savings $ _____

Personal Financial Statement

• Round all amounts to nearest $100. • Attach separate sheet if you need more space to complete detail.

Assets (assets you own)	Amount	Liabilities (debts you owe)	Amount
Cash in this bank: Checking		Loans payable to banks (schedule 2)	
Savings		Loans payable to others (schedule 2)	
C.D.s		Installment contracts payable (schedule 2)	
IRA		Amounts due to dept. stores and others	
Cash in other banks		Credit cards (MasterCard, Visa & others)	
Due from friends, relatives and others			
Mortgage and contracts for deed owned		Income taxes payable	
Securities owned (schedule 1)		Other taxes payable	
Cash surrender value of life insurance			
Homestead (schedule 1)		Loans on life insurance	
Other real estate owned (schedule 1)		Mortgage on homestead	
Automobiles (year, make, model)		Mortgage or liens on other real estate owned	
		Contracts for deed	
Personal property		Other liabilities (detail)	
Other assets (detail)			
		TOTAL LIABILITIES	
		Net worth (total assets less total liabilities)	
TOTAL		TOTAL	

Schedule 1 Securities Owned and Real Estate Owned

No. Shares/Bond Amt or RE Type	Description of Bond/Stock or Address of Real Estate	Names Bond/Stock Registered or RE Title In Names Of	Cost	Present Market Value	L - Listed U - Unlisted RE Yr Acquired
		TOTAL			

Schedule 2 Loans Payable to Banks and Others, Installment Contracts Payable and Mortgages on Real Estate

To Whom Payable	Collateral Description or RE Address	Secured Unsecured	How Payable	Maturity Date	Unpaid Balance
			$ Per		
			$ Per		
			$ Per		
			$ Per		
			$ Per		
			$ Per		

To Be Completed By Bank

This application was taken by: ☐ Face to face ☐ Mail ☐ Telephone

Loan officers who have been in the business of evaluating loan applications for decades offer this advice: Don't be vague. Don't estimate. Get the actual numbers. They want account numbers and balances. If you make $28,000 a year, don't say you make $30,000. If you expect to earn some overtime, put it down, but don't say you will be getting an extra $5,000 when it will only be $500. Don't minimize your expenses and debts. If your rent is $525 a month, say so. Don't say it's $500. If you owe various department stores and other businesses, divulge the extent of what you owe. If you have had a credit problem in the past, disclose and explain it. If the cause of past money troubles has been a job loss, layoff, divorce, medical emergency, or bad judgment with credit cards, you need to say so. According to an attorney, to be less than accurate may be fraud.

It can take an hour or two, perhaps longer, to accurately complete a loan application even when you have all your papers available to you.

Free Advice From a Long-Time Loan Officer

"When the information on a loan application is incomplete, inaccurate or misleading, I automatically think the person is being dishonest. I can't help it. I've been in this business for more than 20 years and feel that I've helped a lot of people. But if they can't be honest on their loan application, I don't want do business with them."

Every lender's application is different. Still, all ask for similar information. All ask for your name, address, social security number, how long you've lived at your present address, where you work, how much you make, where you bank, how much money you have in your savings and checking accounts, who you owe, how much you owe to each, and how much longer it will be until each of your loans is paid off. They want to know the same information about your spouse if you are married and if this will be a joint loan. Loan applications require you to provide a complete financial profile. Give it to them.

Loan officers say they pay as much attention reviewing your assets as they do looking into your debts. They want to know what you own. They want to know the make, year and model of your car(s), what kind of investments you own, your insurance policies, even stamp and coin collections. They want to know what assets you have that you can sell if you get into trouble repaying your loan.

These same loan officers go on to say that ideally they are looking for loan applicants who have:

- A solid history of repaying loans they have had in the past.

- A pattern of making their payments on time.

- No judgments and liens filed against them.

- A clean record when it comes to repossessions.

- A year or two at the same address.

- No history of overdrafts.

- A stable job.

Count on the fact that a loan officer will require you to authorize her to pull a copy of your credit bureau file. Also count on the loan officer to carefully review all the information that is reported in that file.

One loan officer remarked, "A loan applicant should know whether or not they will get a loan before they ever walk through the door. They know how much money they earn, where they work, how long they have been there, what their personal financial position is, and how they have handled their finances in the past. They know if they are a good credit risk."

"If there are black marks (and few people are completely squeaky-clean these days) they should own up to the problems they have had in the past, explain what happened and what they have done to make sure that the same mistakes are not repeated. We don't expect a person to be perfect. In fact, we have found that someone who has faced some tough times and has come through it, is often an ideal borrower. They won't let the same problems affect them a second time."

Not all lenders hold the same belief, but it is comforting to know that past problems and even outright bad judgment may not be held against you for the rest of your life.

Ted had always been a hard worker. After high school, he joined the military. After his discharge, he went to work doing physical labor. He got into a little trouble, but nothing serious. He was making good money, but lost it all when he started drinking. His wife divorced him. He lost his job. He defaulted on his bank loan. He was ordered to pay child support but didn't have the money.

Ted bounced around for a couple of years and eventually got his life in order. He owed $4,500 in child support and needed another $5,000 to get his car up and running so he could get to work. Ted was turned down by 3 lenders before he found one who would work with him. The lender who agreed to help happened to be the same one which Ted stiffed some years back. When asked why he would take a second chance on someone like Ted, the loan officer replied, "He's learned what he did wrong. We have title to his car, so if he defaults this time, he's on foot. But that's not going to happen. Ted's a model citizen now. He made a mistake in the past but we're not going to hold that against him, now that he has his life in order."

He went on to say, "I probably wouldn't have agreed to work with Ted but he came to me with a strong personal reference. His boss, who happens to be someone I know personally, vouched for Ted's job security and his personal character. That's what really convinced me to go ahead with the loan."

By the way, the loan officer's assessment has proven to be correct. Ted has never missed a payment and is not likely to miss one in the future.

The Interview

Completing the loan application is only the first step in the process. After you fill it out, you need to hand it to a person who is in a position to act on it. These loan officers are experienced interviewers. They will visit with you. They will go through the application with you to make certain that it is complete. They will want to verify some of the information with you, just to make certain that you have not overlooked something.

Probably the first question the loan officer will ask is, "What do you want the loan for?" Whatever you do, don't say, "It's none of your business." Lenders need to know. They can't lend for illegal purposes. Knowing the purpose of the loan helps the lender structure the loan — term, interest rate, etc. For example, you will usually get a lower interest rate on a car loan than on a personal loan. And just as important, you don't want to come across as an uncooperative borrower. It doesn't make much sense to be antagonistic with someone who controls your financial future.

You should be ready to provide your most recent pay stubs covering at least a 30-day period. You should also have copies of your last 2 year's income tax returns. (Lenders figure that you won't lie about your income to the Internal Revenue Service.) If you are borrowing to make a purchase, you will want to bring with you some paperwork showing what you are buying and what it will cost.

The real question the loan interviewer has on his mind is one that he will not ask. He really wants to know if you as a borrower will take responsibility for the loan and if you will make it a priority in your life to see that it is repaid according to the terms of your agreement.

The Role of the Lender

Lenders have the job of determining who is creditworthy and then lending money to these people. They make their money on the loan fees and interest they charge. If they make loans to people who do not repay, they will soon be out of business. If they do not make loans, they won't make any money.

They are not the money police. They are not in business to tell you if your loan is a good deal for you or a bad deal. They are not there to tell you if you can afford a loan or not. They are there to lend money to the creditworthy.

One lender says if he had his way he would never lend money to people who use the funds to buy a snowmobile. He doesn't have any problem with people buying them for cash. He just thinks it's wrong to finance the purchase.

Another says the same for boat loans.

A third says borrowing to pay for a vacation should not be allowed.

And a fourth would like to refuse everyone who wants to borrow against their home (home equity loans).

But they all do it despite their personal feelings.

If you think about it, borrowing money for these 4 purposes is not very smart money management.

If you want to buy big, expensive adult "toys" such as snowmobiles and boats, pay cash for them. They are luxuries, not necessities.

The same is true for a vacation. If you can't afford to pay cash for your recreation, do something enjoyable close to home during your time off work that you can afford.

Home equity loans put your house at risk. If you don't make your loan payments, you could lose your home.

These lenders have seen it happen.

Nevertheless, lenders are not the police. They will loan money for any legitimate purpose as long as you meet the lender's guidelines.

One lender says she reviews the loan application and credit bureau report. If everything checks out, she then looks at the applicant's income and compares it to his or her debt. As long as monthly debt, including the payment on a new loan, does not exceed 50 percent of the applicant's net income or 35 percent of a person's monthly gross income, she will process the loan application. Nine times out of 10, that means the loan will be approved.

Personally, the loan officer may have reservations about the purpose of the loan. But, as long as the purpose is legal, that won't stop her from lending the money. Business is too competitive. She says that if she lets her personal beliefs get in the way of giving a loan to a qualified applicant, the lender down the street will write the loan and get the business.

Although one loan officer thinks that it is bad judgment to borrow money to pay for a vacation, and another says that it's a bad idea to borrow to buy a snowmobile or a boat, or to invest in a small business just starting up, none of these loan officers will think twice about approving loans for any of these purposes when the loan applicant is qualified and has shown an ability in the past to repay what they borrow.

All Loan Applicants are Created Equal, but They Don't Stay That Way

Everyone has different personal financial circumstances. That's no one's fault. It is just a fact that people have different jobs, different incomes, expenses, and so on. Common sense tells you that a lender will look more favorably on the loan application from a person who has a steady income and little debt than an application from a person who has recently declared bankruptcy, is unemployed, and just had a car repossessed.

The point is, different loan applicants may all be granted loans by a lender, and all may be offered different terms.

For example, Applicant Alex has been at his present job for more than 2 years, has been in his house for the past 4 years, earns about $4,000 a month, has no derogatory information in his credit file, has a past credit history spanning more than 5 years with 4 different lenders, including credit card issuers, car loan, and a mortgage, has a net worth of more than $50,000 (that's assets minus debts) and has a banking relationship already established where he wants to get the loan.

Applicant Bob's background is not nearly as shiny. This applicant has been on the job for only a year, has been renting an apartment for 2 years, earns $2,500 a month, has a past credit history of 2 years with only a car loan and an appliance loan, and has a net worth of $12,000. While there is no bad information on his credit report over the past 3 years, there is something from further back.

Applicant Carol is getting started in life. She has just started work and has a salary of $2,000 a month. She rents an apartment and has no past credit history, good or bad. She has no debts, but has no assets either. There's no information on the credit report. The landlord has verified that she lives there and has paid her rent on time.

Applicant Doug is trying to rebuild his life. He's working, earns $2,500 a month but has been on the job less than a year. He has a negative net worth, a prior bankruptcy, and the credit report shows a pattern of slow payment on his debts. "Slow payment" means just that. Creditors report to the credit bureau not only the fact that someone makes a payment but also if that payment is made on time or if it is late.

All 4 of these credit applicants may get their loan applications approved. However, all 4 will likely be offered different terms.

Applicant Alex will get the best deal simply because he exhibits the best ability to repay the amount he wants to borrow. He has the best credit history, best job stability, and lowest debt to income ratio. The fact is lenders offer the best deals to those who demonstrate the ability to repay. Usually that is the person who has established a solid credit history. One lender says applicants like this get the best terms because they have earned the right to it. Most have worked hard to get where they are today.

Applicant Bob will also probably get a loan, although the interest rate will be somewhat higher and he may have to pay more in loan fees than Applicant Alex.

The same is true for Applicant Carol. A lender may be concerned, but will probably make at least some offer. The loan amount may be less and the repayment terms tougher, but the loan will be offered.

As for Applicant Doug, he may or may not get a loan. If he does, the terms will be even tougher than with Applicants Bob or Carol because he poses the greatest risk of default.

Lenders set their loan terms based on their assessment of the applicant's likelihood to repay. The lower the risk to the lender, the lower the interest rate and the better the terms for the borrower. The higher the risk of default to the lender, the higher the interest rate and the worse the terms for the borrower. Terms are based on the risk the lender takes in extending the loan to the borrower.

Discrimination

You may have noticed that something very important has not been mentioned up to this point. The subject is discrimination. When it comes to whether or not a loan will be approved and under what terms, the only issue of any relevance should be that of repayment risk. Granting a loan and determining its various terms depends on a person's creditworthiness, and creditworthiness, like justice, is blind.

Creditworthiness has nothing to do with whether you are male or female. It has nothing to do with your race, religious beliefs, ethnic background, or whether you are able-bodied or physically challenged. This is not to say that in the past there was no discrimination. There was. Fortunately, it is largely a thing of the past. If you are shopping for a loan, you can get one if you have the financial strength to show a lender that their money is not at risk, without regard to sex, race, age and all those other biases that at one time were used to deny credit to certain classes of people. That's the law.

Not only is it correct and proper that discrimination has been eliminated from the credit-granting process, lenders have found that it is just good business.

Some may argue that loan discrimination still happens, although not as often as in years past. They may say that they have seen it. Some may say they have actually experienced it. If that's true, it is wrong and should not be tolerated. Fortunately, there are enough lenders in town and around the country who do not practice discriminatory lending. The lenders interviewed for this book are adamant when they talk about discrimination. They all say that the financial organizations they represent follow the letter as well as the spirit of the law, and that their organizations will not tolerate even the hint of discrimination when it comes to lending.

One long-time loan officer explains, "Every once in a while, I get someone who feels they were discriminated against by another lender. I listen to what they say and have them fill out a loan application. I have to admit I am skeptical, because today lenders are careful about being charged with discrimination. I always assure them that their application will be given a fair review. It has always turned out that there were underlying credit problems."

Still, that's not the end of it. There is obvious discrimination, and there is subtle discrimination. That can be when important information is not offered and options are not fully explained. When there is a loan application without an interview, such as with a credit card application, discrimination is unlikely to occur. Where there is a face to face interview, discrimination can happen.

One lender tells the story of a wonderful young woman who was looking for a mortgage to buy her first home. She filled out the application, and told the mortgage lender that not only had she been turned down by another lender, but had been told in no uncertain terms that she had "no business trying to buy a house on her income." She got her loan.

Another customer was rejected after only 8 minutes into the interview. No explanations were given. No alternatives were offered. When he applied at another lender, the loan was approved because he was counseled to refinance his car and thereby reduce his monthly debt payments.

Why Some Loan Applications Are Turned Down

Credit is denied when a potential lender is unwilling to take the risk that you will not repay what you want to borrow under the terms and conditions of a loan. "Sorry," they say, "but we are not able to give you the loan you want."

There are all sorts of reasons that a loan application is turned down.

They range from the obvious to the obscure. For most people, a loan will be turned down because the application score falls into the unacceptable range.

Loan applications are scored usually by an impersonal computer. Certainly all credit card applications are scored by computer. Loans that are processed by individual loan officers often receive a more human touch. But don't be fooled into thinking that these loans are not scored. They are. Even the smallest of lenders scores a loan application, although it may be done by a human rather than a computer.

The score is based on the amount of your income and debt, length of time at your residence, whether you own or rent, and all the other obvious information that the loan application asks you to provide. The better your score, the more confident the lender is that you will repay your loan. The worse your score, the more likely it is that your loan application will be turned down.

While it is pretty clear what criteria goes into developing a program used to score loan applications, lenders are careful to keep the details private. They won't tell you what you should put down on your application in order to qualify for a loan. It would be inappropriate for them to do so. You need to fill out the application completely and honestly. They will score it and let you know if you qualify for the loan you have applied for.

Chris and Janie applied for a mortgage loan. They had found a starter home and Janie had fallen in love with it. They filled out the application and turned it in to the lender. Within a matter of minutes, they found out that they were not going to qualify for the loan they needed to get the mortgage. They didn't make enough money to support the mortgage plus the debts they had already taken on. They were counseled by the mortgage loan officer to take 3 steps and then to visit her in 6 months. She told them to:

1. Close out old credit card accounts that were still active but had a zero balance. Although they were not using these cards, the credit on these accounts was still available to them.

2. Reduce their various debts so they would qualify under the mortgage lending guidelines.

3. Pay off one of the car loans. That one payment would free up about $400 a month that could go toward the mortgage.

Consider what happened to David. He picked up a credit card application and sent it in. Within 4 weeks, he heard back that he had been declined. The reason was not clear. After visiting with a credit counselor and reviewing his credit bureau report, together they determined that he was denied the credit card because he simply had too many cards and too much debt. This credit card issuer was not willing to add to his debt burden. Doug complained that he wanted the new card because it was offering a lower interest rate, and he was going to use it to consolidate his other high-interest credit cards. It didn't matter to the credit card issuer. Card denied.

Jill was turned down because she hadn't been on the job long enough.

Allie was turned down because she didn't have a stable source of income.

Bill was turned down because of past credit problems.

Frank was turned down for a personal loan simply because he was asking to borrow $15,000 and this particular lender doesn't like to lend more than $10,000 to a first-time borrower.

For whatever reason, you can be turned down for credit. If you are, find out why, and then make every effort to correct the problem.

Too Many Inquiries

Every time you apply for a loan, the potential lender will get a report on you from the credit bureau. Every report is called an "inquiry." If there have been a lot of inquiries about you by creditors in the past 6 months from credit card companies, finance companies and others, the lender may feel you are amassing too much credit in a short period of time. That would make you more of a credit risk than they are willing to take.

One lender offers this advice. "Before you go shopping for a car or other big ticket item, get a copy of your credit report and carry it with you. A personal inquiry by you does not count as an official inquiry. Do not authorize anyone to run a credit check on you unless you are ready to go ahead with a purchase. Do not provide a sales person with your social security number or your driver's license, because your credit file can be checked when they have that information. Lenders pay close attention to the number of recent inquiries and will turn down a loan if, in its opinion, there are too many. It is up to the individual to keep those inquiries to a minimum."

How to Get That First Loan

It is not nearly as difficult to get that first loan as it was in the past because of the way credit cards are issued today. It's unusual to find an individual who has not been offered at least 1 credit card these days. Credit card companies are even sending pre-approved applications to students who are in high school and college despite the fact that the card companies know that students have little or no income. They are relying on the parents to cover the payments. They want the students to become attached to their cards and loyal customers of the credit card issuer. The theory is, today's student is tomorrow's customer.

One father shakes his head in amazement and disbelief when he tells the story of his son who was a junior in high school. "I had been with this credit card company for 24 years and I had a $5,000 credit limit. Out of the blue, my son got a pre-approved invitation to get one of their cards with a $10,000 credit line. Are they crazy? It took me 6 more years, but I finally made it to $10,000."

Every credit experience you have had in the past will help a loan officer when you fill out a loan application for the first time. There's the obvious, like the credit card and student loan. It may be a stretch, but you may have a history of paying your rent on time, or making a purchase on lay-away. You pay car insurance, utilities, telephone. Even doctor bills paid over time can help show a credit history.

Whatever the depth of your credit experience, it becomes your job to convince a loan officer that he or she is making the right decision to lend you the money you want to borrow. The first loan is the hardest to get when you have no track record. After that, it becomes easier and easier if you pay as agreed and honor your financial commitments. Just remember, lenders want to lend money. That's what they do for a living. If you can show that you are a good risk, even for a small amount of money, the lender will probably take the chance.

An Unromantic Walk Down the Aisle

Someone with no credit history can gain access to credit if they marry someone who has solid credit. Typically, one spouse will have already established a credit history. Then, when they marry, they can co-mingle their credit. Someone who previously would have been turned down for a credit card or a car loan because of a lack of credit experience might now qualify because the spouse has a good credit history and a stable job.

Unfortunately, this can work the other way, too.

Julie had a clean credit history, stable employment, good income, and a small amount of debt which she had managed well over the past years. She was an ideal credit risk. Then, Julie fell in love and married Art. Together, they now had the income to qualify for a mortgage on the house they found. Unfortunately, Art's credit history was terrible. Julie's income alone could not support the mortgage, so they were turned down. In this case, Julie had acquired Art's credit problems. Their lender didn't enjoy telling them that they had to put their plans on hold.

It doesn't sound very romantic, but everyone should probably follow this advice: Before two people marry they should discuss their mutual finances in depth, especially the amount of debt each has and how they have handled their debt in the past. Please consider asking your soon-to-be spouse to reveal his or her financial past. After all, you will be taking it as your own, for better or worse.

How to Get a Lender to Say "Yes"

A lender will say "yes" to your loan application when you can show that you are ready, willing, and able to repay the amount you are borrowing according to the terms of your loan. If you can show that, you will get the loan. If you cannot, then you will be turned down. It's that black and white.

Still, there is a bit of what some call "wiggle-room."

Say you want to borrow $19,000 for a new car and the financial information in your loan application and the credit bureau just won't support it. The loan officer will say no.

Instead of walking out in a huff, try a counter offer. First, ask what the problem is. You should get an answer. If the problem is one of misinformation, fix it. For example, if there is some negative information contained in your credit bureau report, respond to it, and get it corrected if you can.

Bill was at wit's end. He was trying to get a mortgage to buy a house. Everything was going along just fine until the lender called and asked why he hadn't reported the judgment that was filed against him.

Bill was shocked. He went to the court house to find out what was going on. It turned out that someone with the same first and last name was the subject of the judgment. Bill clarified the situation and got his loan.

If the problem is you don't make enough money or have too many debts to support the loan, ask for a smaller amount. If the lender feels that the full $19,000 is more than you can afford, what about $15,000? Will they go for that? If not, will they lend $10,000. Perhaps you can find a different, less expensive model, or buy a late-model used car that will cost you less money. Negotiate a little. Find out how much the lender is willing to lend and proceed from there. You may need to adjust your outlook a bit, but it's better than being turned down.

Unless you are a flat-out bad risk, chances are the lender will want to work with you. You may qualify for a lesser amount. You may have to delay your purchase for up to a year until you straighten out some income and debt problems. You may need to be on the job another couple of months. You may only need a letter from your employer stating that you have excellent job prospects. You may need to pay off some nagging debts.

So instead of getting upset and saying some things that you shouldn't say, work with the lender so when you fix the problem, you can come back and reinstate the loan application.

A Substantial Down Payment Can Persuade a Lender

There is nothing quite as persuasive to a lender who is considering your loan application as when you are putting a substantial down payment on your purchase. If you are eyeing that $20,000 car and are willing and able to make a $10,000 down payment, a lender is much more willing to look favorably at your loan application. If you can only put down $500, and the loan application is marginal in the lender's view, chances are you will be turned down.

When the Final Answer is "NO"

So what! The lender said no. Don't let it get you down. There is more than one lender in town. There may be others who want your business and who will look at your loan application in a more favorable light. Try, try again.

If you do go to another lender(s), and you get turned down a second and even a third time, get a copy of your credit report from the local credit bureau. There is no charge for this report when you have been recently turned down for credit. A credit report is a confusing document if you don't know how to interpret it. Once you get your credit report, make an appointment with a non-profit consumer credit counselor. Together you can look at your credit report and probably locate the reason you have been denied a loan.

The Role Collateral Plays in Loan Decisions

There are 2 basic types of loans, secured and unsecured. In the following 2 lessons, you will learn more about them. At this point, however, it is important to understand the role that collateral plays in the loan decision.

Collateral is property or an object of value which a lender can take and sell if you default on your loan. A **secured loan** is one in which collateral is offered as security to the lender. An **unsecured loan** is one where there is no collateral offered, just your word that you will repay what you owe.

All too often, people who are turned down for a loan tend to get angry and blame the lending organization in general and the loan officer individually. You hear all sorts of complaints. One of the most common is "Why would they turn me down for that car loan. After all, they have the car as collateral."

A lender who agrees to a loan that will be used to purchase a car, truck, house, large appliances or similar item will keep the title to the property until the loan is repaid. As a result, the typical borrower can get better terms for a secured loan than an unsecured loan. Nevertheless, the lender doesn't want to take your car or refrigerator. They don't want to claim their collateral. They want you to make your payments.

So while a lender has less risk when it has collateral, it still is not making a risk-free loan. After all, how much money can a lender expect to get when it sells a used washer and dryer or a used car?

Now, there is one type of collateral that lenders drool over. If you put cash on deposit and pledge that cash against your loan, you will almost always get the money you are asking for, as long as you don't exceed the amount on deposit.

This is the concept used by issuers of secured credit cards. "Put your money on deposit," they say, "and we will let you have a credit card with a spending limit equal to the amount you have on deposit with us." That way their loan to you is absolutely secure.

You might ask why would you apply for a loan when you have the money you need in the first place? The answer is simple enough. You may want to establish credit. You may want to repair credit. You may decide that it is in your best interest to borrow money to buy something rather than deplete your savings.

Local lenders have programs where you can borrow money and pledge your savings account. Some of the best loan rates are available under these programs. They are especially handy when you have short-term borrowing needs and yet you don't want to invade your savings.

The Role Co-Signers and Co-Applicants Play in Loan Decisions

When you have a damaged credit history or no credit history at all, a lender may be unwilling to take a chance on you. Still, you want to borrow money for a worthwhile purpose, and you honestly believe that you will be able to make the loan payments on time and in full every month.

A lender may favorably consider your loan application if you can get someone who is more creditworthy than you to co-sign the loan with you, or if you can find someone who is creditworthy to be a co-applicant.

Credit counselors are almost unanimous when they say that it is a bad idea for a person to co-sign a loan.

They tell story after story about the parent or employer who was asked to co-sign and ended up saddled with making the payments. One loan officer sums it up best. "If you were a good credit risk, I would loan the money to you. But you are not, so I can't and I won't. If you get a co-signer, chances are that is the person who is ultimately going to make the payments. Is that what you want?"

When this particular lender meets the co-signer, he lays it on the line. He explains that there is every likelihood that the co-signer will have to make the payments. He also explains that the co-signer will have the amount of the loan count against him in the event he should want to borrow some money. He doesn't come right out and tell people that co-signing a loan for a family member, co-worker, or neighbor is a terrible idea, but he comes close to it.

A co-applicant is similar to a co-signer, but not exactly the same. A co-applicant is someone like a husband or wife who will benefit from the loan just like the main applicant. When a couple goes to buy a car, both the husband and wife are usually co-applicants on the loan. Same for a mortgage. Credit cards may be in one name or two.

When there are co-applicants, the lender will consider the combined income and debt, along with all the other financial details of both applicants, combined. Where one may not have enough income to qualify for a loan, together they may have more than enough.

How to Build a Solid Credit History

There is nothing quite so valuable as a solid credit history. Just ask someone who has either no credit background or a damaged one.

There are 2 age-old complaints. The first is "How can I repair a bad credit history?"

The second is "How can I establish credit when no one will give me a chance?"

Both are difficult issues which will be addressed in great detail in Lesson 12. However, the topic requires some immediate attention.

Let's first tackle repairing a bad credit record. If you have derogatory information on your credit report, if you have a record of slow payments, defaults, collections, judgments, repossessions, and perhaps even a bankruptcy, you will be denied credit at every turn. You can't blame lenders for not wanting to lend to you, not with that kind of track record.

If the information is true, it will haunt you for years. There are firms across the country that boast that they can clean up your credit report, that they will challenge all that negative information and get it erased from your file. Usually there is a substantial fee involved before they will even talk to you. That should make you very suspicious. The fact is, they can't do it. No one can. **If you have bad credit for whatever reason, no one can eliminate your past history.**

People have the mistaken belief that if they pay on an account that has been in default or bring a past due account current, that information will be removed from their credit history. It won't.

If you have a collection on your record, and you pay it, it will still appear on your credit report for 7 years, perhaps longer.

Nevertheless, there are steps you can take to repair the damage.

You can enroll in a secured credit card program.

You can take out a secured loan for a small amount from a local lender and prove that you can repay what you have borrowed on time.

You can stay with your job and in your home for a period of time.

You can pay down existing debts, even those that have been written off by lenders who grew tired of waiting.

You can establish a savings account and borrow against it (a secured loan).

Over time, you will be able to repair some if not all of the damage you have done to your credit rating.

The other complaint about establishing credit for the first time is actually easier to address than the one concerning repairing bad credit. When it comes to establishing credit, you don't have a huge hurdle to overcome.

Start locally. Make an appointment with a local lender and visit with them. Tell them about yourself.

Establish a banking relationship (checking and savings account.) They can tell a lot about a person by how they handle their checking account.

Show them job stability.

Apply for a small loan, and when it is granted, make a point of dropping by in person to make your payment. Remind the loan officer that they made the right decision when they approved the loan.

Beware of Predatory Lending Practices

No matter what kind of finacial deal you enter into, you need to be aware of potential predatory lending practices. That means you need to take the time you need to read and understand the terms of the deal you are looking at. If you don't, you may wind up paying unnecessarily high interest rates and fees. There are many people who have made it their business to take advantage of your willingness to accept what they are offering, preying upon your trusting nature.

According to the Consumer Federation of America, some businesses such as payday lenders, title loan companies and check-cashing establishments offer short-term loans that can range from 39 to 871 percent.

Bill needed some extra cash to get him through the weekend, so he got into the car and visited the corner payday lender. He wrote a check, post-dated of course, for $115. In return, he received $100 in cash and the promise that his check would not be cashed for two weeks. Bill thought that the $15 fee was reasonable. Yet, when you calculate the Annual Percentage Rate on this two-week loan, Bill is paying more than $300 percent interest to use the payday lender's money.

How can these businesses get away with charging what they do? It is easy. First, it is not illegal, so the government is not involved. Second, they rely on the fact that most people don't read the loan papers and they tend to write their agreements in such a way as to confuse people. They also depend on the fact that you will accept the terms they are offering.

What to look for:

You can protect yourself against potential predatory lending practices by watching for warning signs.

• A lender asks you to sign papers that contain blanks.

- A lender asks you to sign papers without allowing you to read them first.

- The sales person tells you that, "You need to act quickly. If you wait until tomorrow, you will miss out on this opportunity."

- The lender does not disclose the loan costs up front, provide you with a Good Faith Estimate, or give you a Truth-in-Lending Statement.

- The lender adds life insurance at the closing, without discussing it or getting your advance approval.

Borrower Beware

Some lending practices, even though they are not necessarily predatory, are not in your best interest. A lender may offer to lend you more money than what your property is worth. Although this is not predatory, it can be dangerous. Some lenders will lend you up to 125 percent of the value of your property, a deal that may sound good until you have to sell. You could owe more than you could get from the sale of the property. That's asking for trouble.

Another lender may offer to refinance your loan at a lower interest rate or offer you a loan for remodeling or repairs at "no cost to you." They can offer you a "no up front cost loan" by including the closing costs into your new loan. So, while it may seem you are getting something for free, you will pay interest on the closing costs that you will include in the loan.

Summing Up

Knowing what you know now, would you lend to yourself? If someone asks to borrow money from you, will you do it? Under what terms and conditions?

Knowing when it is appropriate to borrow isn't easy. Knowing when someone will lend you the money you want isn't easy either. Still, there are steps you can take to ensure that when the time comes to borrow, your loan application will be approved.

One final point. A lender isn't doing you any favor granting you a loan that you can't afford to repay.

LESSON FIVE
(Rev. August 2003)

THE TERMS OF THE DEAL

When it comes to your money, you have a choice. You can trust luck and someone else's sense of fair play or you can educate yourself so you know with certainty whether or not you are being offered a good deal. If you are not familiar with all the things you need to know about taking out a loan, you again have a choice. You can make the deal happen immediately although you will have to trust someone else to look out for your best interests, or you will have to put off the transaction until you are comfortable with all the details.

"Trust Me"

Trust is an important concept when it comes to your money. Many lenders pride themselves on the trust they have developed between themselves as individuals and their customers. Every time you borrow money, you will be working with a financial professional. It is wonderful when you like the person you are dealing with. It is also nice if you trust them. However, it is not essential. What is, is that you understand the terms and conditions of the deal.

The term "trust" often means different things to different people. If you are sitting across the table from a loan officer, you want that person to be trustworthy. To you, that may mean that you want to be able to trust the person to look out for your best interests. To the lender, it may mean that the loan officer can be trusted to look out for the lender's best interests. To the loan officer, it may mean that he or she can be trusted to do a competent job of pulling the deal together and disclosing all important terms and conditions to both parties.

Sarah's situation is typical. She was new to town and wanted to buy a car. She didn't know where to go for a loan so she asked a couple of her co-workers and friends. They gave her all sorts of recommendations. Sarah called several lenders and heard the same thing from each of them. "Come on down," they all said, "and we can talk about it."

Ken was looking to buy a small home. He asked for a referral from his parents. He found out who they used and made the call.

Should Sarah or Ken trust the referrals? Should they just pick one and be confident that the person will look out for their best interests? Obviously the answer is no. Both Sarah and Ken need to educate themselves as to the terms of the deal they are looking for. They need to look out for their own best interests.

Trust is a wonderful concept but it does not play much of a role when it comes to financial dealings. You cannot look in the yellow pages of the telephone book under the heading "Lenders" and identify the trustworthy ones because they have three gold stars by their names. You cannot look under the heading "Trust" and see who is included and who is not. You have to trust yourself to learn the terms of the deal.

Don't Allow Yourself to Play the Victim

It may be difficult to believe but there are still people who allow themselves to play the role of victim. They say, "I'm too old to learn this stuff," or "I'm not smart enough to understand," or, "My parents, spouse, or friend will take care of all the details," or, "I don't have the time to check this out."

No one will stand for age, sex, race or other kind of discrimination. Yet, there are still those individuals who insist they are not up to the task of negotiating their own financial deal because they feel they are too old, too young, the wrong gender, not smart enough, or some other excuse.

Shame on the people who allow themselves to fall into that trap. You wouldn't allow anyone else to practice this kind of discrimination against you.

Bonnie was 65, widowed, and used to letting her husband take care of all the financial aspects of their life together, but he is gone now. So when it was time to collect the life insurance and attend to all the other financial details required when someone dies and leaves an estate, she did not know where to turn. Instead of trusting her finances to the lawyer, banker, insurance agent, real estate agent, and stock broker, Bonnie set to work learning about financial matters so she could make informed, intelligent decisions about her money.

She was bright, healthy, and fully capable of understanding financial terminology. She was not about to be placated, patted on the head and told that she needn't worry her pretty little self about these things and to just let the professionals do it for her.

Bonnie didn't know every question to ask, but she was not afraid to ask anyway. She listened, took notes and learned what she needed to know. She also asked questions of more than one financial professional and compared their answers. This gave her more information to help her make good decisions.

The "Yes" Syndrome

There is a trap which too many people can fall into. Watch for it. It's called the "Yes" Syndrome and it works like this.

You are visiting with someone about a technical subject. It might be life insurance, investments, mortgage financing, or car leasing. The person is going on and on about the subject at hand. You find yourself rocking back and forth, nodding "yes, yes, yes" every time he or she asks if you understand what is being said, which of course you do not. Actually, you are thinking to yourself, "If the salesperson would only stop, I'll buy the product just to get out of here."

Watch for the tell-tale rocking and nodding motion that goes on as the "Yes" Syndrome kicks in. Guard against it. Don't allow yourself to fall into its trap no matter how boring or tedious the subject.

Refuse to be Embarrassed

When someone explains something highly technical which may be difficult to grasp, and then asks "Do you understand?", the response usually is "yes." Of course you don't have a clue as to what is going on, but you don't want to be embarrassed by saying so. That is a huge mistake.

If you don't understand, please say so.

If you still don't get it, say so again. Remember, it is up to you to educate yourself about what is being discussed.

Jennifer is probably the best when it comes to insisting on understanding the terms of the deal. She will sit with the loan officer, investment counselor, or insurance agent and listen intently to the presentation. When it is over and the financial professional asks "Do you understand?", she will say, "No, can you explain it again" if she is unclear.

Jennifer feels it is her job to listen and learn as much as she can so she is comfortable with the terms of the deal. If she doesn't understand, then it is the fault of the financial professional who did not do a good enough job of explaining. Jennifer wants and needs to be clear on the terms of the deal so she is just giving them another chance to do it right.

Jennifer will make people explain something two, three, or more times until she understands all the details. Jennifer refuses to be embarrassed. In fact, she has mentioned more than once that she feels that financial professionals would do a better job of explaining things if more people were honest when answering the question "Do you understand?"

More people should be like Jennifer. She requires a full understanding and explanation. She will not be put off. She guards against the "Yes" Syndrome. She is not embarrassed to say she doesn't understand.

Jennifer is a terrific role-model.

The Price is Important and So Are the Other Terms of the Deal

Two people can buy the same clothes at the same store, select the same cars at the same dealership, run up the same doctor bills, order the same meals from the same menus at the same restaurant, and still pay vastly different amounts. The prices are the same. The difference is in the way they pay for it.

The one who pays cash pays less than the person who finances the purchase and pays interest over time.

The one who pays a lower rate of interest pays less than the person who pays a higher rate.

The person who takes a loan without administrative fees pays less than the person who is charged various fees.

The person who finances and pays those monthly bills on time pays less than the person who falls behind and is assessed late fees and penalties.

When you look at the price tag for an item, keep in mind that the amount you see is not necessarily what you may ultimately pay. There is a lot more that goes into determining the final price of an item. As a consumer it is up to you to ask all the questions necessary to complete the picture.

Kim's Car Was a Beauty

Kim went car shopping. He had a pretty good idea of what he wanted to buy but was still not prepared when he saw the sticker price of $22,500.

He walked around the showroom. He left and he came back, twice. Finally he and the salesman negotiated a deal. Kim could have his dream car for $14,000 plus his trade-in.

Kim was pleased. He was willing to pay the $14,000, but of course, he didn't have $14,000 in his checking account. Kim was going to finance the car. He agreed to take out the loan for 3 years at 9.5 percent. Kim didn't count on $800 in additional sales tax, title fee, registration fee, and license plate fee that went with buying and financing the car. Next time Kim will know better.

Working Through Any Deal Involves a Four Step Process

You may not consciously think of each separate step every time you buy something but the process is there nonetheless.

Step 1: You decide that you want or need to purchase a particular item or basket of items. You might go to the mall to pick up all sorts of things. Or you might go to a particular store to purchase one thing.

Step 2: You find what you are looking for at a price that you think is fair and that you are willing to pay. Sometimes the price they are asking and the price you are willing to pay are one and the same. Other times it is not. If the price is too high, you won't buy it. If it is an emergency, you will pay almost any price. If you find a bargain, you might buy something earlier than you had planned.

Step 3: Once the decision to purchase has been made, you decide if you are going to pay cash or finance (charge) your purchase. It's the old "Cash or Charge" question that always comes up.

Step 4: If you decide to finance, you decide on the terms you are willing to accept.

When a Tank Of Gas is Not Just a Tank of Gas

Here's a simple example of the four step process. You are driving along and you glance at the fuel gauge. It's getting toward empty and you know you need to find a gas station. (Step 1: You have made the decision that you will buy gas for your car.)

Naturally, you don't want to pay more than you have to, so you look at the sign listing the current price for gas. If there is a neighborhood station you frequent, that's where you go, if you have enough gas to get you there. If you are running on fumes you pull into the nearest station no matter what the price. (Step 2: You decide what is a fair price and what you are willing to pay.)

You look in your wallet to see how much cash you have on hand. (Step 3: You decide how you are going to pay.) Actually, you may have lots of options. You may decide to pay with cash, write a check, or use a debit card, gas card, or credit card. If you opt to pay cash, the amount of money in your wallet determines the amount of gas you will buy. If you decide to use a gas or credit card you will probably fill your tank.

If you use a gas or credit card you will have to decide which card you want to use if you have more than one. If you make it a practice to pay your gasoline charges in full every month, then it really doesn't matter very much. If, on the other hand, you carry a balance, you will want to use the card which carries the best terms. (Step 4: You determine if you will use a credit card which carries a 6.9 percent introductory annual interest rate, a 12.9 variable rate, an 18.9 fixed rate, or a 21.9 regular rate.)

The point is, every time you put gas in the car you have made a series of choices. The cost at the pump may come to $15. If you pay cash, that's that, unless you are at a station which gives you a discount for cash. If you charge the gas, you may still only pay $15 if you pay the bill in full when it comes in. If you drag out the payments, you could pay $18 or $20 or more for that same tank of gas because of the accumulating finance charge.

This same process applies when you buy clothes, eat out, go to the doctor, shop for a car, look for a house, or decide to attend college. Once you decide to buy and determine the price you will pay, you have to figure out how you are going to cover the tab. If you want to pay with cash, then you must have the money available right now. If you decide to pay by taking on debt and repaying that debt over time, you need to understand the terms you are agreeing to.

The Case of the Leaking Dishwasher

Kate had had it. Every time she turned on the dishwasher, she had to mop up the puddle of water that ran through to the basement. Finally, she called a plumber (at a cost of $45 for the visit). He told her the dishwasher was shot and that a new one would cost between $200 and $400 plus installation.

She thanked him for his visit and advice and paid him the $45. Then she looked in her checkbook. There was not an extra $400.

Kate wanted a new dishwasher, but she didn't want to go into debt for it. She felt that although she wanted a new dishwasher she would get along without one until she could afford to pay for it. She thought she could put away $50 a month. Five or six months wasn't so long. She could do dishes by hand until then.

Then the Sunday paper arrived with a big ad for dishwashers at $50 to $100 off the regular price. Kate decided it was too good a deal to pass up and decided to go shopping. She bought the dishwasher that was on sale for $250. (Installation was going to be another $50.) The fact remained that she didn't have $300, so she borrowed it. While she got the dishwasher she wanted, and she got it without waiting and $50 off the regular price, she turned a good deal into a lousy one. The reason the deal was bad was despite the $50 savings off the regular price, she ended up paying $80 in interest and $50 in installation charges.

Perhaps the biggest mistake that people make when they finance a purchase is that they fail to take into account the true cost of the purchase. They don't know what the loan is going to cost them from beginning to end. They don't ask about the interest rate, how long they will pay, and what happens if they fall behind in their payments. They just want to know what it is going to cost them every month.

Some lenders say they honestly feel that some people don't really want to know. They tell themselves that it's only so many dollars every month so the interest rate doesn't really matter.

Every Loan Has Four Common Criteria

These 4 criteria determine if you are getting a good deal on what you finance. You must understand these criteria and how they work. A lack of understanding can cost you tens of thousands of dollars, perhaps more. A clear understanding of loan terms can save you those dollars. The four criteria are:

• **Loan fees.** Lenders will tell you what you are being charged for them to process the loan. Sometimes you have to ask. In fact you should ask at the very beginning of the loan process so there are no nasty surprises later on.

• **Interest rate.** When you borrow money, you have to pay it back, plus interest. The interest rate you agree to pay should be competitive with what other lenders are charging someone with your financial history, work background, savings, and so on.

• **Length of the loan.** The longer the loan, the lower your monthly payments but the more interest you will pay over time. You may be better off taking shorter loans, assuming you can afford the higher monthly payments.

• **All the other fine print.** This is where people get into the most trouble. They fail to read all the terms and conditions of the loan they are taking on. If and when hard times arise, they find themselves in a heck of a mess.

When you understand the terms of your loan and you are happy with what you are agreeing to, you are getting a good deal. When you do not understand the terms, there is every chance that you will be unhappy with the deal should you find out what you agreed to.

Remember Kim and his car? He came up with the extra $800 he needed to close the deal, but he wasn't happy about it. Like most people, Kim really dislikes extra charges that are not disclosed right up front. He financed the $14,000 car loan over 3 years at 9.5 percent. His payments came to $448.47 a month. The grand total of all those payments came to $16,144.92. So the true cost of the car was not the trade-in plus $14,000, but rather $16,144.92. Kim will pay $2,144.92 in interest over 3 years, or almost $60 a month more.

Two weeks later Kim was visiting with a couple of his friends. He was showing off his new car. One of his pals asked him about the financing. Kim learned that he could have financed the deal through a different lender at 8.75 percent rather than the 9.5 percent he agreed to. At first Kim was really angry that he was saddled with the higher interest rate for 3 long years. Later, when he put pencil to paper he calculated that his monthly payment at the lower interest rate would have been $443.57. He would have saved $4.90 a month. Kim decided that it only amounted to the price of one lunch a month. But over the life of the loan, he is out $176.40. Maybe that's worth being upset about. Maybe not.

Still, he thought, why didn't someone tell me that I could have gotten a better interest rate elsewhere? The answer is easy enough to figure out. **It was Kim's job to shop for the best terms.** It was not the lender's job to tell Kim to take his business down the street to the lender's competitor where Kim might get a better deal. Still, all is not lost. Kim can investigate refinancing elsewhere to see if he could save the $176.40.

A Dramatic Example of What You Can Save

Pat always wanted a house of her own. Finally, she found it. The price tag was $165,000. She had been saving her money, and combining what she had saved plus $2,500 she got from her parents, she was able to come up with a $15,000 down payment. That meant she would look for a $120,000 mortgage. She has the income and debt-to-income ratio to qualify for this size loan.

Pat wanted to know what the $150,000 mortgage would mean in terms of monthly payments. Assuming a mortgage of 6 percent over 30 years, Pat will pay $899.34 a month. The grand total she will spend on the mortgage to buy her $165,000 house comes to $323,762.40. Over the years, Pat will pay $185,762.40 in interest.

Is this the best deal for Pat? Let's change the terms just a little bit. The price of the house remains the same and so does the interest rate. But instead of making payments over 30 years, Pat agrees to a 20 year mortgage loan. Now the monthly mortgage amount is $1,074.66, an increase of $175.32 a month. However, the grand total she will spend on the mortgage is $257,918.40, which represents a savings of more than $65,844. So the question becomes, would Pat rather stretch her budget a little bit by paying $175.32 more each month for 20 years so she can save $66,000? Sounds like a pretty good deal, assuming that she stays in the house that long.

Let's shorten the loan term another 5 years. How much would she save by paying the loan off in 15 years rather than 20 years? A 15 year mortgage at 6 percent means a monthly payment of $1,265.85, or $227,844 over the life of the loan. So for another $191.14 a month over 15 years, Pat could save herself another $30,074.40 in interest charges.

Administrative Loan Fees Can Break a Deal

Carlos needed a loan. He wanted to consolidate some of his credit card debts. He didn't owe a lot of money, just a bit over $4,000. He wanted to pull everything together and get a lower interest rate than he was paying.

Carlos had the right idea. He went to a local lender and filled out a loan application. He told the loan officer how much money he wanted and what he wanted to do with it. He was honest about his job, his personal history, and his past history with credit and debt. Everything was going along fine.

The loan officer explained that Carlos would probably be approved for a loan under the following terms: He would have to repay the loan over 2 years and pay a 12 percent interest rate. The monthly payments would be $188.30. In addition, he would have to pay a loan processing fee of $125, a credit bureau fee of $35, and a recording fee of $25.

The extra $185 in fees was enough to nix the deal. Over the 2 years of the loan, Carlos would pay $519.20 for the privilege of borrowing and repaying $4,000. When you add in another $185 in fees and charges, the entire equation changes. Now the true cost of the loan over the 2 years is $704.20.

Administrative fees and charges that lenders may require in order to process your loan can be substantial. They run up your cost of borrowing. They can turn a good deal for you into one that you may not be willing to accept. These fees and charges show up under all sorts of different names, like origination fee, commitment fee, underwriting fee, and processing fee. Whatever a lender calls them, they mean the same thing to the borrower — more money out of your pocket.

Sometimes a lender will allow the borrower to add

these fees and charges to the amount of the loan. That in itself may sound enticing because you don't have to pay for them immediately. Just be aware that you will have to pay later, plus you will pay interest on these fees and charges over the life of the loan.

Obviously borrowers are better off keeping these administrative fees to a minimum. Often these expenses are negotiable. You may be able to get some fees eliminated or at least reduced.

Typically, lenders know each other quite well. Each lender knows what their competitors are charging borrowers to rent their money. As a result, loan terms and conditions tend to be comparable.

However, on a daily, weekly or monthly basis, there will be one or more lenders in town who will actually run special promotions, just like your favorite retail store in the mall. You have seen sales on shoes and shirts. Lenders do the same thing with money. "Step right up. This week only we have a special rate on loans for new and used cars and trucks."

If you are not certain what terms you can get from a lender, stop by and ask. That's right, shop for the most favorable loan terms.

Carlos was not happy with add-on fees he was being asked to pay. He tried to get them reduced but the lender was adamant.

So Carlos left and went elsewhere. He found the same loan amount at 15 percent rather than 12 percent but without all those extra charges. It was going to cost him $193.95 a month ($5.65 a month more), but the administrative cost was only $50 (a savings of $135). The interest over the life of the loan comes to $654.80. When he added in the $50 fee, he found that the total cost of the loan was $704.80, the same as the other loan.

Carlos found out that the 2 deals were almost exactly the same. Carlos took the one that didn't require him to pay all those administrative fees up front.

The Interest Rate is Only One of the Keys

When comparing loan terms, most people first think of finding the lowest interest rate. Carlos found that the lowest rate doesn't always mean the best loan, or put another way, he found that the higher rate does not always mean a bad loan. Nevertheless, the fact is the lower the interest rate on your loan, the lower your monthly payments will be.

The federal Truth-In-Lending law requires lenders to present all the terms of the loan in a uniform manner. Lenders quote the Annual Percentage Rate (or A.P.R.) on the loan. That way borrowers can compare rates from one lender to another. **The A.P.R. takes into account the initial interest rate, how the interest is compounded, and the fees the lender is charging.**

One thing to keep in mind is that the A.P.R. may not be the same as the interest rate quoted on the loan contract. That's due primarily to the additional fees and expenses charged by the lender.

Another way to compare interest rates from one lender to another is to ask the lender to calculate the total amount of interest you will have to pay over the life of the loan. They have to do that on all loan documents. All other things being equal, you should be able to compare various loan deals and make an informed decision.

Fixed Versus Variable Interest Rates

The amount of interest you pay on your loan depends on the interest rate you agree to in the loan document. In years past, the rate was set, just like all the other terms of the loan. You might have to pay 9 percent on a car loan, or 8 percent on a home mortgage, or 14 percent on a personal loan, or 18 percent on a credit card balance.

Today, it is not quite so simple. Now there are fixed interest rate loans and there are variable (or adjustable) rate loans.

With a fixed interest rate, the rate will stay the same for the life of the loan.

With a variable interest rate, the rate can change every so often. The frequency depends on what the loan document says.

Credit cards come in the fixed or variable rate varieties. Check the statement which comes with the credit card offer. If it's variable, see how they calculate the rate. Chances are it's going to be complicated. This is how one credit card issuer figures the interest rate on its variable rate accounts. If the account is in good standing, it charges a rate which is 11.43 percent above the 3-month London Interbank Offered Rate published in The Wall Street Journal on the third Wednesday of March, June, September and December "LIBOR"). The rate for cash advances on this particular card is 14.24 percent above LIBOR, or 19.8 percent. If your account is not in good standing, meaning that you do not meet the repayment requirements described in the Cardholder Agreement, the variable rate jumps to LIBOR plus 15.21 percent.

Where can you find a quote on the current LIBOR rate? Check the business section of the newspaper.

With a variable rate, credit card issuers will also tell you how frequently the rate can be adjusted.

Mortgages are another place where you can choose between a fixed and an adjustable rate loan. Again, determine the frequency of the adjustment period (1 year is typical), how high or low that adjustment can be (usually 1 or 2 percentage points), and the ceiling or floor for the interest rate (perhaps the rate cannot vary by more than 5 percentage points above or below the original rate.) The interest rate on a business loan is usually variable.

Then there is the introductory (or teaser) rate being offered by many credit card companies. You start with an interest rate as low as 0 percent for 3 months to a year and then the rate increases to the standard rate which is usually substantially higher.

One difficulty with a variable rate loan is it can foul up your long range planning. If interest rates increase, the monthly payment on your adjustable rate loan will increase, too, and that can throw your budget into chaos.

The Length of the Loan

How long is it going to take you to repay what you borrow? One year, 2 years, 30 years? This is a question worth considering before you borrow.

Mortgages typically run for 15, 20 or 30 years. However, the length can be customized to suit the borrower.

Car loans can run as long as 7 years or be as short as a year or 2.

Personal loans can be for 1-5 years.

Credit card balances can take up to 30 years to repay if all you make is the minimum payment. That's why it's always in your best interest to pay more than the minimum payment.

Installment and Revolving Loans

There are 2 basic types of loans. There's the **installment loan** like Carlos is seeking. It is for a certain amount ($4,000), a fixed interest rate (15 percent), and a set period of time (2 years.) Assuming Carlos makes his monthly payments, at the end of the 2 years, the loan will be repaid.

The rule of thumb is, the longer the loan term, the smaller your monthly payments but the more interest you will pay over the length of the loan. The shorter the loan term, the larger your monthly payments and the less interest you will pay over time.

Then there's the **revolving loan.** The best example of a revolving loan is the well-known credit card. Here you take on debt. The card issuer lets you know what the current rate of interest is on your unpaid balance. And there is no time frame imposed by the lender for you to repay what you owe. As long as you make at least a minimum payment, you can go on for years.

Lenders will usually tell you that when given a choice, you are better off with an installment loan simply because your loan payments serve to reduce the amount you owe. With a revolving loan such as a credit card, the balances tend to stay the same.

Secured and Unsecured Loans

When you take out either an installment or a revolving loan, you promise to repay what you borrow. What's more, you acknowledge in writing that if you fail to keep your promise, the lender is permitted to try to collect from you all that you owe, plus interest and the cost of collection, by all means allowed by law and spelled out in the loan agreement you signed.

When making loans, lenders prefer to make secured loans. The reason is simple enough. When you agree to a secured loan, you give the lender more than just your written promise that you will repay what you are borrowing. You are also pledging certain property so that if, for whatever reason, you default on your loan, the lender has something it can easily find, take physical possession of, and quickly sell. Don't for a minute think that the lender won't go after property that you have pledged as collateral. It will do just that if you fall too far behind.

It's Usually With Regard to the Length of the Loan That People Fool Themselves

Let's say you are in the market for a car. You start shopping. You visit 3 or 4 car lots to get a feel for what you'd like. If you are like most people, you have a figure in mind. Unfortunately, the number you are thinking of is not the price of the car. Rather it is the amount of monthly payment you feel you can afford. If you are comfortable making a monthly payment for a vehicle of $300 a month, you are asking the question, "how much car can I get for that amount of money?" That all depends on the other terms. It's enough to cover a $6,500 car loan at 9.5 percent over 2 years, or $12,000 over 4 years, or $16,500 over 6 years. So, what will it be?

Since most people want to know what they can afford at a given price (say $300 a month), that is the precise question that the sales person at the car lot will ask. "So, you're looking for a car? What do you want your monthly payments to be?" Armed with that information, the sales person can steer you to what you can afford.

Most advertising today is geared toward monthly payments; often times the actual price is not even mentioned.

All the Other Fine Print

Without question, this is the part of the loan that presents the most difficulty. People understand that they need to ask if there are administrative fees and charges, how much they are, and what they are for. They also need to know what the interest rate is so they can compare one loan with another. The term or life of the loan is not a difficult concept. You should know how long you are going to pay for that car. The same holds true for a mortgage and any other kind of installment loan. You also know what the general terms are for credit card loans.

Perhaps you have heard the cliché "The devil is in the detail." It's true. When it comes to borrowing money, whether it is a mortgage loan, a car loan, a credit card, or other loan, you have to understand the details. And there can be a lot of them.

Have you ever noticed the ads that appear in the newspaper and on television, touting the great terms for this or that loan? The interest rate appears in bold letters. The fine print is so tiny that you cannot read it without great difficulty, and that's with a magnifying glass.

Stop down at a local lender and ask for a copy of the loan document that they use. They should be willing to give you one. Take it home and read it, carefully. Make sure you understand all of the terms that appear on it. Go through all the fine print. When you do, you will actually see just what it is that you are agreeing to.

When some lenders make a loan, they use two forms; they have the promissory note and they have a security agreement. Other lenders use a single form combining both the promissory note and security agreement onto one long sheet of paper. It doesn't really matter from the consumer's standpoint which one they use.

The language contained in the note and security agreement doesn't vary much from lender to lender, although there are differences in the language from state to state because the laws are slightly different.

- There's information about your name and address.

- There's the promise you make to pay the lender a certain amount of money plus interest.

- The document talks about interest charges.

- The payment schedule.

- Charges for late payments.

- If the note can be renewed.

- A penalty for paying the note early.

- If there is security or collateral required on your part.

- Whether or not the loan can be extended.

- What happens if you default.

- What happens if you try to pay with a bad check.

- Who pays legal and collection costs.

- If the lender can take money from your other accounts and apply it to the loan.

- Information about co-signers and guarantors.

- The terms of your security interest in the loan.

- A place for the signatures for all the parties involved.

That's a lot of information and fine print.

It doesn't matter. When you are asked to sign a loan document, you must take the time to read and understand the terms.

The details on a car loan can run page after page. They are usually pre-printed on the back of the forms that car dealers use.The contract has been drafted by the lender's attorneys and the terms are not negotiable. Just be aware of what you are agreeing to.

Mortgage loans are full of fine print. Just ask Paul who took the time to read all of it.

Whatever loan you take out, check the details of the fine print. If you don't you won't know what you are agreeing to.

Paul and Debbie signed a contract to buy their first home. Settlement day finally came, and they showed up at the appointed place and time. They had the check they were told to bring. They had also been warned that they would be signing a lot of papers.

There must have been 50 pieces of paper in the stack requiring signatures in at least 20 different places. Much to the dismay of everyone at the settlement, Paul settled in to start reading. When asked what he thought he was doing, he replied, "Exactly what every consumer protection advisor tells you to do. I'm reading the fine print so I will know exactly what I am agreeing to. After all, a whole battery of lawyers thought it was important enough to write all this stuff down. The least I can do is read it and understand it."

"It's just standard stuff," said the lender, the title company representative, the real estate agents, and the clerk.

"It may be standard stuff for you, but not for me," was Paul's reply. "If the fine print wasn't important, you wouldn't require that I agree to it. I want to know what it says before I sign."

His wife was embarrassed, and the people around the table shrugged their shoulders and called him a "reader", a derogatory term which describes people who take their time reading all the documents. But Paul didn't care. He read and read and read. It took nearly 2 hours. He marked all the areas he didn't understand with yellow post-it notes. Then he started asking questions.

Paul did the right thing, despite fouling up everyone's schedule.

When you are called upon to sign a credit card agreement, a car lease, a car loan, a mortgage, or any other loan document, you had better spend the time reading what you are signing, and understanding exactly what you are obligating yourself to do. If it's going to take you some time to read and digest all the details, then you should ask for the loan documents a day or two in advance so you can study them. That way, if there is a problem, if there is something that you disagree with, or if there is a requirement you are not willing to accept, you will have time to discuss it with the lender and perhaps negotiate more agreeable terms.

Negotiate? As a practical matter, you can negotiate some loan terms and not others. But if there are terms which you simply cannot accept, then you had better know that before you sign. There may be terms so unacceptable to you that you decide to walk away from the deal.

In Paul's case, his eye for detail resulted in the discovery that the interest rate was 1/8 percent more than he had originally agreed to, there were $349 more in closing costs, and the address of the property was wrong.

Today, the terms of the agreement are written much more clearly than they used to be. It doesn't take a team of lawyers to figure out what a loan document says. If you have a high school education, you can understand what is required. Just take the time to read all the fine print.

Credit Card Terms Are Among the Most Variable

How many credit card applications do you receive in the mail during a typical month? Some people get dozens, each touting the benefits of one card over another. Remember, credit card balances are revolving loans, not installment loans. As long as you make the minumum payment, you may pay for decades.

There are at least 12 different terms you need to know about when deciding on a credit card:

- The annual fee (if any).

- The Annual Percentage Rate (APR) for purchases and balance transfers.

- Whether the interest rate is fixed or variable. If variable, what the terms are for the adjustment.

- The grace period for repayment of purchases, if any. Some cards make you pay interest from the date of purchase whether or not you have an outstanding balance. Others won't charge you interest on this month's purchases as long as you paid last month's balance in full.

- The minimum finance charge.

- The method of computing the balance on which interest is charged.

- The amount of your credit limit.

- The penalty for late payment.

- The penalty for exceeding your credit limit.

- The fee for cash advances.

- If there is an introductory low interest rate, what it is and how long it will last.

- What interest rate you will be charged if you do not keep your account in good standing by making timely payments.

Shop For the Right Deal

If you don't like the terms and conditions offered by one lender, visit another. Perhaps you can do better. And if you don't like what you find at the second lender, see a third.

Don't think for a minute that the deck is stacked against borrowers and in favor of lenders. The facts simply do not justify that conclusion. Get a telephone book and turn to the yellow pages. Look up the heading "Loans." You will find listing after listing of banks, credit unions and finance companies. All want your business as long as you are creditworthy. Credit card issuers continue to flood the mail with one introductory offer after another.

Car dealers offer on-site financing.

So do many furniture and appliance dealers.

Many of the major department stores have their own credit cards and installment repayment programs.

Gasoline retailers have their own credit cards.

As a consumer you are being courted, wined and dined, and proposed to on a regular basis. "If you are creditworthy, please, please, please come see us when you want to borrow some money. We will give you the best deal, the lowest interest rate, and the most lenient terms," they say. "We'll meet and beat any deal in town."

Well, perhaps it is not quite that easy, but almost.

The Gentle Art of Negotiation

You can get the deal that best fits your needs if you are willing to shop a little, pay attention to all the details, and negotiate. Of course, you have to have good credit.

Picture this. You are sitting in front of a loan officer applying for a loan. You tell her what you want the money for and how you will repay it. You supply all the information that she asks for. Then she tells you that your application looks fine and that you should be able to pick up the money by noon the next day.

Now you get into the terms, interest rate, fees, and length of the loan. You know you can do better. So you tell her that the interest rate is 1/2 percentage point too high and the lender down the street will offer you the same deal but at a better rate, or that you don't want to pay all those fees and another lender will do the deal without the fees.

"So what can you do for me? Cut the interest rate? Reduce the fees? If not, I'll go elsewhere. Nothing personal. It's just business. I work too hard for my money to pay more for a loan than I have to."

That's not being mean or nasty. It's not that you are being disloyal to the place you conduct your regular financial affairs. It's just shopping for the best deal.

Recall Kim the car shopper. He found the right car for the right price, but he didn't shop for the right loan terms. When he found out that he could have financed the car at a lower rate, he was angry at the lender for not telling him. Kim was angry at the wrong person. He didn't do his homework. He should have made a few calls to find out what the going interest rate was.

He should have asked if there were any special financing programs coming up. Yes, specials. Lenders are always trying to get new business so they run advertising campaigns. "Step right up and get your special car loan today. Interest rates are good only through the end of the week." It sounds like a barker at a carnival and in essence it is. Lenders are competing for your business. So shop for bargains.

Pick Your Spots

Negotiating the fine points on a small loan may not be very effective. When the difference is only $5 or so a month, it may not be worth the haggling.

One lender offers this example. You want to borrow $1,500. You need to know that loans of that size are usually not cost effective for most lenders. They will do them but usually as an accomodation to you. If you want that $1,500 for 12 months, you may be quoted a 13 percent interest rate, and a monthly payment of $133.98. You may have been quoted 12 percent by another lender down the street. That 12 percent rate would mean $133.27 a month for a savings of 71 cents a month.

That's not worth haggling over.

Legal Rights of the Lender if You Fail to Keep Your Promise

Listen to the language contained on a typical "secured" loan document. These contracts used to be written in technical language that was terribly difficult to understand. Today the verbiage is much clearer. Still, if you are not familiar with the terminology being used, you may need to study what is being said. If you still have trouble, remember Jennifer who refused to be embarrassed. Get some help from a person who understands these contracts.

Remember Paul who insisted on reading all the fine print before he was willing to sign all the mortgage papers? Imitate him. Don't let people pressure you into signing a contract that you have not read or that you do not fully understand. Read what you are agreeing to especially when it comes to pledging your possessions against a loan payment.

Here's a typical series of promises required by a lender.

"To protect you (the lender) if I (the borrower) default under this loan agreement (or any extension or renewal of it), I give you a security interest in the following property. (Here's where the description of the property goes. Things like your car, house, other real estate, bank accounts, investments, and so on.)"

"I will keep the secured property insured if you require it, and I will pay all related taxes when due."

"If I am in default, you have my permission to repossess and sell my property that you hold as security and use the money from the sale of the property to pay my loan. If you get more than I owe, you will send me the difference. If you don't get enough to cover my outstanding debt, I will owe you the difference despite the fact that the property has been sold."

"You may also exercise any other legal rights you may have."

"In addition, I agree to pay any reasonable attorney's fees, legal expenses and costs of collection that result from my default."

"If I am in default, you may take the money from any of my accounts I may have with you to pay what I owe. My accounts include all accounts to which I am a party, so if I have a joint account with another person, you can use the money in that account. You may do all this without notifying me."

"I own the property securing this loan, free and clear of competing interests (except recorded liens that I have told you about.)"

"I promise that I will not sell or give any of the property that you have a security interest in to anyone else or surrender possession of it without your written permission. I understand that you don't have to give me your permission. In fact, you probably won't."

"I will keep the property in good repair."

"I will provide you with financing statements at your request."

"I will give you 30 days advance written notice before changing the address where the property securing this loan is kept, including removal to another state."

"Your security interest covers all proceeds from the sale of the property or the insurance proceeds payable as a result of the damage or destruction of the property. Your security interest also includes all goods installed or attached to the property." For example, if I borrow money to buy a car and I put in a $800 stereo, that stereo becomes part of the security for the car loan.

Wow! If you are going to promise all that, you better not fall behind in your loan payments.

Default

Now you know specifically what the lender can do with your property if you break your promise to make each loan payment in full and on time. Technically, if you miss making a full and timely payment, you are in "default" on your loan. But what does a lender really consider to be "default?"

Are you in default if you are a month late with your payment? Yes.

A week? Yes.

A day? Yes.

Are you in default if you make only a partial payment? Yes.

Can you get back in the good graces of a lender by making up missed payments? Can you make up a payment and bring a loan current? Perhaps.

The fact is, bringing your account current does not necessarily cure the default. Check the specific language in the loan document before you sign it to determine exactly what a lender means by the term "default." Here's what one lender requires that you agree to before it will make a secured loan.

I am in default when:

"I do not make a payment when due or do not make a payment in the full amount." Notice it doesn't say anything about being given any grace period, and it doesn't give you any leeway to make a partial payment.

"I made misstatements on my loan application." Yes, a lender can demand full repayment of the loan balance if it finds you have lied outright on the loan application. The same holds true when it finds you have exaggerated the truth, or even failed to disclose material facts about your finances.

"Someone tries by legal proceedings to get money or property I have on deposit with you." You are in default if someone sues you and tries to attach either the secured property or your savings account.

"I do not make a payment when due on any other loans I may already have with you or on any other loans I may have with you in the future." If you fall behind on one loan, the lender figures you could fall behind on other loans, too, so it will want its money.

"A case under the U.S. Bankruptcy Code is started by me or against me or any guarantor of this loan." A bankruptcy proceeding is a red flag to a lender.

"I do not keep required insurance on the security for this agreement or I fail to pay any related taxes on the security when due, or I use the security for an unlawful purpose."

"I die." That's the ultimate default.

"You believe in good faith that I may not be able or willing to pay you as promised." No proof required.

If I Default, What Are You Going to Do About It?

Again, check the loan document to see what the lender can do. Read on:

"If I am in default, you may require immediate payment of the unpaid balance on this loan, including the interest I owe."

"You may repossess and sell my property that you hold as security and use the proceeds to pay my loan. You will notify me at least 10 days before the sale."

"If I am in default, you do not have to accept any payments from me unless required to by law. If you do accept payments, you do not waive any of your other rights, including the right to demand that I immediately pay all I owe you."

The point is, when you take out a secured loan, you will probably have to agree to let the lender claim certain property that you have, sell it, and apply what it gets from the sale against what you owe.

Now, this bears repeating. If the lender gets enough cash to cover your debt (plus all of its expenses associated with the default and sale), it will mark your loan "Paid" and that will be the end of the matter, except, of course, for the black mark on your credit record. If there is extra money, you will get it. If the cash from the sale is not enough to cover your debt, you are responsible for the difference.

Generally, you will apply for a secured as opposed to to an unsecured loan when you:

- Finance a new or used car or truck. The lender will keep title to the vehicle until the very last payment is made.

- Finance the purchase of big ticket items such as appliances, furniture and home electronics. Again, the lender will want to keep title to the property until you repay what you have borrowed.

- Finance a mortgage loan. The lender will keep the title to the property until the mortgage is paid in full. Miss your payments and you stand to lose the house, including any down payment and equity you may have built up.

- Borrow against the equity in your home with a home equity loan. Not all states allow home equity loans, although most do. Where permitted, the lender will file a lien at the court house to secure its interests. If you fall behind on your home equity loan payments, the lender can enforce the lien and you could lose your house.

- Refinance existing secured loans. A lender will want clear title to the property when it refinances a loan so it can be first in line just in case you fall behind with your payments.

- Pledge assets against the outstanding loan balance of a loan used for other purposes. You can ask a lender to borrow money that would otherwise take the form of a personal, unsecured loan and get better terms for the loan by offering a security interest in certain property.

Security

Security is a simple enough concept. If you do not make your payments as you promised you would, you stand to lose what you have pledged as security for the loan. If you default, the lender can take the property and sell it for whatever it can get.

What is the lender willing to take as security? That depends on the lender of course; however most lenders agree that some property will qualify as security for a loan while other property will not.

Ideally, a lender will want property that it can get its hands on easily, has a measurable market value, and can be sold relatively quickly.

Residential, rental, and commercial real estate qualifies. So do stocks and bonds which are traded on the major stock exchanges. Savings accounts will do. So will certificates of deposit, and cash value life insurance contracts.

IRAs and other tax-qualified retirement accounts do not qualify. Neither do U.S. Savings Bonds.

Lenders are not likely to lend against artwork, hard-to-value specialized equipment, and household goods. Don't expect lenders to lend against coin collections, stamp collections, Mom's award-winning county-fair quilts, collectibles, antiques, and similar stuff. Usually they won't lend against jewelry either because it will rarely fetch more than 25 percent of its retail cost and there is a limited market.

A Case of Overkill

Not only are some forms of property unacceptable to lenders when it comes to pledging security for a loan, lenders will usually require that you pledge assets that are worth substantially more than you are borrowing. In addition, lenders won't usually loan you 100 percent of the market value of the property you are using as security. Typically, they will lend you between 50 and 80 percent of the market value of the property. That way they are covered if you default and they have to hold a quick sale during a soft market.

Danny wanted that truck. The lender told him that they would lend 80 percent of the purchase price and no more. The lender wanted Danny to put some of his own money into the truck. When he came up with the money for the down payment, the lender made the loan, securing it with the title to the truck.

Danny won't get the title to the truck until he makes the very last payment, even though the lender has less and less risk of losing its loan with every payment that Danny makes.

It may not seem fair, but that's the deal. Buy a $20,000 car. Put $4,000 down, and take out a $16,000 loan for 48 months (4 years.) Make payments on time for 3 1/2 years. At that point, the loan balance is less than $3,000, and the lender still has title to the car which is probably worth well over $10,000.

Sue wanted to start her own business. She approached a lender and asked for $45,000. The lender agreed because Sue had the income to support the loan and was willing to pledge a piece of real estate that the county assessed at $100,000. Why did the lender demand security worth so much more than the amount being borrowed? Because real estate is tough to sell quickly.

Don wanted a business loan of $120,000 to upgrade some equipment and expand the property. The lender was willing to make the loan, but demanded security worth $200,000. That's not the least bit unusual.

Summing Up

It's the terms that make or break a deal, along with the price of the merchandise of course. What's a good deal and what's not? That all depends on what you are willing to pay and what financing terms you are willing to accept.

Perhaps the biggest mistake people make is that they rush into a deal despite price and terms because they want instant gratification. They want it now. They don't want to wait. Don't let this happen to you.

Angie perhaps said it best. "No deal is so good that it won't wait until next week."

Remember, the better your credit, the better the terms you can get. The end result is you will pay less for what you purchase. That's important because the less you have to pay for things, the more money you have available to realize your dreams.

LESSON SIX
(Rev. June 2004)

AUTO LOANS AND LEASES

The last time you bought (or leased) a car, did you get a good deal? How do you know? Would the dealership have charged less if you negotiated harder? Was your financing the best you could find? Are you sure?

Do you know all that you need to know about buying or leasing a car? Chances are, you are among the 99 out of 100 who do not. Nevertheless, you will probably still go car shopping, find the make and model that strikes your fancy, and ink the deal even though you know you are terribly unprepared.

Setting up a car deal requires a lot of knowledge, especially as it relates to the terms of your loan or lease. Let's face it. A car is a very big-ticket item, very big indeed. While you probably buy and sell a home only a couple of times between your 20's and 70's, you will, most likely, find yourself at the car lot at least once every 4-5 years, if not more frequently. Today, new car prices average over $25,000 and used cars are holding their value. The prices on new and used cars continue to go up with no end in sight.

Let the Buyer Beware

Do yourself a favor and review the beginning of Lesson Five where it talks about "Trust." The fact is there is a lot to learn about car deals. The old cliche — **Caveat Emptor, or Let The Buyer Beware** — is as true today as it was when it was first uttered centuries ago, and they didn't have cars back then.

Car dealerships are in the business of selling cars and trucks. Banks, credit unions, finance companies and others make their money by financing the deal. The dealership's finance office wants to help arrange the financing because they get fees and commissions, plus they sell things like warranties and credit insurance. That's how everybody makes money on the deal.

It's your money that pays everyone. So that you don't overpay, you need to spend the time it takes to investigate the make and model that suits your needs as well as the financing terms that work best for you. If you overpay, it's your choice, not the dealership's or the lender's. If you don't ask all the questions about financing, it's your fault again.

For example, Michelle recently bought a car and financed it with her lender where she does all of her banking. She asked what the rate was for a $16,000 car loan over 4 years, and the loan officer told her. The rate seemed competitive with what she had heard, so she accepted the deal. Two months later Michelle found out that she could have gotten a 2-1/2 percent lower interest rate because she qualified as a "B" credit risk, rather than a "C" credit risk, which this lender put her in.

Whose choice is it that Michelle is paying more each month than she had to? Michelle's, and no one else. She didn't ask all the questions she should have.

The Love Affair We Have With Our Vehicles

The reality is people own and lease cars so they can get around, go to work, school, shopping and vacation. But cars are more than just basic transportation. Ours is a mobile society and we treasure the independence that driving provides. Public transportation just doesn't satisfy the need people have to go where they want and when they want. On average, people drive about 15,000 miles a year, and whether or not they realize it, folks pay a small fortune for the privilege.

In addition, cars also provide an identity. Don't laugh. Some people "love" their cars. What you drive often makes a statement about who you are and how well you are doing in your career. Cars have become something of a yardstick, certainly they can be a status symbol.

In a recent episode of a television series, a waitress finishes work and jumps into her new BMW. When asked how she could afford such a pricey car, she replied that she had to give up almost everything else in her life in order to get the car. But it was worth the price. The car was the statement she wanted to make and she was willing to do without a lot of things just to have it. Not everyone feels that way. Some people drive their cars until they won't go any further. Some refuse to spend the money on new cars, opting instead for cars that cost only a couple of hundred dollars. They don't care what others think. They prefer to spend their money elsewhere.

Questions You Must Answer

There are at least 7 financial decisions you face even before you start to shop for a car, and they can be daunting. You have to decide:

- How much can you afford or are you willing to spend to purchase a vehicle. This includes your down payment and the monthly payment you will have to make on the balance of your loan.

- How much can you afford or are you willing to spend to operate the vehicle. That includes everything from gas and insurance to tires and repairs.

- If you can afford a down payment, and the amount.

- Whether you will buy or lease.

- If you buy, whether you will pay cash or finance your purchase.

- If you finance, the terms that will work best for you.

- If you lease, the terms which will work best for you.

By the way, each of the decisions, choices and options which come into play when you are ready to purchase or lease a new or used car also applies to trucks. For purposes of this lesson, we only talk about cars, although you can substitute trucks if you prefer.

Can You Afford to Operate a Car?

First things first. When it comes to cars, nothing is free.

Before you even start thinking about buying or leasing a car, you should know what it will cost you to keep the car on the road. As every parent and adult knows, there is more to having a car than just making a down payment and driving away from the showroom. You have to be able to put gas in the tank, keep up your insurance, pay for routine maintenance (unless you do it yourself, and even that costs money), pay for new tires, brakes, and other parts that wear out, and pay city, county and state automobile taxes and registration fees. Finally, you have to be able to afford to park your car.

There are a lot of dollars needed to operate a vehicle. The price of unleaded, regular gasoline has been more than $2 a gallon, depending on where you live. Part of the price is made up of federal and state gasoline taxes. In addition, if you live in a tourist area, gasoline prices tend to increase (sometimes substantially) during the summer season. With the average usage of 15,000 miles a year on a car, you will pay for 600 gallons of gas (assuming 25 miles to a gallon.) You can do the math to calculate how much gasoline is costing you each year. The more you drive, the more you will pay for gas.

The cost of auto insurance can run hundreds of dollars a month, depending on a number of factors:

- The make and model you drive (Corvettes are more expensive to insure than Chevettes).

- Your driving record (accident free drivers pay lower rates than those who have accidents).

- Age (older drivers tend to pay less than younger drivers).

- Gender (females often are charged lower rates than males).

- Locale (some areas of the country are more expensive when it comes to car insurance than others).

- Your liability insurance coverage (the more insurance you want, the higher your insurance premium will be).

- Your deductible (the higher your comprehensive and collision deductible, the lower your premium).

A 45-year-old woman who uses her 6-year-old Toyota Camry only for personal driving may have to pay only $500 a year (or $42 a month) for insurance.

The 17-year old male high school student who does not have terrific grades and who has not bothered to take drivers education will pay $5,000 a year to insure a high performance so-called "muscle" car. (Students can get discounts for good grades and drivers education courses).

There is the cost of keeping your car running safely and smoothly. That means changing the oil, checking the brakes, replacing old batteries, having good tires and keeping the wheels aligned. A new set of steel-belted radial tires can cost $400. Snow tires are not cheap either. Newer cars and cars under warranty will cost their owners less to maintain than older cars which have been driven hard for many miles.

Taxes and registration fees can run from as little as $50 a year to thousands of dollars. In some areas of the country, car owners have to pay an annual tax based on the value of the cars they drive. The tax can amount to 5 percent of the book value of the car each year. On a $10,000 car that's "only" $500, while on a $50,000 luxury car, the tax would be $2,500.

In some cities, it can cost you $300 a month or more simply for the privilege of parking your car in a garage.

Many New Yorkers and residents of other large cities choose to forgo automobile ownership simply because of the cost of parking in the city. They find cabs to be a cheaper and more convenient alternative. When they want to travel, they rent something for the weekend.

If you commute to work from the suburbs and parking is expensive and difficult to find downtown, you may opt to take public transportation. Meanwhile the car sits at home. Nevertheless, you still have to make your car payment, insurance payment, and so on.

How much are you spending to keep your car on the road these days? Go ahead and add what you pay for gasoline, insurance, repairs, maintenance, taxes and parking. You may be shocked at the total. Most people are. Did you have any idea you were spending that much? Still, most people want access to their own transportation and they are willing to pay $600 a month or more for the convenience of being able to go when and where they want.

Stan was in his early 80s and still going strong. His daughter, Audrey, wanted him to give up the car and his driver's license. The reason was understandable, but Stan insisted on maintaining his independence. Strictly from a financial standpoint, Stan and Audrey found that he was paying about $3,000 a year for the privilege of keeping his car, or about $8.20 a day. (The car loan was paid off long ago.) For that amount of money, Stan could take a lot of cabs to the grocery store, the doctor's office and elsewhere around town without being a road hazard. And that's what he did. He got rid of the car, started taking taxis, saved himself a lot of money, and saved Audrey a lot of worry.

Nick was like most teenagers. He wanted to drive. His parents had an older pick-up that they had told him would be his once he was old enough to drive. Nick begged and pleaded for permission to get his license. His parents sat him down and tried to explain that it was more than a matter of just letting him get his license. They went through what it was going to cost to insure a vehicle that was going to be driven by a teenage boy. They told him about the cost of the annual registration fee as well as all the other expenses, including gas, that Nick was going to have to take on himself.

Nick got his license but he had to work in order to pay for all the expenses associated with his driving. That meant an end to all of his extra-curricular activities at school.

The cost of operating a car includes a lot of things. But one thing that has not been included in the total operating cost is what you have to pay for the car itself. That comes next.

How Much Car Can You Afford?

Now that you know what it will cost you to keep a car running as well as parked in front of the house or in the garage, and you have decided that you can afford to spend what it will cost you for gasoline, insurance, repairs and all those other expenses, you still have to purchase or lease the car. That's going to cost you plenty. So, the next decision you have to make is how much you are willing to spend to get your car.

You know the balance in your savings account, and you know if there is some wiggle room or flexibility in your budget. You know how much you make, how much you save, and how you spend what's left. Given that, **you can determine if you want to invade your savings to pay for the car, or use some savings for a down payment and finance the remainder. If you finance, you can calculate what you are willing to spend each month on a car payment, including interest.**

Most people do not pay cash for their cars. Vehicles are simply too expensive. That leaves some sort of financing as the only other alternative.

Lenders use various formulas to determine if you will qualify for a car loan. One formula says that you can spend up to 20 percent of your income on debt service (other than your home.) Here, income means what you make before your taxes and other deductions are taken out of your paycheck. For example, if your income is $3,000 a month, 20 percent is $600. If you are already spending $200 on credit cards (minimum payments) and another $100 on student loans, you have $300 available for a car payment.

Another formula says to take all your debt and divide it by your income. You're fine as long as your debt to income ratio is under 40 percent.

Still, other lenders make a chart of debt and income ratios and charge different loan rates to those who have better debt to income ratios.

These formulas are used by lenders who finance car loans, and they are reluctant to lend you money to finance a car if it means you will exceed their limits.

Twenty percent is the top end. There is no rule that says you must spend 20 percent of your income on debt service, including car loans. You certainly have the option of spending less. While the formula may say that you can afford $300 a month, you may decide that you are uncomfortable spending more than $200 or $250. That is up to you.

Frank and Carol were doing nicely enough. Between them, they earned $4,500 a month and had impeccable credit. They already had one child and wanted another. They had one car (it was 2 years old) and thought it would be nice if they had a second. Before heading for the car lot, they sat down to review their budget to see what they could afford.

They went through the exercise. They took 20 percent of their income ($900), and subtracted what they were already paying on one car loan ($280), the VISA and a store credit card ($175), and his student loan ($155). That left $290.

They talked about it. Finally, they decided that although they probably would qualify for a car loan, they just were not willing to go to the extra expense (along with the extra operating expenses). They decided to put off buying a car until one of them got a raise and they had put more money into their savings so they could make a more substantial down payment. They decided to suffer the personal inconvenience of being a one-car family for the time being until they felt their finances could support a second car payment. They decided all this despite the fact that they had impeccable credit and most lenders would be more than happy to loan them the money to buy a car.

What About A Down Payment?

Two people can purchase the same make and model car, everything can be the same, right down to the paint job and interior trim. Yet the two people can pay vastly different amounts, and it is all because of the amount of the down payment.

Say the car goes for $25,000 "out the door." That means you get everything for that price — the car, taxes, tags, prep charges, everything. Both people take out 4-year loans at 7 percent interest. If one person makes a down payment of $5,000 and finances the $20,000 balance, the monthly payment is $478.93. If the other person goes for a deal where he or she finances 100 percent of the purchase price, the monthly payment is $598.66.

The larger your down payment, the smaller your monthly payment and the less interest you pay over the life of the loan.

Down payments come in 2 forms. You can save month after month until you have enough money to make the monthly payments affordable for your budget. Or you can trade your present car and use what you get on the trade as your down payment. You might even add to it by taking money out of savings. If you want that $25,000 car, and have a car that is worth $10,000 (and you own it free and clear), you can trade the old one in on a new one, using your $10,000 car (or whatever the dealer will give you for it) to reduce the amount you have to borrow to get the new car. Actually, there is a third way to make a down payment. You can sell your car outright and use some or all of the cash you get for the down payment.

The point is, you (not a lender or salesman) should decide what you can comfortably afford, given your income, obligations, personal circumstances, and the amount you can spend on a down payment. This is something you should know before you step on a car lot to look for a car. Visit a lender to see what amount of car loan you qualify for. Review your budget to see what loan payment you can afford. It may be quite a bit less than what the lender will qualify you for. Then go looking for a car.

Make Your Financing Plans Before You Shop

You may be in the market to buy your first car or you may already have one. You may have been given a vehicle some time ago by a parent or other relative, or you may have purchased your first car for $1,500 cash. You may have your brother's or sister's or grandma's hand-me-down. But when the car you are driving wears out, when it breaks down once too often, or when you decide it's time to buy a car just because you want something new, you will find yourself at the car lot. Everyone does.

Actually, you may find yourself at the car dealer because you can no longer resist the enticing advertising message. "Come on down. We have a deal you can't pass up. No money down. Six years to repay. $199 a month. No hassle on-the-spot financing, no matter how bad your credit. No reasonable offer refused. We pay big bucks for your trade-in. We finance anybody."

You have probably heard or read all these ads before, and you will continue to hear them month after month, year after year, simply because these are the marketing buzz words that bring people onto car lots. This kind of advertising works. It gets people to shop for cars. You shouldn't be surprised. After all, car dealers are in the business of selling cars.

If you carefully re-read the advertising messages listed in the preceding paragraph, you will realize that a great deal of a dealer's advertising message talks about financing terms, not the price of the merchandise. Don't you find that interesting?

A young Airman went car shopping one Sunday after-noon and found a new truck that he really liked. The sales-man made him an offer he couldn't refuse. No money down. Payments of only $425 a month. He thought that was great, until Monday morning when he called to change over his car insurance. He found out the insurance on the new truck was going to cost him $100 a month more than he was presently paying. Suddenly his great deal was no longer affordable. He tried to return the truck, but the dealer wouldn't take it. In the end, the Airman ended up trading the truck in on a less expensive one for a large loss. It was a hard lesson to learn, but he should have checked all the details before signing the purchase contract.

Before you go car shopping, not only do you need to know what you are willing to spend each month on the

car you want and the amount of down payment you can afford, but you also need to have a pretty good idea of how you intend to repay what you are going to borrow.

Since you will probably not pay for the car outright, you need to know your price range before you go shopping. Do you have good enough credit to qualify for the amount you will want to borrow to buy the car? If you don't have strong enough credit to qualify for a car loan on your own, you should have a creditworthy co-signer lined up who will step forward to complete the deal. (If you don't have the credit you need to qualify for a car loan, you may want to rethink your car buying plans.) You need to ask your bank, credit union, finance company, and car dealership about the current interest rates and other terms on car loans.

Cooling Off Period

You should not be impulsive when buying a car. It's one thing to splurge for that pack of gum or magazine at the grocery store check out counter. It's quite another to come home with a $25,000 car that you may or may not be able to afford. If you don't have a great deal of will power when it comes to car dealers, you can take one of two precautions. If you are married, shop without your spouse. Then when its time to close the deal, you have the opportunity to leave so you can get your spouse. Or shop but don't bring your checkbook. You can't buy a car if you don't have a way to pay for it.

Buy or Lease

Today, there are 2 ways to get that new or used car of your dreams. You can buy it or you can lease it. Not so many years ago, leasing was not an attractive financial option. Today, it may be.

When you buy a new car, it has its full useful life. You don't have to worry about buying someone else's problems. You have a full factory warranty and a car with the latest equipment and styling. On the other hand, you have a high initial cost, the car declines in value (depreciates) over the years, and because of the high cost of the new car, you will pay higher insurance rates than you would with a less expensive car.

Leasing also has its pros and cons. Your monthly payments are lower. The down payment is low too. You get to drive a new or almost new car almost all the time. On the other hand, you never own it, you have mileage restrictions, and you have to understand the terms of the lease contract so there are no surprises when the lease expires.

Is it better to buy or lease? There is no simple answer.

When you buy, you are making a purchase. You pay the price that you have agreed to pay. If you finance, you pay the price plus interest over the length of the loan. Once the loan is paid off, the car is yours to do with as you please.

When you lease, you strike a different deal. With a lease, you are paying primarily for the amount the car depreciates while you have it, plus an interest charge. At the end of the lease, you can turn the car in, buy it for about half of the sticker price, or lease another. The choice is yours.

If you are someone who buys a car by taking out a loan, and as soon as the car loan is paid off, you rush to the dealership and buy another, you may want to consider leasing. Essentially you are doing the same thing, only with a lease your payments are lower.

If you buy and drive the car for 6, 8, or 10 years or more, you are probably better off buying than leasing. If you want or need a newer car all the time, leasing may make the most sense.

Leases have become easier to understand and have become more consumer-friendly. Still, leases have a language all their own. You have to know terms such as: acquisition fee, capitalized cost, closed-end versus open-end leases, disposal or disposition fee, GAP insurance, purchase fee, purchase-option price, residual value, and subvented lease. If you don't, you need to find someone who will explain them to you and what they mean in a lease you may be considering. It's the job of the people who lease cars to explain the terms. Make them go over all the details with you until you understand everything. Don't be embarrassed to ask for an explanation. Remember Jennifer from Lesson Five.

When you buy a car, it's yours. You pay for it with cash from some source. It may be from your savings account, or, more likely, it will come from a lender in the form of a check made out to the dealership. You drive away, and that's that.

When you sign a lease, you sign a contract with the dealership, which is representing the leasing company. The dealership actually sells the car to the leasing company for the exact price you negotiated. Your monthly payments go to the leasing company.

If You Buy, Will You Pay Cash or Will You Finance?

Most people finance the cars they purchase. They are either unwilling or unable to pay cash. Most don't have the cash. Those who do would rather pay for their cars over a period of months rather than invade their savings or investments.

If you had the money available to pay cash, should you do it? Or would it make more financial sense to borrow what you need to buy the car and finance the loan?

Here's the rule of thumb. If the interest rate on a car loan is higher than the interest rate you can earn on your savings, then you are better off taking the money out of your savings to pay for the car. If you earn a higher rate of return on your savings than you will have to pay on your car loan, you are better off financing the car and leaving your savings intact.

Ed found one of those financing deals that was too good to pass up. He and his wife had always saved, and they had a substantial nest egg put away. At the time, they were getting about 8 percent on their savings. So when the lender explained that they had a special deal where Ed could buy the car and finance the deal at 2.9 percent, Ed knew that he was better off paying the interest on the car loan and leaving his savings in the bank.

But times change. Some years later when Ed found himself back in the market for another car, interest rates on savings had dropped to 3 percent while the best deal he could get on a car loan was 6 percent. This time around, Ed paid for his new car with money from savings rather than financing a higher interest loan.

So all you have to do to determine which option (cash or charge) is in your best interest is to compare the interest rate being charged on car financing against what you are earning in your savings account.

This same procedure holds true when it comes to your down payment. If your car loan interest rate is high and the savings account interest is low, you want to make the largest down payment that you can afford. If the loan interest rate is low and the savings account interest rate is high, you want to put as little down on the car purchase as possible. It's just that simple.

If You Finance, Which Terms Work Best for You?

Car dealers say that 9 out of 10 people who buy cars finance their purchases either through the dealer's business office or their own borrowing resources. The amount of down payment varies depending on the person's personal finances and the cost of the car. The question becomes, which financing terms work out to your advantage? The answer is it depends on your personal circumstances.

When it comes to a car loan, there are 4 essential terms you need to keep in mind. First is the cost of the car. Second is the down payment. Third is the interest rate you are being charged. Fourth is the length of the loan.

You can arrange for your car loan at any number of lenders. You may already have a personal relationship established at your bank, credit union, or finance company. Even if you don't, you can approach any of these traditional lenders and ask about their rate on car loans, or you can let the business office at the dealership do your car loan shopping for you. They will know the interest rates that most lenders in town are charging. They will also know about any costs charged for establishing the loan.

The bottom line is, the lower the interest rate, the less interest you will pay over the life of the loan. However, it is not quite that simple because lenders often charge different interest rates depending on the length of the loan. You may be offered a 2.9 percent loan over 2 years, 5 percent over 3 years, 7.5 percent over 4 years, and 9.5 percent over 5 years or longer. The longer the loan, the higher the rate because the lender assumes more risk of default.

Some lenders offer lower interest loans to those who agree to make their monthly payment through an automatic withdrawal from their checking accounts. Lenders do this because they know they will get their money on time every month.

The length of the loan has a direct bearing on the

amount of money you eventually pay for the car. On a $15,000 car loan, if you get a 9 percent interest rate over 3 years, you will pay $477 a month or $17,172. If you buy the same car at the same interest rate, but take out the loan for 5 years, you will pay $311.38 a month or $18,682.80. You are exchanging a lower monthly payment for a longer period of time to repay the loan.

Some lenders are stretching car loans out for as long as 7 years (84 months). Before you agree to a loan of that length, you need to have some confidence that the car you are buying will last that long.

When you finance a car, the length of the loan carries another important consideration. The longer the loan, the longer it will take you to gain "equity" in your car.

Equity is defined as today's value of your car minus the amount you owe on the loan. If you have a 3-year loan, you typically start to gain some equity in your car about 18 months into the loan. On a 5-year loan, the value of the car will exceed the amount you owe around year 3. On a 7-year loan, it's anybody's guess when the car will be worth more than you owe.

Having some equity in your car is important when you approach a lender about a personal loan (which we'll get to in Lesson Eight.) Lenders want people to have assets. Your car is an asset, but only when its value is more than what you owe on the loan. The sooner you gain some equity, the better off you will be from a creditworthy standpoint. When you owe more on the car loan than it is worth, those in the lending profession say, "you are upside down" on the loan. They mean you owe more than you could get if you were to sell the car. You won't find yourself "right-side up" on a financed vehicle until the last year or so of the loan.

There are other financing terms you may want to explore. For example, instead of buying that car and making equal monthly payments over 36 or 48 months (or whatever other term you choose), you may want to look at a special term loan where you make smaller monthly payments and have a large (balloon) payment at the end of the loan. This makes the car payment more affordable during the loan. However, you will have to make arrangements to pay off the balance at the end of the loan. That can be tricky, unless you can refinance the car loan at that time, and there's no guarantee the lender will be willing.

When you finance a car, you don't have to wait to pay

the loan off. If you come into some extra cash, you can always pay the loan off early. Of course, you want to make sure that you don't have to pay any "prepayment penalty" for the privilege of paying off the loan ahead of time.

In addition, if you owe on the car loan and you are in the mood, for whatever reason, to buy another car, you can do it. The dealer will calculate the present value of the car you are trading and the amount you owe on the loan, and incorporate that information into the deal on the new car. It can be difficult to find these numbers, but it is important that you do just that. Buying a replacement car when you still owe on the old car is the norm rather than the exception. It happens all the time. Just make the dealer show you the numbers, and have an idea of the value of your car before you negotiate. Lenders have "blue books" that can serve as a guide for your "trade-in" value.

Refinancing Your Car Loan

Car loans don't have to last forever. You can always refinance if you are unhappy with the terms especially if you have equity in the vehicle.

Carol wanted her house, but the mortgage lender said she had too much debt. What the lender meant was her monthly payment on her debt was too high. Her best way to qualify for the mortgage was to refinance her car loan. She bought her car for $15,000 3 years ago, agreeing to a 4-year loan at 9 percent interest. The monthly payment was $373. Today the car is worth $7,500 and she owes only $4,480. She refinanced the car loan by taking out a 2-year loan at $205 a month. By refinancing, Carol reduces her monthly debt payment by $168 a month. That was enough to qualify for the house loan. The car will cost more, but she will get her home loan sooner.

If You Lease, Which Terms Work Best for You?

Leasing terms can be quite a bit more complicated than the terms you have when you buy, but only because most people are not familiar with them. You need to first negotiate the price of the vehicle, just like you were going to purchase it. In fact, you may not want to tell the salesperson that you are considering a lease just yet. Once you have agreed upon a price, you can then investigate the difference between buying and leasing.

If you opt for the lease, you have to decide on the length of time you will be leasing the car and the number of miles you will be driving it each year. The typical lease lasts for 2 or 3 years. The number of miles you can put on the car may be 12,000 or 15,000 miles a year.

If you put a down payment on the car you want to lease, the monthly payments will be less than if you don't put any money down.

You may have to make a security deposit equal to one or two month's lease payments. You should get the security deposit back at the end of the lease. Check to see what the contract says. You may be able to reduce your monthly payment by agreeing to a lease contract with a balloon lease payment at the end of the lease term. It's usually called a "lease buyout" payment.

You have to read the terms of the lease carefully so you fully understand what you are agreeing to. The terms must be fully disclosed.

Many people who lease do so with the warranty in mind. They know that if they lease a vehicle for up to 36,000 miles, they will be covered by a full warranty. Essentially, they will be driving a new or nearly new vehicle with little chance of costly breakdowns.

Study after study shows that when it all comes down to it, buying and leasing come out just about the same from a financial standpoint.

Still, there are some very special leasing deals that become available from time to time which can make leasing very worthwhile.

At the end of the lease, you have some options:

• You can turn the car in, along with the keys.

• You can purchase the car for its residual value, as stated in the lease contract.

• You can lease another car.

You can refinance the car you have been driving the last 2 or 3 years. Most car lenders will do that if you have made all your payments on time.

Today, leasing a newer used car or what's called a "pro-

gram car" by the car dealers may be one of the better bargains around. These cars typically have low mileage on
them, and yet a major part of the depreciation on the vehicle has been taken care of by the earlier owner. It is something worth considering.

Shop a Little, Negotiate a Little

Now that the general idea of financing your purchase is
set, you can visit the car dealer. You walk around the lot
and the showroom. You meet a sales associate. You test
drive a couple of vehicles. Eventually, you find the make
and model you like and agree on a price you are willing to
pay for the car and the dealership will accept. That's right,
you found the car and you have haggled over the price tag.

Interestingly, dickering over the price of a car is one of
the very few times you get to negotiate these days. When
you walk into a department store to purchase a pair of
shoes, you pay what is marked on the tag. When you go to
a grocery store, the price is clearly indicated on the shelf.
You can say, "I'm willing to pay $35 for those shoes even
though they are marked $85." Or, "I'll give you 89 cents for
that carton of milk." But it doesn't usually do any good.
The clerk will probably look at you like you have lost your
mind. With cars, it's a different story. At most, although
not all, dealerships, you are expected to negotiate.

First you look at the sticker price. Then you ask the
sales person, "How much is this really going to cost me?"

He or she responds, "Make me an offer I can't refuse."

You say, "I don't know. How much will you let it go for?"

So the negotiation begins. It's a little game. Some people
like it. Others dread it. It can be enjoyable once you know
the ground rules. It can be a terrible source of irritation if
you do not. If you have never negotiated a car deal before,
read up on it. There are lots of good books and magazine
articles written by car sales people on how to go about it.

Eventually you agree on a price. The fact is, you probably would have been willing to pay a little more and the
dealership would have been willing to accept a little less,
but that's okay. As long as you feel you got a good deal,
everyone is happy.

Some very savvy consumers suggest that before you sign
on the dotted line, you should do a little outside reading.

There are many books available to consumers.

Did You Negotiate the Price or Did You Merely Agree on a Monthly Payment?

Are you in the market for a Chevette or a Corvette? A Mazda or a Mercedes? A junker or a Jaguar? Are you willing to spend $15,000, or are you looking for something a little more pricey, or something a little less expensive? It all depends on your personal finances, the kind of financing terms you can find, and how deep the dealer is willing to cut the price.

For most people, the car they eventually buy depends on the monthly payment they can afford. It is not surprising, then, that one of the first questions a sales associate is likely to ask you when you first meet is, "How much of a monthly payment are you looking for?"

You might say $200 to $250 a month. Or you might say $400. Or you might be honest and say that you are looking for a car in a certain price range. **Shop for the car, not the monthly payment.** You are not trying to be sneaky. You are just letting the salesperson know your price range rather than monthly payment amount. After all, the salesperson needs some idea of your price range so he or she can show you a selection.

There is not much of a relationship between the sales price of a vehicle and the amount of the monthly payment because of the many variables involved.

Let's Make a Deal

Selecting the make and model you want to drive home and negotiating the price are really the two easy parts of closing a car deal. Now you have to pay for the car in order to drive it home. That means you will have to stop by the business office to sign the required papers, make arrangements for recording the title, pay any taxes imposed by the city or county, and finally get the license plates. Oh, of course, you have to pay for the car, too.

Frankly, the dealer doesn't care how you do it, just as long as you do. Dealers sell cars; they don't finance them. You may be one of the fortunate few who can write a check to the dealership, hop in the car, and drive away. Not many can. Most need financing.

If you do need financing, the person in the business office is in an ideal position to help. The dealer's business office is offered to people as a convenience. The staff works very closely with most of the lenders in town as well as one or more national lenders. They are familiar with the terms lenders are currently charging on car financing.

If you tell them that you have already made arrangements for financing through your bank or credit union, you won't get any argument, although the good ones will ask you if you mind them checking around to see if they can get you a better deal. But when it comes right down to it, they don't care where you finance your car. Anywhere is fine, just as long as it means you can write a check for the purchase price, including taxes, tags and registration. Remember, the dealer's job is to get the car out the door. Only if you indicate that you want some help finding financing will the business office step forward.

Keep in mind that the dealer's business office will know the specific terms being charged by at least 5 different lenders, which is probably 4 more than you know.

Kathy made arrangements for financing with the lender where she keeps her checking and savings account before she even starting looking for a car. She visited with a loan officer and explained that she was thinking about buying a car. She was told what the current loan terms were and that she probably would qualify for a car loan based on her credit history. The loan officer told her to go shopping and to come back when she found what she wanted.

After a week of shopping, she found the car. She found out that a different lender in town was offering a slightly better rate than the one where she was pre-qualified.

Billy was in a similar situation only he found that the dealer's business office was able to find him a lower interest rate with the same lender which had quoted him a higher rate only 2 days earlier.

The business office of a car dealer is not in the business of financing cars. However, it is the job of the people who work there to find you a financing source and payment plan that will enable you to drive away with the car you want. They are not paid to be your financial advisor.

The terms of your car loan will depend on the strength of your credit history, and whether you are buying a new car, a newer used car (something less than 3 years old) or an older used car (something 4 years or older.)

The process works like this:

- You get pre-qualified for a car loan by visiting with your local lender.

- You find the car.

- You negotiate the deal.

- You visit with the business office.

- You fill out a credit application.

The business office electronically sends your loan application to a number of potential lenders. Usually 3 to 5 lenders will see it, depending on the experience of the people in the business office. By the way, nothing at this point has cost you any money.

Each lender who receives the loan application will score it based on your credit report, income level, and debt. If you score an "A", you will be offered the best terms. If you score a "D", you will either be turned down or you will be offered the worst terms. If you score a "B" or a "C", the terms will fall somewhere in between.

The terms of your car loan will also depend on whether you are buying a new car, a newer used car, or an older used car.

For example, the terms being offered require that a new car may be financed for at least 3 years but for no longer than 7 years. When an "A" quality borrower wants a 3-year loan, the interest rate may be as low as 4 percent. If a "D" quality borrower wants a 7-year loan, the interest rate may be as high as 18 percent.

If you're looking at a newer used car, the interest rate may be as low as 6 percent on a 3-year loan or as high as 15 percent on a 6-year loan.

On an older used car, lenders want you to pay more interest for a shorter period of time because older used cars won't last as long before they completely wear out.

Some lenders won't lend on vehicles that are over 8 years old. Some lenders won't lend on vehicles that have more than 100,000 miles on them. Others will.

In addition to local lenders, the dealer usually has access to one or more national lenders such as General Motors Acceptance Corporation or Ford Motor Credit Corporation. Usually the national lender is associated with the dealership. For example, a Chevy dealership will deal with GMAC.

These lenders can sometimes offer deals that are simply too good to pass up. When they talk about zero percent financing, they really mean it.

Sometimes they will offer extremely low financing on makes and models that are not terribly popular or are late in the model year. Sometimes they will offer special financing when they introduce a new model. Sometimes they will offer special financing in addition to a customer rebate or other special consideration.

In any case, ask at the business office if there are any special financing deals going on right now that they have access to. Then consider what's the best place to finance your car.

This part of the deal is yours to negotiate, just like you did on the price.

Once you find the financing terms which best suit your needs, sign the papers, and drive away happy.

One final point to keep in mind when you visit the dealer's business office. In the industry, it is often referred to as "F&I." The "F" stands for financing, the "I" stands for insurance. The business office doesn't sell auto insurance.

However, it does sell credit life and disability insurance as well as extended service warranties. So don't be surprised if the staff makes it a point to offer these products to you at the time you are being asked to pay for the car.

If you want them, that's fine. If you do not, you can just say no. It's that simple. You will have to determine if they are a good buy or not.

Summing Up

Buying or leasing a car doesn't have to be a hassle. In fact, it shouldn't be. Before you go car shopping, calculate what it costs to operate a vehicle and what you will pay for it (including interest) every month. Then figure out how you will pay for everything. With all that in mind, you can shop to your heart's content. In fact, a lot of people get to the point that they enjoy the challenge of bargaining for the best deal possible.

(Rev. June 2004)

HOME SWEET HOME

Three of the most important loans you will ever apply for concern your home. The first, of course, is your mortgage. The second is refinancing your mortgage. The third is the well-known home equity or home improvement loan. There are all sorts of rules and requirements that apply to all of these loans, and you need to know what they are before you fill out your loan application.

Financing a Home

At some point, you will probably decide that you want a home of your own. Good for you. There will be a lot of people who will encourage you to own rather than rent. Home ownership is considered by many to be an important part of the American dream. It shows stability and commitment. It shows that you want to become a part of the community.

Buying a home is probably the most expensive purchase you will make in your lifetime, so you don't want to make a mistake. Buying a home is not just a purchase, but it is also an investment (which should increase in value over time) and it has definite tax advantages. Buying a home requires that you have a very good credit history because chances are you are going to have to take out a mortgage loan.

Buying a home is often an extremely emotional experience. It doesn't have to be. Buying a home is just like buying a car only more expensive. You can be happy in a lot of different homes. If one doesn't work out for you, there are others. There is no single house that you just have to have or you will die. Buying a particular piece of real estate is not a matter of life or death. The property and the financial terms have to be right for you at that particular time. If they are not, then keep searching for the property and deal that work for you.

There are people who have shopped for a home for years. They feel that the longer they shop, the better the deal they will get. They wait until they find the right property at the right price, with the ideal financing terms. Of course, they could end up waiting forever.

There is a lot to learn before you actually purchase

your home. There are strange new terms that you will need to understand and a whole new group of professionals you will meet. You will deal with larger numbers than you are used to. Prepare yourself for the adventure called "buying your home."

Notice that doesn't say "buying your first home." You may buy your first home when you are in your mid-20's. You may sell that place and buy another when you are in your 30's or 40's. You may find that you actually buy and sell a half dozen or more homes during your lifetime, starting small, getting larger as your family and income grow, and then downsizing as the kids leave the nest and you get older. Each of these transactions will be different. Certainly, the general structure of the deal will remain the same, but the details will change from home to home. You have to pay attention to the terms which are in effect at the time of the transaction. Every time you buy or sell a home, you will need to reacquaint yourself with the ins and outs of buying and selling.

Identifying the Players

When you are in the process of buying a home, you have to know who all the players are (and there are at least 10 of them) and exactly what is expected and required of each.

• **Buyer.** The buyer is the person who is out looking for a home. She should know what she is looking for, the number of bedrooms, the size of the house she wants, the location, school district, potential resale value, and, of course, what she can afford to spend. The buyer is the one paying the tab. She should have a price in mind, although she may be willing to go higher.

• **Seller.** The seller is the one who has a place and wants to sell it for money. The seller may have any number of reasons for wanting to sell. She may be moving out of town. She may be buying another place so she needs to sell the one she is in. The seller has a price in mind. She will tell you what it is, although chances are she is willing to negotiate a lower price or make certain concessions.

• **The Mortgage Loan Officer and the Lender.** The lender is a bank, credit union or mortgage company which is in the business of lending money to people so they can buy a house. The mortgage loan officer is the person who arranges the financing and assembles the loan package for you and the lender. It is the loan officer who asks you about your job, how much you earn, what you owe, and all that other personal financial information. The mortgage loan officer usually charges fees for his services. You should ask how much you are expected to pay. (See the discussion under "Points" later on in this lesson.) The information you share with the mortgage loan officer is personal and will not be shared with any other parties to the transaction. The loan officer will not tell your real estate agent or the seller's real estate agent how much money you make or any other details of your financial affairs.

• **Buyer's Real Estate Agent.** Finding a real estate agent to help you buy a home is vital, so request references and check them out. Use only that person you are extremely comfortable with. Today, a prospective buyer is shown house after house by a licensed real estate agent. This is the person who will help you prepare a contract offer which he or she will then present to the seller and her real estate agent. Buyers need to know who is paying the buyer's real estate agent. Traditionally, it is the seller. If it is the seller who is paying the fee, that fact needs to be disclosed to the buyer. There are real estate agents who exclusively represent buyers, and in that case the buyers have to pay for them, although the fee is usually included in the offer price of the home. Otherwise, the buyer's real estate agent is paid by the seller which means that the buyer's real estate agent, by law, represents the interests of the seller. It's a bit of a conflict for everyone concerned, but those are the rules of the game. If you want to share your personal financial information with your real estate agent, that is up to you.

• **Seller's Real Estate Agent.** This is the real estate agent who lists the property and represents the seller in the negotiation for the sale of the property. The seller signs a listing agreement which describes the property, sets the sale price and the amount of commission she is willing to pay to the real estate agent. The amount is usually represented by a percentage of the sales price.

• **Home Inspector.** Most buyers insist on a satisfactory home inspection, as well they should. They want to know what condition the house is in, so they hire someone to poke into all the corners, check the plumbing and electrical system, and climb up on the roof. The buyer pays for the report. If there are problems with the property that haven't been disclosed, the seller usually will be given the choice of fixing them or letting the buyer out of the contract.

• **Home Appraiser.** Just because the buyer and seller agree on a purchase price doesn't mean the lender agrees that the property is worth that price. The lender wants an independent appraisal of the value of the property so it won't wind up lending more than the property is worth. The lender will require that a licensed and experienced home appraiser, approved by it, checks out the property and determines what the fair market value really is. The buyer usually pays for this service, although the seller may agree to pick up the expense. The appraisal in no way guarantees the condition of the property.

• **Mortgage Insurance Agent.** Unless the buyer puts down at least 20 percent of the purchase price on a conventional loan, the lender may require that the buyer pay for private mortgage insurance (PMI) to cover the lender in case the buyer defaults on the loan. It's not a huge expense, but over time it can amount to thousands of dollars. This mortgage insurance does not pay a missed payment. Instead, it covers expenses for foreclosure on a defaulted loan.

• **Settlement Agent.** This is the person who takes care of all the paperwork and details. He handles the money, schedules the meeting, and gets the buyer and the seller to sign all the proper papers to finalize the sale.

• **Title Insurance Company.** It guarantees that the seller is selling property that he actually owns and that there is no problem with the title to the property. It also insures the lender that there are no problems with the buyer that would attach to the house.

A question that often comes up is "Do I need a lawyer to help me buy or sell a house?" The answer is, "Maybe not," if you are using an experienced real estate agent. However, if you are buying or selling without using the services of a licensed real estate agent, then by all means spend the couple of hundred dollars it will cost you to hire an attorney who is well-acquainted with local real estate law. Although the buying and selling of residential real estate sales has become so commonplace and standardized these days, there is always the chance that something could be amiss. That's where professional legal help can come in handy. If you will feel more comfortable with an attorney looking over the paperwork prior to putting your signature on the bottom line, then by all means do so. However, find an attorney who does a lot of real estate deals because you want someone who is familiar with real estate law as opposed to someone who is primarily a litigator or someone who practices corporate law.

Keep in mind that real estate agents usually work for the seller or are put in the position of representing both the buyer and the seller. Only by hiring an attorney will you have someone who is entirely on your side.

When it comes to commercial real estate transactions, both parties should consider legal counsel.

Pre-Qualifying For a Mortgage

Perhaps the best place to begin the process of buying a home is in the office of a mortgage lender, not in the car driving through neighborhood after neighborhood. If you don't know where to go to find a mortgage lender, ask friends and relatives for recommendations. Check the listing under "Mortgages" in the yellow pages of the telephone book. Select one and call the office for an appointment. Explain that you want to talk about "pre-qualifying" for a mortgage. The people in the office should be happy to help you.

One mortgage loan officer says that she thinks it is a good idea for people who are thinking of buying a house to come in for a pre-qualifying visit perhaps years in advance of the purchase, simply because it allows sufficient time to plan finances, save for the down payment, and establish a solid credit history.

By the way, you should understand that there is an important difference between "pre-qualifying" for a mortgage and asking to be "pre-approved" for a mortgage. Pre-qualifying means you visit with a loan officer who will look over the information about your income and expenses which you provide. Then based on that quick appraisal of your finances, he will give you a ballpark figure of the amount of mortgage that you will probably qualify for. The loan officer will cover himself by saying that the amount you pre-qualify for depends on the accuracy of your financial information.

A "pre-approval" on the other hand is when you go to a mortgage loan officer and have him run a credit check and pre-approve a fixed amount for a mortgage, by submitting the information to an underwriter. With a pre-qualifying visit, you won't have to pay for the service. For a pre-approval, you probably will.

At your first visit with a mortgage loan officer, explain that you want to buy a home, although you haven't found one yet, and you would like to know:

- What would be the best kind of mortgage loan for you?

- How much money you can qualify for?

- How much cash you will need?

While the loan officer may not be willing to go out on that proverbial limb and tell you what would be the best kind of mortgage loan for you, he should be willing to explain the various types of loans that mortgage lenders are making. In any case, he will be ready, willing and able to explain how much the mortgage company will lend you based on your income, various debts, work experience, job prospects, and credit history, once you complete the process.

The lender will ask you to fill out a loan application. You will have to answer some specific questions. You will be told that when you make the mortgage loan application, you will need to provide copies of your last 2 or 3 federal income tax returns along with your last few pay-stubs covering a 30 day period so the loan officer can verify your income. At this point, he will take your word for your income. (A pay-stub and a W-2 form from your tax return would be helpful here so you don't have to estimate.) The loan officer will access your credit bureau report to check on your credit history. You will have to provide a run down of all your debts, including credit cards, car loans or leases, student loans, personal loans from your parents, child support payments you make or receive, and so on.

The mortgage loan officer will take all the information, process it, and come up with an answer as to how much the lender might lend to you under various loan programs.

The loan officer will go through your many options with you, including:

Conventional Financing. These are regular, mortgage loans that are not guaranteed or insured by a government agency. These loans contain standardized terms and requirements set out by the Federal National Mortgage Association (better known as Fannie Mae) or the Federal Home Loan Mortgage Corporation (or Freddie Mac), both located in Washington, DC. FNMA determines the acceptable ratios between monthly income and monthly mortgage payment (commonly referred to as PITI — for principal, interest, taxes and insurance), as well as the ratios between monthly income and total debt. These ratios have been adjusted from time to time to reflect current economic conditions throughout the nation. Ask the loan officer to calculate how much loan you can qualify for based on your income and your current debts using the current ratios.

There are 2 basic types of conventional loans — conforming loans and jumbo loans. The regular, conforming loan is for an amount that falls below a level set by FNMA. The jumbo is the larger loan. The terms on each vary.

FHA Financing. This is government insured financing through the Federal Housing Administration (FHA). It only applies to loans up to certain amounts. The FHA sets the ratios and terms for loans that it insures. Again, ask the loan officer for details. Borrowers who use FHA insured loans have to pay a monthly premium for the FHA mortgage insurance. The good news is that they don't need much of a down payment.

VA Financing. This is government guaranteed financing for those who have served in the armed forces or national guard. One of the benefits of a VA guaranteed loan is that you may not have to make any down payment. There are all sorts of detailed rules governing VA guaranteed loans which the loan officer will go over with you, if you qualify for this type of loan.

Various State Government Mortgage Programs. States may participate in their own mortgage programs. Most are specifically geared to help low-to-moderate income residents acquire their first homes.

Down Payment. With conventional financing, you may need a down payment of 5 to 20 percent of the purchase price or more. Conventional financing programs for low income allow for as little as 2 percent down in some cases.

With FHA financing, the down payment is approximately 3 percent or so. With VA, there is no down payment requirement.

The larger your down payment and the longer the repayment terms on your loan, the lower your payments will be.

With conventional financing, if you do not make a 20 percent or larger down payment, you will probably be required by the lender to take out Private Mortgage Insurance (PMI). That will add $25 to $100 a month to your mortgage payment, depending on the amount you are financing.

Interest Rates. Each of the types of mortgage loans (Conventional, FHA, and VA) carries its own terms and conditions. Perhaps none is more important than the interest rate. The question you have for the mortgage lender is, "Once you determine the amount I can borrow, what will the interest rate be?"

Depending on the type of loan, whether it is fixed or adjustable, the length of the loan, the number of points you are willing to pay (see "points" below), the amount of your down payment, and other variables, the loan officer will quote you the lender's interest rate.

Don't hold the lender to this rate. By the time you find the house you like, make an offer, and go through the give and take of contract negotiations, 6 months may have gone by. The interest rate originally quoted to you by the mortgage loan officer during your pre-qualification session may not be the current rate being charged by lenders to borrowers who take out loans that day. Mortgage rates can actually change several times a day when interest rates are volatile.

The loan officer will probably not "lock in" a mortgage rate for you until you actually turn in a loan application or at least a signed purchase agreement, although there are exceptions. Even then, the rate will not be locked in for more than a couple of months.

Do not strictly shop interest rates. Some mortgage lenders may advertise promotional rates that are stunningly low. What's going on here is that you will find in the fine print that you will either have to pay a great deal of money up front to qualify for the exceedingly low rate, or that that you will have to finance the fee in the mortgage for up to 30 years.

Fixed Versus Adjustable Rate Mortgages. A fixed-rate mortgage will carry the same interest rate throughout the term of the loan. With an adjustable rate mortgage (ARM), the lender adjusts the interest rate periodically to reflect changes in current interest rates. For example, a typical ARM will adjust the interest rate by no more than 2 percentage points on each anniversary date of the loan. The adjustment over the life of the loan may be no more than 6 percentage points above or below the original interest rate. The initial rate on an ARM is usually lower than a fixed-rate mortgage.

Which is better? That's up to you to decide. People in the housing industry, particularly real estate agents and mortgage lenders, have their personal preferences and ideas about fixed versus adjustable rate loans and they will usually tell you their opinion. Just keep in mind that there are as many who favor ARM's as those who do not like them, so the decision is up to you.

The initial (first-year) interest rate on an ARM may be significantly lower than a fixed-rate mortgage. As a result, you may be able to qualify for a larger mortgage with an ARM than with a fixed mortgage. On the other hand, after the first year, the rate may go up, stretching your budget. With an ARM, you may pay a lower rate when the loan balance is highest.

One of the details you want to discuss if you are interested in an ARM is whether or not it is convertible to a fixed mortgage at some point in time in the future. And if it is, at what cost to you.

Your decision requires you to do a bit of gazing into the proverbial crystal ball. If you feel that interest rates are stable or going down, an ARM can save you a lot of money, especially for a shorter-term mortgage. If you feel that interest rates could rise, then a fixed-rate mortgage may be your preferable option.

Choosing an ARM or fixed-rate mortgage should be based on your personal situation and the plans you have for your home. For example:

(1) Do you have a job in which you get annual raises, or do you rarely get raises?

(2) Do you have a spouse who is not working now but will be in the future?

(3) Do you plan to stay in the house for 3 years, 5 years, 10 years, 30 years?

(4) Are you willing to gamble what interest rates will be in the years to come?

(5) Do you have enough savings to refinance your loan if interest rates climb too high?

(6) Can you handle higher payments?

Loan Origination Fee. When it comes time to actually take out a mortgage loan, home buyers are usually charged a small percentage of the amount borrowed, typically 1 percent of the loan or so. For example, if the amount of the loan (not the price of the house) is $150,000, and the mortgage lender charges a 1 percent loan origination fee, that comes to $1,500 for putting the financing together. This fee is rarely negotiable. The loan officer will tell you what the lender charges. If you don't like it, you will have to go elsewhere for your mortgage.

Points. The loan officer has to explain "points" to you. Points are fees charged to you by the lender under various types of loans (Conventional, FHA, and VA) which help establish the interest rate on the loan. A "point" equals 1 percent of the amount being borrowed, so the less you borrow, the less you may have to pay in points. You pay this fee when you close on the loan.

The loan officer may explain that you have 3 basic options.

> *You can get a mortgage loan at 7 percent and pay no points; or*
>
> *You can get a mortgage at 6-3/4 percent and pay 2 points;*
>
> *You can get a mortgage at 6-1/2 percent and pay 3-1/2 points.*

What's going on here is you can "buy-down" the interest rate on the loan by agreeing to pay more "points" at settlement. Typically, if you plan to stay in the house for a decade or more, you will come out ahead by "buying-down" the interest rate, assuming you can afford to do it. If your home is what's known as a "starter" home, and you intend to be in it for only a couple of years, the buy-down may not be effective. In any case, you should go over your options with the lender so you can figure out which deal makes the most sense to you.

The fact is, points can be used to help you to buy-down the better interest rate. This affects your total interest cost over the life of the loan and your monthly payment. An experienced mortgage lender can show you the actual cost savings to you by running a printout comparing your total costs.

Length (or Term) of the Loan. Pay off the loan over 30 years and your monthly payments will be lower than if you take out a loan that calls for repayment over 15 years. The shorter the loan, the less interest you will pay over the life of the mortgage.

For example, if you borrow $150,000 at 7 percent over 15 years, your monthly payment will be $1,348.26. The total amount of interest you will pay over the life of the loan is $92,686.80.

If you borrow that same $150,000 at 7 percent over 30 years, your monthly payment will be only $997.96, but the total interest you will pay over the life of the loan will be $209,265.60. That is a sizeable difference.

Lenders are flexible when it comes to the length of a mortgage. Although 15 year and 30 year loans are the most common, they can make the loan 20 or 25 years if that's what you want. Some lenders can make a loan for whatever length you would like. This is particularly important for people who are selling one place and are replacing it with another. They may want an 11 year, 4 month mortgage term for the new house loan because that was the remaining length of time on the mortgage on the home they are selling.

However, like most things involving buying a home, determining the best term is not quite as simple as it seems. Some advise that you should take out the shortest loan that you can afford. Others say that you should take out the 30 year loan and if you have extra money, you can double up on your mortgage payments (although that seldom happens.) There are all sorts of ways to reduce the length of your mortgage and save yourself a significant amount of interest. If you add an extra $50 or $100 to your monthly payment, you may reduce a 30 year loan to 20 years, saving yourself tens of thousands of dollars. If you can find a lender who offers bi-weekly mortgages (you have to make half your mortgage payment on the first of the month and the other half on the 15th), you can save a pile of interest, too.

There is a lot of information available to you if you want to bone up on what you can do to reduce the amount of interest you will pay on your mortgage and the number of months you have to pay.

Other Fees and Expenses. Although you are only asking a lender to pre-qualify you for a loan, you should know that there are other expenses associated with buying a house that the first-time home buyer may know nothing about. They are commonly called "closing costs," and they can include everything from "points" (explained earlier) to recording fees, title insurance, loan origination fees, and so on. The loan officer will give you a rundown on each expense you may have to pay at closing and what he estimates it will cost you. Usually the estimate is fairly accurate; if anything, it will be on the high side. The idea here is that you shouldn't be surprised at these expenses. Rather you should include them in your

financial planning as you go out in search of your new home.

Now You Know

When you walk out of the meeting with the mortgage loan officer, you should know 4 things. First, you should now know how much the lender may be willing to lend you based on the information you provided. Second, you should know how much of a down payment you need to save or have available to you from other sources like a parent or other relative. Third, by adding these 2 numbers together, you should know the maximum price you can afford to pay for a home. And fourth, you should know approximately how much money you will need to cover your closing costs.

Room to Negotiate

The reality is, mortgage lending is not nearly as flexible as auto lending. The ratios required by one lender are likely to be the same ratio required by another lender. If you are quoted rates and terms for 15 year and 30 year loans at one place, it's likely that the competitors down the street will have the same rates. You can negotiate until you are blue in the face, and it's not going to do you much good. Sorry.

The Process

The main players are Dan and Sally (the buyers), Jan (the mortgage loan officer), and Chris (Dan and Sally's real estate agent.)

Dan and Sally have been married for a few years. They have been renting the same apartment for 2 years and she is ready for her own place. They are both working and they feel they have the income to be able to afford a home. So, they make an appointment and go to a mortgage company. They fill out all the information they are asked to provide, and then they get the bad news. They learn that they will not be getting a loan, at least not at the present time.

Jan was the loan officer. She politely explained to them that she wouldn't be able to give them a loan right now primarily because of their debt, but if they are willing to pay attention to just a couple of things, they would probably qualify within 6 months. She explained that they should do the following 3 things.

First, they should make sure that they do not add any more debt than they already have.

Second, they need to pay off some of their present debt.

Third, they need to stay on their jobs and collect the raises at work which both of them said they had been promised by their bosses. The fact is, a person cannot qualify for a loan based on projected or promised increases to their income.

Instead of being upset and angry, Dan and Sally were relieved to find out what the ground rules were, exactly what they were going to have to do with their personal finances in order to qualify for a mortgage, and how long it was likely to take to accomplish the goal.

"Both of you need to spend 6 more months working with your current employers. Don't change jobs. Get your raises which will boost your combined income. Don't add any more credit card debt. Pay off 1 car loan which has only 4 more payments to go. Do all that and you should qualify for a house loan." That's what Jan told them.

They followed her advice, and 6 months later, they were back in the office. Jan once again checked the credit bureau report, and after going through the numbers, pre-qualified them for a $180,000 mortgage. She also warned them that when they were ready to buy a house and take out the mortgage, it was going to cost them approximately $4,500 in closing costs.

Sally had put off looking for 6 months, and now she was ready.

There is one more item that Dan and Sally need to keep in mind. **While they know how much they can borrow for a home mortgage loan, they still haven't determined exactly how much of a house they can afford to buy, and how much of a house they were willing to buy.** In Sally's and Dan's case, they have $5,000 to use as a down payment, plus Sally's father had promised that he would kick in another $10,000 when it was time for them to buy their first home, and he was willing to pay the closing costs. That's pretty generous.

Using these numbers, this couple could be looking at homes costing up to $195,000. That's $15,000 down, with a mortgage of $180,000. That doesn't mean they have to buy a $195,000 home. They are certainly permitted to purchase something less expensive. However, because they have been pre-qualified for a mortgage, they know what their maximum spending limit is.

Once you know what you have available for a down payment and what someone is willing to lend you, you should decide what you are willing to afford. Dan and Sally have been told by the lender that they will qualify for a $180,000 mortgage, over 30 years, at 7 percent. That will cost them $1,200 a month. In addition, they will have to pay real estate taxes and homeowners insurance every month. For purposes of our example, that will bring their monthly payment to $1,550. They are presently paying $750 a month rent on their apartment, so they are facing an immediate increase of $800.

They will have to decide if their budget can afford it.

They should also have a reality check because what the mortgage lender tells borrowers they can qualify for may be far different from what they actually can afford. Here, they are a young couple, both working, and have not yet started raising a family. What will happen if Sally gets pregnant and has to leave work? Can they still afford $1,550 a month on Dan's salary alone?

Are they willing to stretch their monthly budget to the limit just so they can get into a house? Where will the money come from to pay higher utility bills? Will they do without their membership at the health club? Will they put their old furniture in the new house or will they want to replace the old stuff? How about appliances, like a washer and dryer? Will the new house have a refrigerator or will they have to buy one?

Sally and Dan have gone over their budget carefully and feel they can afford a monthly payment of $1,200. Working backwards, they subtract $350 for real estate taxes and insurance, so they will make a $850 payment on the loan. That $850 monthly payment for 30 years at 7 percent represents a loan of $125,000. They have $15,000 that they can put down on the house, so they will be looking for something priced around $140,000. They know that they will have to save more money from their salaries if they want to put even more money down.

They start looking. Sally has a friend, Chris, who is a real estate agent. Sally tells Chris that she and Dan want something between $130,000 and $150,000. She doesn't explain that she could get a larger loan and a more expensive house. Instead, she tells the real estate professional exactly the price range that she is willing to afford.

Chris takes Sally around town, looking at 20 or 30 different houses in Sally's price range. Sally finds 3 that she really likes, tells Dan, and together, they go through them. They finally decide on the one they want. It's offered for sale at $140,000. They drive around the neighborhood. They talk about it.

They tell Chris, and together, they make an offer, in writing, of $134,000.

Once they make that purchase offer and it has been accepted, they are legally bound by its terms, conditioned on a satisfactory home inspection which they request.

If they didn't have Chris, they would have been wise to go to a real estate attorney to help them draft the purchase offer. In fact, there are many cases where an attorney is brought in just to go through the purchase offer to explain all the fine points to the person making the offer, whether there is a real estate professional involved or not.

The offer is much more detailed than just putting down a price on a slip of paper. Dan and Sally want all the appliances to be left with the property. They want the wood in the wood pile. They want the dining room chandelier. They want the window treatments. They want to move into the house within 90 days. They specify a settlement date.

Finally, after attending to all the details, they send Chris to present the contract to the seller, along with a check for $1,000 (that's called earnest money and can be for any amount), made out to the real estate company, to show good faith.

The seller says no, that he will accept $138,000, and he wants to keep the refrigerator and chandelier. Sally and Dan and the seller go back and forth a couple of times with offer and counter offer, through their real estate agents, of course.

Finally both parties agree on a purchase price and all the terms.

It's a done deal. Sort of.

Now everyone gets busy.

Sally and Dan meet with Jan and fill out a mortgage application. They will have to pay around $400 immediately. This payment covers the credit bureau report and appraisal. Remember, they were pre-qualified by Jan, but they were not pre-approved.

Jan sends for all the verifying financial information she will need to process the application. She tells Dan and Sally what they need to bring to her so she can make copies, things like their 2 most recent tax returns, pay-stubs, credit card statements, car payment booklet, and so on. She arranges for the appraisal which will come directly to her. Because Jan is an experienced mortgage loan officer, she should have a pretty good idea if the loan application she is preparing will be approved. Remember, she is not in the practice of doing all the work necessary to assemble a loan package and have it turned down.

The approval process used to take 4 to 8 weeks. Today, thanks to computers, the approval process for a mortgage loan application is much quicker than it used to be. Once the complete package is assembled and sent to the people who make the final determination, it's only a matter of a day or two. Some lenders can approve electronically in a matter of minutes once all the data is verified.

The lender lets you hold the title to the property, but the property is subject to a mortgage. That's what makes this a secured loan. The lender will file a lien against the property at the court house until the mortgage loan is paid in full.

At the same time that Jan is getting the loan application together, the real estate agent will help the buyer find a home inspector, to be paid for by the buyer. If the real estate agent isn't any help here, the buyer will have to do it on his own. Look in the telephone book. It's a good idea for Dan or Sally, or both, to show up when the inspector does his work. Wear jeans because you will be poking into corners.

This may be the most important thing a consumer can do. Start to worry if someone tells you that a home inspection isn't necessary and will only cost you money. Always afford the cost of a home inspection. Make your offer conditional on a satisfactory inspection. If the inspection turns up some problems, then you can negotiate a new deal, or walk away in the event there are major problems with the house.

Rarely does everything go like clockwork. There are

always hassles and delays. But usually, through the efforts of the mortgage loan officer and the real estate agents, everything works out.

A week before settlement, Sally calls the settlement office and makes arrangements to get a copy of all the papers that she and Dan will have to sign. Too often, buyers are told that the papers won't be ready until the day of settlement. Don't be put off. You want those papers a couple of days in advance so you can review them. You don't want to be pressured into signing paper after paper without having read every word. Sally also learns the exact amount of the certified check she will have to bring to cover the down payment.

Sally finds out how much settlement costs will be. Settlement costs shouldn't come as a surprise because chances are you have been forewarned of what each expense would come to at the time you applied for the loan. Settlement costs cover everything that everyone is charging to make the sale go through. It lists who is paying for title insurance, taxes and city or county recording fees, the termite inspection, the loan origination fee, and all the other fees and charges that have to be paid.

It's not that people don't trust you, but you will probably have to pay your down payment and the settlement fees with cashier checks.

Sally checks with her homeowners insurance agent to make sure that the property is covered with enough homeowner's insurance. She will need proof that the insurance premium has been paid for 1 full year when she shows up at settlement.

At the appointed time, all the parties to the settlement (or their legal representatives) meet, and after a flourish of paper shuffling, signing, and the passing of checks to the settlement agent, Dan and Sally become homeowners. For the next 30 years, they will make their payments, and eventually the house will be theirs. By the way, buyers and sellers rarely are together at closing because of financial confidentiality.

Actually, they will probably find themselves at a real estate closing any number of times during their lives, buying and selling as they go. When they sell this house and buy a replacement, they will pay off the mortgage lender with the proceeds from the sale. Any money they make can be used to cover the cost of the next place they want to buy.

Buying and selling a house doesn't have to be difficult or scary. But it does take being informed of the process and understanding the role of each of the players in the transaction.

Refinancing

Homeowners are constantly checking current mortgage rates to see if they can get a better deal. Just because you took out a mortgage loan at, say 7-3/4 percent over 30 years, does not mean that you are stuck with it. In fact, you have the best of both worlds. If interest rates go up, you still have a 7-3/4 percent interest rate. But if rates go down, you have the option of refinancing the existing balance on your loan under more favorable terms. Your lender does not have this option.

Refinancing has its advantages and disadvantages. On the plus side, you may be able to reduce the interest rate you have to pay and therefore your monthly payment when you refinance at a lower rate.

When refinancing, you may want to tap some of the equity in your home and use it for other things, such as college expenses, to remodel your home, or to pay some nagging bills. Of course, you realize that this loan reduces the equity you have built up in your home.

Let's say that you bought your home 10 years ago. At that time, the price of the home was $125,000. You took out a $100,000 mortgage at 9-1/2 percent over 30 years. You have been faithfully making a monthly payment of $840.86. Now, 10 years later, you have 20 years remaining on the loan with a mortgage balance of $80,000. The house now has a market value of $200,000. You want to refinance.

You visit the lender and find that it is willing to write a new loan for 75 percent of the present value of the house. That comes to $150,000. Your personal finances are in good shape, and you are quite creditworthy. You tell the lender that you want to borrow $110,000, use $80,000 to pay off the existing loan and use the $30,000 for "other" things. The lender agrees to make the loan. The new terms are a $110,000 loan at 6 percent over 20 years, or $788.08 a month.

Another reason to refinance is to either reduce the number of payments you have to make or to reduce the amount of the monthly payment. If this homeowner didn't need the $30,000, but instead wanted to take advantage of a lower interest rate, this is what would have happened. The new loan would have been for $80,000 over 20 years at 6 percent and the monthly payment would have been $573.16, a savings of $214.92 a month. Or, if the homeowner wanted to keep the payments close to what they have been over the past 10 years, the new $80,000 loan at 6 percent would be paid off over 11 years at $829.38 a month. The refinancing would reduce the length of the loan by 9 years. Wow.

There is only one real disadvantage to refinancing. It's not free. Essentially, refinancing means you are selling the house and buying it back with a new mortgage. The lender will run another credit bureau report, have the property reappraised (unless it's been done very recently), prepare another loan package, and so on.

There will be closing fees similar to what you paid the first time. Overall, the cost of refinancing an existing loan can run thousands of dollars. Some people finance these costs, including them in the cost of the new mortgage. Whether or not that is a smart idea depends on your personal finances, how long you will be living in the home, and the decline in interest rates.

To calculate if refinancing your present mortgage makes financial sense, you need to compare your present monthly mortgage payment amount with the new payment amount. The difference between the two is your potential monthly savings.

In our example, that comes to $268. Divide the amount of your monthly savings ($268) into the cost of refinancing (fees, credit check, appraisal, points, etc.). They may come to $4,000. That result is the number of months it will take you to recoup your refinancing costs. In this example, it will take almost 15 months. If you plan to stay in your home more than 15 months, then you will save money by refinancing.

Another way to figure out if refinancing makes sense is to determine your monthly interest savings and divide that number into the cost of refinancing.

Anytime the current mortgage interest rate is 1 to 1-1/2 percent lower than what you are paying, you should look into the advantage of refinancing a mortgage. Otherwise don't bother.

Home Equity Loans

Home equity loans are a relatively new type of loan. The concept is very similar to refinancing. First, we need to define the term "equity." Equity is the difference between what a home is worth today and what you still owe on the mortgage. For example, let's say you bought the house for $125,000 some years ago. Today, the home has a market value of $175,000, while you still owe $80,000 on the mortgage. Your equity is $95,000. It's just that simple.

Lendable equity is a percentage of your equity.

Instead of refinancing the entire amount of the outstanding loan ($80,000), you can take out a loan based on the amount of equity you have in the property. That's called a home equity loan. You can use the loan for all sorts of purposes. Just be aware that it has to be repaid.

The interest rate is usually higher than what lenders charge on mortgage loans.

The term may be for as long as 20 years, depending on the loan amount.

Just like with a regular mortgage, you are pledging the house as collateral for the loan.

The original purpose of the home equity loan was to use the money to pay for home improvements which increase the value of the home.

These days, a lot of people want to take out home equity loans and use the money to pay off credit card balances. Lenders may be willing to make these loans because they are fully secured. However, lenders warn that unless you are willing to change your spending habits, chances are you will run up your credit card balances all over again, only this time you will not only have the credit cards to pay but also the home equity loan.

Home equity loans are not something to commit to lightly. If you default, you can lose your house. Remember, this is a second mortgage.

Tax Ramifications

One of the benefits of home ownership is that you will probably be able to deduct the interest you pay on your home mortgage and your home equity loan, along with the real estate taxes you pay, from your income when you file your tax return. That assumes, of course, that you itemize these deductions on your tax forms. These deductions are quite valuable, especially as your income increases and you find yourself paying ever higher income tax rates. In effect, the deductions homeowners get for interest and tax payments are subsidized by the federal tax law. That's neither good nor bad, it's just the way things are. There is every reason to believe that these deductions are as safe as they can be. Unless the entire tax system is overhauled, homeowners will be deducting their interest and tax payments for many years to come.

The rules on tax deductions get very detailed, but for the most part, you will gain a full deduction for what you spend on interest and real estate taxes.

Reverse Mortgages

The ideal plan is to buy a house, or two, or more and live in them while you pay off the mortgage. Most people try to own their homes free and clear (without any loan balance) by the time they retire from the workforce. By having no mortgage payment, you can substantially reduce your monthly expenses.

A new mortgage product has come out over the past couple of years, and it is increasing in popularity and practicality. It's called a **Reverse Mortgage.**

Two things happen as you pay down your mortgage loan. You reduce the amount of debt you owe on the house, and you build equity in the property. Your equity is the difference between what the house is worth and what you owe on the loan.

When you retire and the mortgage is completely paid, chances are you have a lot of equity in the house. Unfortunately, while you have a valuable asset, it does not generate any income to you at a time when you have retired and may need the money.

So, people are entering into a reverse mortgage. You go to a mortgage company that offers these mortgages. The property is appraised so everyone knows what it's worth. Then you and the lender will agree on the amount of money you will receive each month, and for the length of time you will receive it. The amount depends on the value of the house, if you have any existing mortgage or home equity loan, etc. Or the lender can agree to pay you a lump sum. Whatever you decide, you can get some money to pay bills or receive a monthly income. The lender only has to be repaid at your death, or the death of the second to die (if you are married), or you sell the place.

If you have interest in learning more about the pros and cons of a reverse mortgage, contact a mortgage company in your community and they will tell you if they offer them. If they do not, chances are they will be able to direct you to someone who does.

Summing Up

When you find yourself in the market for your first home, a replacement home, refinancing a mortgage, or taking out a home equity loan, there are a lot of things to learn. Just because you may have learned them once does not mean that you know what the current rules are. You need to relearn them each and every time you find yourself in this highly specialized market.

LESSON EIGHT
(Rev. September 2002)

CREDIT CARDS AND OTHER LOANS

As a consumer, you will be exposed to many different kinds of loans. They come with different terms and interest rates. It is up to you to sort through all the fine print to determine which loans best suit your needs.

There are a number of things you should look for when comparing one loan against another. One difference concerns whether or not you, the borrower, have to provide the lender with collateral in order to get the loan. Another difference concerns whether you are taking out an installment debt or a revolving debt.

Secured Versus Unsecured Loans

Collateral, or security, is a very important concept. A loan secured by collateral is a loan where not only do you promise to repay the money that you borrow, plus interest, you also give the lender the right to sell a valuable piece of property that you own if you fail to keep your promise. This property is often referred to as collateral. Car loans, home mortgages and home equity loans are secured loans because the lender can sell the property in the event you do not make your payments. Remember, even though a lender has collateral, you still must make your monthly payment.

On the other hand, an unsecured loan, like what you owe on a credit card, is a loan where the lender has only your promise that you will make your payments. If you don't make your payments, he may be able to take you to court and get a judgment against you, but there is no property against which he has a claim.

Revolving Versus Installment Debt

Revolving loans such as what you owe on credit cards or lines of credit, are loans where there is no fixed period of time within which you must repay what you borrow. Usually you are required to make a monthly payment, which may be a minimum amount or only the interest which has been added for the month. You can add to the loan, up to your pre-approved maximum credit limit by continuing to charge your purchases.

An installment loan, such as a home mortgage or car loan, calls for a fixed monthly amount to be repaid (including interest), over a set period of time.

Both revolving loans and installments may be either secured or unsecured.

Collateral is King

When you can provide the lender with collateral or security for what you are borrowing, loans can be easy to get, sometimes too easy. Even if you have had a bad credit history, you can probably still get a credit card. It may not be a regular credit card account. You may have to sign up with a credit card issuer who insists on securing the credit card line with a savings account equal to the amount you want to borrow.

If you want a car loan, you pledge the car as security. Of course it helps if you make a substantial down payment. This will give you equity in the car. Equity is the difference between what the car is worth and what you owe on the loan.

If you want a house loan, you pledge the house as security. The same down payment situation exists here, too.

If you want a boat loan, you pledge the boat as security.

However, don't get the idea that just because you have collateral the lender will be anxious to give you the money you want. Today, banks, credit unions, and finance companies are not solely "collateral lenders." If your credit is bad or your repayment ability is questionable, they probably will not want to make a loan to you no matter how much collateral you have. There is an exception, however. That is when the loan is secured by your savings or investments. In that case, lenders will look at your loan application much more favorably because they can get to the money with a minimum of trouble. They will not have to sell an asset at auction, for example.

The Most Common Revolving Loan

Credit card loans are the most common revolving loans. A credit card involves a line of credit, approved by the credit card issuer, which you can access when you want. Once the credit card application has been approved and you have been given a credit line, you don't have to ask for the money. It's there waiting for you. The difficulty with a revolving loan is that it tends to be the last bill you pay each month. It can take a great deal of self-discipline to fully repay a revolving loan quickly.

Credit card loans are usually unsecured. However, there are at least a handful of credit card issuers, typically those associated with retail stores, which hold what is called a **Purchase Money Security Interest (PMSI)** in what you purchase. Most people don't realize that these are secured loans, and that if they fail to make their payments, the store will demand the return of everything that you have purchased on the card back to the last time you had a zero balance. There is nothing wrong with using a credit card where the lender keeps a security interest in what you buy, as long as you know about this important detail prior to the time you use their card. It just reinforces the fact that you need to read the fine print of every credit card and other loan agreement before you sign on the dotted line.

Applying for a Loan

There are a lot of ways you can borrow money these days. Some loans are easier to apply for than others. Some loan applications can take quite a bit of time and effort on your part and the part of the lender to fill out, such as when you apply for a mortgage loan. Other loans can be detailed, but relatively easy to get, like a car loan. Still others are as simple as filling out a 10 to 15 line credit card application and dropping it in the mail.

You may apply for a personal loan from your bank, credit union, or finance company and assuming it is approved, use the money for a wide variety of purposes. Take that route and you will have to fill out the loan application, sit before a loan officer, and make your case. These days, you may be able to send in a loan application by using the Internet. A lot of financial institutions have made this option available to borrowers. If your credit history, income, and debt ratios check out, you should be approved. One caution for those who apply on-line: On-line terms and rates may not be as good as what you can get when visiting a loan officer in person.

You can ask to borrow money to pay for your purchases by using a credit card. Again, you will have to apply, but this time you are not really asking for a loan. Technically, you are requesting a line of credit that you will be able to use any time you want. This credit card line of credit will usually be approved or declined depending on your computer-scored application. There is no face to face meeting with a loan officer to explain about a few black marks on your credit report or that time you were out of work.

Credit Cards

Credit cards have become the primary source of borrowing for millions of people. Typically, those who have been approved for a credit card have 3 or more in their wallet. In fact, it is not uncommon for people to have a dozen open credit card accounts.

People use their credit cards to pay for everything from small ticket items costing a few dollars to cars, vacations, and other things costing tens of thousands of dollars. Credit cards show up in almost every type of purchase you can make these days. Merchants selling all types of products and services accept credit cards. Hospitals and doctors accept cards in payment of their bills. You can charge meals and groceries. You can charge gasoline, tires, and repairs. You can charge a vacation, including transportation costs. You can even use a credit card to charge the expenses of attending school, including tuition, room, meals, and books. There is very little that you cannot use a credit card for these days.

Unfortunately, repaying credit card debt has become a major problem for many individuals and a national problem for card issuers. Personal bankruptcies set an all-time record recently, approaching 1.5 million cases a year, and if the trend continues, there will be even more personal bankruptcies in the years ahead. Some of the blame for these personal bankruptcies is placed at the feet of credit card issuers for making credit too easily available.

Those who use the cards are not blameless. Credit card issuers may entice people to charge their purchases, but no one is twisting their arms, forcing them to run up huge credit card balances. Card issuers are making credit available. It's the individual who is using it. The consumer is making the purchases, not the credit card lender.

This is all about personal responsibility. The cold, hard fact is, you have to take responsibility for the use of your credit cards. How wisely or how unwisely you use them will determine the ease you will have in gaining access to credit in the future.

The Obligation of Credit Card Borrowing

Credit cards are actually misnamed. More properly they should be called "line of credit" cards," or perhaps "loan" cards."

Think about the terminology for just a minute. A credit card implies that you are getting credit. That's true. The credit card issuer is granting you credit. However, when you use the credit card, you are taking out a pre-approved loan. When you are approved for a credit card, the card issuer is extending to you that line of credit. Whether you use it or not is up to you. How you repay it is also up to you, although you are required to make a minimum payment every month.

To get a credit card, you first have to fill out a credit card application. You provide the card issuer with all sorts of personal, family and financial information. You tell the credit card issuer all about yourself. You write down your name, address, social security number, where you work, how much you make, how much you owe, who you owe, and such information. Although you may be completely honest about your personal, financial and credit information, the credit card issuer will verify your story against what the credit bureau has on file about you. If everything checks out, and you fit the profile that the card issuer is looking for, your application will be approved and you will receive your credit card in the mail.

If you alone sign the application, you will get only 1 card. If you ask for additional cards for others and you agree to be responsible for what they charge, you will get those cards, too. If you and your spouse sign the application, you will get 2 cards, and both of you will be fully responsible for all the charges made by either one of you. If you live in a community property state, both parties are equally responsible for the charges made by the other whether or not both have signed. Responsibility for others charging is especially important if you are involved in a pending divorce or separation.

For the most part, credit card companies will not send you one of their credit cards unless you have applied for it. In years past, credit card issuers were known to send out pre-approved cards by the truck load with the instructions to sign it and use it. Today, they only send you a pre-approved credit card application, but you still have to fill in the blanks, sign it and return it to the issuer. If you do, chances are good that you will get the card along with the approved line-of-credit. You will be told exactly how much credit they are willing to extend to you and how you will have to repay what you borrow.

Whether you fill out a pre-approved credit card application that you have received in the mail, or you fill out a standard application that you pick up at your local financial organization, you will hear, one way or another from the credit card issuer. Your application will either be turned down or it will be accepted.

If you are turned down, you will get a letter in the mail that politely explains that you don't fit their criteria.

If you are accepted, you will get a different letter, along with the card.

"Congratulations," they say, or words to that effect. "Your application for our credit card has been approved. We have checked your credit history. We feel you have the capacity to repay what we are willing to lend to you and we feel that you have demonstrated the responsibility to repay what you have borrowed in the past. Because of your income and your past history, we are willing to lend you up to $5,000 (for example). Should you wish to use the card and therefore the credit we are extending to you, you will, of course, have to repay what you are borrowing, plus interest."

They go on to explain precisely what is required of you. They tell you about the minimum payment you must make each month, the interest rate you will have to pay, the annual fee (if any), the penalty if you are late or if you exceed your credit limit, exactly how they compute the interest they charge you for borrowing their money, how they can change the terms and conditions of the agreement, and more. They are required by law to explain all these terms and conditions to you in writing. It is up to you to read the fine print and decide if these terms are acceptable to you. You cannot plead ignorance. You can not negotiate terms. Once you sign the back of the card and use it to charge a purchase, you have agreed to accept the terms of the card issuer whether you understand them or not.

If you do not like the terms, you should shop for a card which offers terms more to your liking. If you feel the interest rate is too high, shop for a card with a lower rate. If you are unwilling to pay an annual fee, shop for a card which does not charge one.

Later in this lesson you will find a section which discusses the various loan terms you have to deal with. The only way to determine if you are using a credit card which offers decent credit terms is to compare everything from the annual percentage rate, grace period, and annual fee charge to fees, credit limits, and the method used for computing balances for purposes of charging interest.

Why Anyone Would Want to Use a Credit Card

With all the potential problems that a credit card can cause, you have to wonder why people are so anxious to use them in the first place. The answer is simple enough. Credit cards are convenient, perhaps much too convenient for those with little or no self-discipline. Susan writes, "My husband got a Discover Card and racked up over $1,600 before I even knew he had it. By then it was too late."

Credit cards provide a great deal of flexibility when it comes to paying for things, and they can provide you with an instant loan any time you have the need, but you have to take care of the bill when it arrives in the mail.

Having a credit card when you want to buy something certainly beats carrying a lot of cash. It's safer to use a credit card, plus you gain certain valuable consumer protections when you charge a purchase and later have a problem with it.

Using a credit card also makes it much easier to keep a record of your purchases which can help tremendously when it comes to sticking within your budget.

Having a credit card is almost a necessity when you travel. It's not impossible to travel without a credit card but it certainly is inconvenient. Life is so much simpler when you use a credit card to reserve your room. It's next to impossible to rent a car without a credit card.

Having a credit card can be a godsend if you have an emergency and cannot get to your banker. Paying for emergency repairs to your car while traveling can be almost impossible unless you have a credit card. Surveys show that the potential for emergencies are the main reason people carry credit cards. While some credit professionals acknowledge that's why people carry credit cards, they point out that that is not the reason why they use them. People use credit cards because they are convenient.

Just because you have a credit card does not mean you have to use it for every purchase you make. You should be able to write a check for what you buy when you are in town. When you need to use the card, and you use it responsibly, you will be glad you have it.

Credit Cards Are Really "Loan Cards"

When you have a credit card available to you, you know that you can take out a loan, or a series of loans, just by presenting your credit card to merchants who accept it for payment of goods and services. You don't have to go to a loan officer. You don't have to fill out a loan application. You don't have to wait for loan approval. It has already been approved, in advance.

That credit card, or **Loan Card**, is so very convenient. After all, you wouldn't ask a banker to borrow $35 so you could purchase a pair of shoes, or $200 for back-to-school clothes for the kids, or $20 for a tank of gas. Yet, every time you reach for that piece of plastic, that is exactly what you are doing. You are taking out a loan. It may be a loan for only $5, but it is a loan nonetheless.

That's not all you can do with your credit card. As you are probably well aware, you can use your credit card to take out a cash advance. That's right. You can walk into any financial institution which honors your card and get some money. From a financial planning and budgeting standpoint, it is usually not a good idea to take out a cash advance. It means you have exceeded your budget and your income. Nevertheless, people do it all the time. Cash advances usually result in a sizeable loan fee, plus, of course, interest charges from the date you get the cash. The cash advance feature of a credit card has become a very popular way for people to borrow small (and sometimes not so small) amounts of money, instead of going to the boss and asking for an advance against their paycheck.

Another feature the credit card issuers have gone to in recent years is the **Credit Card Check**. If you have a credit card, chances are you have received in the mail, a handful of checks from the credit card issuer. They say "Go ahead and use these checks just like you had the money in the bank." You don't of course, but people use them anyway and then are suprised when the credit card statement arrives in the mail with these charges on them. One credit counselor tells the story of a woman who came to see him. She had run up more than $130,000 in credit card debt on 35 cards. He asked her how she could lift her purse with so many cards in it. She replied that she didn't actually carry any credit cards. All she did was use those checks that the nice people had been sending her.

People who are not careful with their money can get themselves into too much debt by taking out loans they cannot afford to repay. They usually have the best of intentions of repaying their debts, but somehow things happen. That is something to guard against.

Guard That Card

Once you have a credit card, you are legally responsible to pay for all charges you make on it. That seems straight forward enough, but there can be a problem if you are unaware of your responsibilities. For example, if you let a relative or friend use your card, you are responsible for the charges. If your card is lost or stolen, you can also be held responsible for the first $50 worth of fraudulent charges. If you are married and you and your spouse have signed the application, both are responsible for all the charges made by the other person. In some states, you can be held responsible for the charges made by your spouse even if you have not signed the credit card agreement. The point is, if you have a credit card, you need to protect it from unauthorized use.

Develop a Repayment Plan Before You Borrow

Using a credit card is just like taking out any other type of loan. When you approach lenders for a car or mortgage loan, they want to know how you intend to repay what you would like to borrow. They want to know that you can afford to make the monthly payments, and that you are, in fact, likely to make those payments each month until the balance of the loan, plus interest, is repaid.

But mortgages, car loans and similar debts are supposed to be repaid in equal amounts each month. These installment loans have a beginning and an end. You borrow a certain amount of money. You know what the interest rate is. You know what you will pay every month. You know when the loan will be paid off.

That's far different than the debt you take on when

you use a credit card.

When you use a credit card, you are taking out a revolving loan. You know what you owe, and you know what the minimum monthly payment is. You can pay more if you want, but there is no requirement that you do so. The minimum amount is usually 2 percent of the outstanding balance. At that repayment rate, plus interest, and assuming you do not add to your balance, it can take 30 years to repay your revolving loan balance. If you continue to add to your balance, the loan may never be repaid in full.

The fact of the matter is with a revolving credit card loan, you charge a little, you pay a little, and you continue to charge a little more. That's how people typically use their credit cards. And that is precisely why credit card balances tend to creep ever higher.

So that you do not find yourself with too much debt and no way to repay, you need to first ask and then answer this question each and every time you use your credit card — "When do I intend to repay what I am about to charge?"

Shirley had a bad tooth. The dentist told her that the crown and other dental work was going to cost her $695. Shirley didn't have the money but needed the dental work, so she charged it. Shirley doesn't have enough to pay this credit card balance in full when the bill comes in. But she is smart enough to pay the minimum plus an extra $60 plus interest every month to the credit card company until it is paid off.

Credit counselors advise that you should plan to pay off small purchases that you put on your credit card on a monthly basis. They say that if you use your card for a big ticket item, you should plan in advance to pay it off within 12 months. If it will take you longer than that, take out a loan at your local lender.

Sally has been using her credit cards for more than 20 years. She charges everything. She knows that she pays interest when she does not pay her charges in full at the end of the month. She tries to do just that, but doesn't always succeed. She uses her card, month after month, even when she fails to pay the balance in full. Over the years, her credit card balances have moved up and down. When she gets a little extra money, they decrease a little. Over all, they stay pretty much the same from year to year.

Sally wants to repay what she owes. She says she would have plenty of money to cover her living expenses if she didn't have these revolving credit card bills. But she never seems to have enough money to make a serious dent in them.

Sally would probably be better off with an installment loan from her local lender rather than the revolving credit card loans she presently has. An installment loan is a regular, fixed bill which has to be paid each and every month for a certain number of months. It's just like clockwork. Most people with an installment loan look forward to the day when the last payment will be made. When you send in that last payment, there often is a great sense of accomplishment, satisfaction, and even a bit of relief.

If you are disciplined enough to repay your credit card balance in full each and every month, then you have no problem. More than one-third of all credit card users do just that. These self-disciplined individuals account for 50 percent of all charging that goes on. They charge clothing, meals, everything and anything. Then, when the bill arrives in the mail, they write a check for what they have charged during the preceding 30 days.

Make it a point to be among this elite group.

One couple, Connie and Jack, have used their credit cards exactly that way ever since they married 15 years ago. Instead of carrying cash around with them, they charge their purchases. Each carries a small note pad so they can jot down what they charge, the date of the purchase, and the amount. Each keeps a running total. Their family budget allows for $800 a month in discretionary purchases, so between them they do not charge more than that amount. It's a system which works well for them.

Carrie, on the other hand, doesn't have discretionary income to spend at this time. She earns enough to cover her rent, car payment, gas, food, insurance, and the utilities, but not much more. There is very little left over at the end of the month.

Carrie's friend asked her, "Why don't you get a credit card?" Her response was, "If I can't afford to pay for something now, I won't be any better able to pay for it later. What if I go ahead and charge what I want. How in the world will I be able to pay for it when the bill comes in at the end of the month?"

She's right. Before you pull out that credit card to pay for a purchase, you better have a good idea of how you are going to pay the bill when it arrives next month. If you don't have the money now and you won't have it when the bill comes in, then put that credit card away.

Cards May Look Alike, But There Are Important Differences

There are at least 5 different types of plastic cards. Because of those differences, you need to understand exactly what you are reaching for when it is time to pay for a purchase. Your local banker and credit counseling agency will have pamphlets which explain the differences between cards in great detail. Pay particular attention.

1. ATM Card. ATM stands for Automated Teller Machine. You use your ATM Card when you want cash. The only place to use your ATM Card is at an ATM machine located somewhere about town. Some locations are directly outside the bank or credit union or in their lobby. Others are located at convenient spots in town where there is a lot of foot traffic.

When you use your ATM Card, you are withdrawing money directly from your checking account. There is no loan transaction although there may be nominal fees involved. If you do not have enough money in your account to cover the withdrawal, the machine will not disburse the money to you.

If you use an ATM Card, be very careful to protect the card from unauthorized use. Thieves have been known to empty people's bank accounts.

Do not reveal your personal identification number (PIN) to anyone.

Do Not Write Your PIN on your ATM Card.

2. Debit Card or Check Card. A Debit or Check Card looks just like a credit card. It is issued by your bank or credit union. You use a Debit Card just like a credit card only instead of taking out a loan, you are paying for your purchase by withdrawing money directly from your checking account. In that regard, a Debit Card is quite similar to an ATM Card. In fact, some Debit Cards can be used for both withdrawing money from an ATM and making purchases anywhere a credit card is accepted. However, the money comes out of your checking account when you use the Debit Card.

Again, be very careful to protect this card because a thief can empty your checking account and you won't know it for some time. By then, the thief is gone and so is your money. This can be especially dangerous for those who have overdraft protection attached to their checking account.

A Debit Card can be an excellent means of getting the benefits of a credit card for travel, convenience and emergencies without the financial dangers of a credit card.

3. Charge Card. A Charge Card represents an account where you are required to pay your account in full at the end of each month. Credit is not extended beyond that period of time. If you fail to make your payment, you stand to lose your charge privileges. Perhaps the best known charge card is the American Express Card. Use Charge Cards to pay for your purchases, but you had better be ready to pay when the bills arrive in the mail.

4. Secured Credit Card. A Secured Credit Card account requires you to put money in a savings account as security against a line of credit. Those who do not have good credit are often required to do this. A credit card secured by a savings account is used just like a regular credit card. No one but you and the issuer know that there is security involved with the account.

5. Unsecured Credit Card. This is the most well-known type of credit card account. The issuer gives you a line of credit. All you do is sign an agreement that contains your promise to repay what you borrow, plus interest. There's no security. It's simply a pre-approved loan issued because of your good word and good credit history. You don't have to pay the balance in full each month. However, if you don't, you will be charged interest on the unpaid balance of your loan.

Prepaid Cards Make Their Debut

Within the past couple of years, a new type of card has hit the market; it is known as the Prepaid Card. Many retailers have them. Perhaps 2 of the best known are Wal-Mart and Starbucks. VISA and MasterCard issuers have them, too. Prepaid Cards work like this. You go to the store or merchant and actually purchase the Prepaid Card. Then, as you use it, the balance on the card declines. Prepaid long-distance telephone cards are very popular. Parents often purchase prepaid VISAs or MasterCards for their college-bound children. Many people use Prepaid Cards as gifts. A couple of words of caution: Prepaid Cards are the same as cash. If you lose it, it's gone. Whover finds it can use it. No questions asked. A Prepaid Card may have an expiration date. Some do, others do not.

Terms and Conditions

Before you select a credit card, you need to become familiar with and understand what each of the terms and conditions of its use means. You should use these terms and conditions to compare one card against another, and then select the one that best suits your needs.

Annual Percentage Rate. The annual percentage rate, or APR, means the rate of interest you will have to pay on your outstanding loan balance. The higher the APR, the more interest you will pay. Many card issuers allow themselves to adjust the APR as often as they please, based on current economic conditions.

Grace Period. You can avoid paying any interest if you pay your bill in full within a certain period of time. Miss it by even a day and you will pay interest.

Annual Fee. Some card issuers charge an annual fee of $50 or more just for the privilege of using their card. Others charge less. Some charge no fee. Those that make you pay an annual fee usually charge it to your account at the beginning of the year. How much are you willing to pay for the privilege of using a credit card? Those cards that charge an annual fee tend to have lower interest rates. Those cards that have no annual fee tend to have higher interest rates.

Transaction Fees. You may have to pay a fee:

- When you take out a cash advance.
- If you are late with your payment.
- When you exceed your credit limit.
- If you don't use your credit card.

Higher Penalties for Late Payments

Over the past couple of years, penalties charged by card issuers for late payments, and when you exceed your credit limit, have soared. Penalties used to be $19 or so for these indiscretions. Card issuers have found them to be a lucrative source of revenue, and have boosted them to $29 and even $35, depending on your balance. Many consider these penalties to be extraordinarily excessive. Card issuers counter, saying they can be avoided just by paying the bill on time.

On-Line Payment and Information Services

Many card issuers will make your account information available to you on-line. You can check on the status of your account, where you have charged, how much you owe, and when your payment has been received. Card issuers also encourage their account holders to pay their bills on-line in order to make certain to avoid those late-payment penalties. Typically, on-line payment of your credit card bill will require you to authorize your bank or credit union to pay the credit card issuer each month on a certain date. It is something that is pretty common these days.

Teasers

Credit cards are a huge business. Issuers make a lot of money on both sides. First, they charge a fee to the merchants each and every time someone uses the card. For example, you charge $100 worth of clothes. The merchant doesn't get the full $100. Instead, the credit card company takes a small fee, something around 2 to 3 percent. They then give the merchant the remainder.

Second, they charge you interest on your unpaid balance, if any.

Third, they charge you fees on late payments, etc.

The key to the success of their business is to have you use their card instead of their competitor's card. The way they accomplish their goal is to offer you a better deal. Typically the better deal is a lower interest rate, at least for a short period of time.

The pitch goes something like this. "We have one of the lowest APR's anywhere. It's the rate you can count on for purchases and balance transfers for the next year (for example). Transfer balances from your high-rate cards to save money on finance charges. Use our credit card to pay off those high interest balances and we'll only charge you 5.9 percent."

What happens after the introductory period is over? The rate reverts to its regular, standard rate.

There's nothing wrong or shady about these teaser offers. You just have to know that once the introductory period is over, the APR jumps, sometimes dramatically.

A word of warning is appropriate. A lot of people take advantage of these low interest rates with the idea of switching to another low-rate card when the introductory period is over. And, by and large, they do just that. If that is your strategy, make sure that you cancel the card that you are paying off through a balance transfer. Otherwise, you will still have an open credit line which could hurt you when you apply for a loan in the future.

Some teaser rates are unbelievably low. There are credit card issuers who are so anxious for you to use their cards that they offer an initial interest rate of zero percent. That's right, zero interest. That's almost too good to be true. However, after checking the fine print, you will find out that the introductory zero interest rate is only for a short period of time, and when that time expires, the interest rate returns to its regular rate. It doesn't make much sense to use a low teaser rate for only a few months, especially when you can use a credit card, interest free for the first month anyway. Some card companies which offer teaser terms take a couple of months to get the card to you, so you get very little benefit.

When you compute how much money is at stake, cards offering teaser rates usually are not worth the time and effort it takes to utilize them.

Easy Credit, Perhaps Too Easy

Many credit card issuers have been accused of blindly granting credit to everyone who has a pulse. Perhaps that's a bit too harsh, but not by much. Some people can't get a credit card no matter how hard they try. Their credit history is just too damaged.

However, for many others, even those people of limited financial means, it is all too easy to get credit card with a credit line of $5,000 or more. That's a lot of temptation for someone who may not be able to refrain from spending money they do not have.

They get the credit card and they use it. They charge this and that and the other thing. Sometimes they go on a spending spree. Sometimes they use their card for emergencies. Sometimes they use a new card to pay off the balance of an old card. The result is the same. They have maxed out their card. They have charged up to the pre-approved credit limit.

Now that they have spent the money, they can look forward to repaying it. All too often, they have little to show for what they borrowed.

In an article that appeared in *USA Today*, the headline read "Cruise on Credit." The first line of the story said it all. "Play now, pay later."

Good advice? No, not if you are a savvy consumer.

Yes, if you are running a cruise line and want to fill cabins.

Yes, if you are a credit card company. This is a big ticket item. You can be pretty certain that people will charge thousands of dollars which can take years to repay, plus interest.

Credit card issuers want you to charge your purchases on their card. The line of credit is available to you. The Madison Avenue advertising firms do everything in their power to entice you to spend your money as well as money that you don't yet have. The credit card people have already approved the loan. Do you want to make the purchase, take the vacation, buy the new furniture, walk out of the store with the new clothes? They tell you that you can have it all, right now. Just remember, they are all trying to sell you something.

It is up to you to show some self-control. If you can afford to buy these things, that's all well and good. If you cannot afford them at the present time, then it is up to you to be responsible and walk away until you can afford them.

Credit card issuers are not bad guys because they extend credit to people who they feel can be trusted to repay what they borrow. They are not bad guys any more than a loan officer is a bad guy because he or she expects you to repay the money you borrowed to pay a car.

What's more, credit cards are not evil. Millions of people use credit cards responsibly every day. They charge what they purchase, and they try to repay the credit card company in full at the end of the month. Most of the time, these people manage to do just that. Other times they carry a balance for a month or 2 or even 3. They use the credit card as a pre-approved line-of-credit, just as it is intended to be used.

Then there are those who do not pay off their credit card balances. They charge, find that they are saddled with terribly high rates of interest, make minimum payments, and charge some more. The cycle goes on month after month. They find that they cannot repay what they have borrowed. Don't let this happen to you.

Be part of the first group of people, those who pay their credit card bill in full each month. Use your credit card instead of cash if that works for you. Just pay it off.

Bill Consolidation Loans

For consumers, bill consolidation loans are a great idea. The problem is, not very many lenders are willing to help you out. A lot has been written about bill consolidation loans in recent years. Much of the advice is good, at least in theory. However, when it comes time to find a lender who will put up the money, most people have their hopes dashed.

There are 2 types of bill consolidation loans. There is the **Unsecured Personal Loan** that you would take out to pay off all your credit card and other debts. Then there is the **Secured Personal Loan** where you will pay off your outstanding debts but in addition to giving your promise that you will repay what you borrow, you give the lender some collateral.

The fact of the matter is, unsecured bill consolidation loans just don't happen very often, at least not in large amounts. Lenders explain that they have limits on what they will lend for unsecured bill consolidation loans. Typically, the amount is something between $2,500 and $10,000 depending on who you approach.

Secured bill consolidation loans are much more common, simply because lenders have collateral they can and will sell if you fail to make your payments.

Pat and Terry have been married for 8 years. They both work, bought a house a couple of years ago, and have one child, Lynn. They watch their budget, although not as closely as they should. Sometimes their spending gets away from them. If they need something, or they want something, they just go a little overboard. This past Christmas, they spent too much and they know it. Christmas is over but their credit card bills have become a constant, nagging reminder of what they did.

Over the past 3 years, Pat and Terry have been using

4 different credit cards to pay for things they couldn't otherwise afford. The result is they now owe $20,000 and really don't have much to show for it. They are making minimum (combined) monthly payments of $715, of that $315 is interest. The APR is a whopping 18.9 percent on all the cards. It could be worse. There are cards with higher rates.

They continue to use their cards, adding to their balances. The result is the amount they owe goes up month after month. They don't see any way they can fully repay these credit card balances, at least not in the immediate future. The best they can hope for is to make their minimum payments, plus maybe $100 or so, and not sink too much deeper into debt. They wish they could pay off at least 1 of their cards, if not all 4. But they can't, and they know it.

If they could pay off 1 of the cards, they say they would use what they paid to that card to more quickly pay off the remaining card balances.

Then, one day, Pat heard someone talking about the wonderful benefits of a bill consolidation loan. Immediately they thought of consolidating their 4 credit card debts into one big $20,000 loan. They would pay a lower rate of interest, perhaps 13 percent instead of the whopping 18.9 percent they are saddled with. That way, they could pay about $455 a month and pay the balance off within 5 years. Unfortunately they pay twice that amount every month and the balances on the 4 cards hardly changes.

So they ask their local lender for a bill consolidation loan, and they get turned down.

Pat and Terry are amazed that their lender isn't jumping at the chance to lend them the money, and honestly they are more than a little irritated about it. They point out that they have a great credit bureau report. They have never missed a payment. They feel that they are an excellent credit risk. Why in the world, they wonder, won't the lender give them a bill consolidation loan?

It makes perfect sense to them to replace their high interest rate loans with a single lower interest rate loan. It seems reasonable to take these revolving loans which never get paid off and replace them with an installment loan which will be paid in full in a couple of years. It makes sense to everyone but the lender, who, unfortunately for Pat and Terry, is the one who has to be convinced to make the loan.

From the lender's stand point, this is not a good loan risk. Everything the couple says is true — they have good credit, have not missed any payments, and would be better off financially paying less each month on a single loan rather than on those high interest credit cards — the fact remains that they have borrowed money over the years and now they are having a great deal of trouble repaying it. Why would a lender want to take on that kind of risk? The answer is, he doesn't.

This lender is like many lenders. They dislike bill consolidation loans, secured or unsecured. These lenders have first hand experience with this type of loan. They and their colleagues have seen it time after time. The borrower combines all the debt into one loan, and for the first month or two, he enjoys the financial relief provided by the bill consolidation loan. Then he starts charging on his credit cards all over again. This isn't true for everyone of course, but it is true for many.

As a result, the lender knows that if he loans the money to consolidate the debt, it is very likely that the borrower will find himself in the same mess within a couple of years, only this time he will have the bill consolidation loan to repay in addition to the new credit card debt. The majority of lenders who agree to make an unsecured bill consolidation loan may agree to a relatively small amount. All too often, that is not enough to pay off all the bills.

That's the case when the borrower has little or no collateral. Lenders are especially reluctant to make bill consolidation loans where there is no collateral, or the collateral is hard to get to. Pat and Terry don't have collateral. They have 2 cars, but don't have more than $500 worth of equity in them. They haven't been in their house long enough to qualify for a home equity loan. They have about $1,000 in savings. Their retirement plans at work don't count since they cannot be used to guarantee a loan.

If they had some collateral, especially in the form of home equity, lenders would view the bill consolidation request more favorably. Chances are they would make the loan because now there is something to take and sell if the loan goes unpaid.

Lenders want security for their loans. You can't blame them for that. Give them that security and they will loan you money for almost every legal purpose under the sun, including consolidating your debt, assuming of course that you can demonstrate your capacity to repay what you want to borrow. But without that security, you're going to find that bill consolidation loans obtained through standard borrowing channels will be few and far between.

Even when you can provide collateral, you may find a bit of reluctance on the part of lenders. That's because of their experience in the field of consolidating bills. They have seen it all. Lenders say that the only way to get out of the cycle is to **change your spending habits and life style so you can cover your bills on a day to day basis without charging and running up additional debt.**

There is a downside to taking out a secured bill consolidation loan. If you fail to make your payments on a secured loan, the lender will repossess and sell the property that has been pledged as collateral. If you fail to make your payments on unsecured loans, the lender has little recourse against you. Lenders will always prefer to substitute unsecured loans with secured loans. It is good business for the lender.

One lender sums up the subject of Bill Consolidation Loans this way. "The habit of spending more than they make must be changed before a bill consoldation loan will be good for either the consumer or the lender."

Delayed Payment Loans

"Buy now. Make no payments and pay no interest for a year!" That's what the ad says. And it's true. Merchants have been using this advertising campaign for a long, long time because it works. It gets people in the store to buy things they want but may not be able to afford, at least at the present time.

Nick wants that television.

Bob's mother is coming for a visit and he needs to furnish the guest bedroom.

Ellen wants to replace badly worn carpeting.

None of the 3 has the money in savings to pay for these purchase. But each goes ahead and orders the merchandise.

They understand that they can have what they want right now and that they won't have to pay for a year.

What they don't understand is that if they don't pay for the goods within the 1 year time frame, they will be charged interest back to the original date of purchase.

So, if you enter into one of these agreements, you should know exactly what you are getting yourself into.

It is not that these are bad deals. It is just that too many people have the best of intentions, but then something happens, and they learn the hard way that good intentions don't get the bills paid. They plan to save their money during the following 12 months so they will be able to pay for the goods when the time comes. But, for whatever reason, something usually happens, and 1 year later, the bill comes due and there still is no money. The better idea is to restrain yourself and save for that special purchase. You will be happier in the long run.

Rent to Own

When you have a need and you don't have the money, you might look into renting what you have to have, and using those rental payments to pay for the merchandise. Financially, this is usually not a very good deal for consumers, but sometimes it is the only alternative, given individual circumstances.

Rent-to-own is not nearly as good a deal as buying on credit. However, if that avenue is not available to you, you may want to check into renting.

One credit executive correctly advises that instead of renting, you may want to consider buying used items instead. The cost of renting is about 4 times as much as buying used.

Summing Up

Credit cards are convenient and provide a tremendous amount of flexibility. But they can be terribly dangerous to your financial well-being. Use them carefully.

Bill consolidation loans can be a good idea for consumers, but you will have trouble finding a lender who will loan you the money you need unless you can provide collateral and can show repayment ability. If you want to consolidate your debts into a single, lower interest loan, do so only if you are willing to change your spending habits.

YOU'VE GOT TROUBLE WHEN ...

It is all too easy to get into financial trouble these days. It can happen to anyone. Financial pitfalls stalk the rich and poor. They follow the young, middle aged, and old. They can strike at any time, quite unexpectedly. The reasons behind financial disasters don't really matter, except to the extent that others can learn from them.

This bad stuff happens more often than you might like to think. Sometimes you can find yourself owing more money than you can afford to repay because of events that are simply beyond your control. However, in too many cases, a person's financial problems are due to the decisions and choices they have made. If you are in trouble with creditors, it may be because you have chosen to live a lifestyle that costs more money than you can afford to spend and now you simply do not have the income and savings to cover what you owe.

It's really not all that difficult to see when you are in trouble. There are the obvious signs. Are you writing bad checks? In some states, that can be a felony and you can go to jail. Are you writing post-dated checks? Are you hoping that a paycheck will make it into your account so the check you have written is good? Are you avoiding telephone calls at home because you know the calls are from bill collectors? Have you had a judgment filed against you? Are you being dragged into court because you are not paying your bills?

Those are the more obvious signs. There are others that are not as easy to recognize. In this lesson, you will learn how to recognize some of the more subtle tell-tale signs of lurking money problems and danger signals. You will also learn to identify poor money management decisions.

The 24 Tell-Tale Signs

This lesson is something like taking your car in for a 24 point check. The mechanic will change your oil, check the oil and air filters, radiator and battery levels, and all those other things that need to be checked regularly to keep your car on the road. You need to do the same thing with your personal finances.

At this point in your credit and personal financial education and experience, you should be able to recognize when you or someone you know is facing a potential problem with money. Right off the top of your head, how many tell-tale signs can you name? What follows are two dozen signs identified by experienced lenders, credit counselors, and regular everyday people. They have seen it all. They have heard every excuse. They have tried to work through every circumstance. While this list is far from complete, it does cover the most common issues people face.

Don't get the wrong idea. Few people are perfect when it comes to their finances. However, the more areas you have problems with, the more likely it is that you are in trouble. Some of these 24 tell-tale signs represent outright devastating money problems while others simply reflect poor money management practices which if left unattended can result in future money problems.

You may be able to get away with one or more and believe you don't have a problem. In any case, you need to ask yourself if you are managing your money as well as you should or could.

1. Lack of a Budget (and Spending) Plan

You may be headed for trouble if you do not have a budget and do not refer to it on a regular basis.

The two most important actions you can take to stay out of financial trouble both involve budgeting.

First, you need to develop a detailed monthly budget for your household which reflects all of your revenue sources and all of your spending. This includes how much money you make, what you pay in taxes, and what you spend on necessities as well as nonessentials.

Second, you need to establish a lifestyle that fits with your income. This may require you to curtail your spending habits. If that's the case, so be it.

Too many people simply do not bother to develop a household budget, and some who take the first step of making a budget do not take the second step of reviewing it regularly. They go to the trouble of preparing a budget, but they leave it in the desk drawer or on the computer. They go through the motions, and that's all. They do not keep up with the financial challenges that occur almost every month. They do not watch their spending. They let their credit cards entice them into unwise purchases.

One counselor is passionate when she says, "This is so true. It is next to impossible to stick to the same budget perfectly month after month because things do come up. But a basic guideline is so important. Otherwise you don't know if you have spent too much."

Because some people do not keep up with the budgeting process, they do not know how much money they bring home each month. They do not know how much they are spending on necessities. They do not know how much they spend on luxuries. They have no idea if they are spending more than they make or if they are making more than they spend. They don't know when their car insurance payment is due, how much they can afford to pay for a car, what they spend at the grocery store, or if they can afford a vacation.

These people are choosing not to know. The fact is, when it comes to their personal finances, they really don't know very much. They need to. Everyone does.

Your budget is a blueprint of your personal finances. Businesses, large and small, have budgets, and smart management follows them religiously. When managers and owners stray from their budgets, they find themselves in financial hot water. The same holds true for individuals and families.

Without a budget, you are operating in the dark. With a budget, you can manage your money responsibly, effectively and efficiently. With a budget, you should be able to plan your household's finances. You should know what purchases you can afford and what you need to postpone because you don't have the money in the bank to pay for them.

If you learn nothing else in this course, acknowledge that it is essential you have a household budget, review it no less than once a month, and work with it as you take care of your personal finances.

2. Little or No Savings Account

If you do not have enough cash in a readily accessible savings account to cover at least three months worth of your household's monthly financial needs, you are not managing your money responsibly. As a result, you are courting disaster.

Stuff happens all the time. It's part of everyday living. Don't kid yourself into believing that bad things only happen to other people. Read the newspaper or listen to the news, and you will find story after story that tells you of the misfortune suffered by this family or that town. You hear about tornadoes and floods. You hear about automobile accidents and factories that close. You hear about one problem after another faced by family, friends, neighbors and colleagues.

Ken had worked for 13 years at the local plant. It happened to be a meat-packing plant but it could have been any place of business. One Thursday morning, he showed up for work and found the building engulfed in flames. By the time the fire was brought under control, the plant was a complete loss. Ken, along with the other 650 people who worked at the plant, were immediately (in this particular case) permanently out of work.

Could something similar happen to you? Of course it could. In fact, something probably will, sometime. No one is wishing you bad fortune, but the fact remains that you need to be prepared, and the best way to be prepared is to have sufficient savings behind you.

Now you needn't sit up all night worrying about being in the path of a tornado or losing your job. However, you do need to make plans to cover yourself and your family, just in case something bad should happen.

That's where a savings account comes in.

Years ago, money experts told people they needed to be able to cover at least six months worth of their monthly expenses with their savings. Today, that number has changed. Some say you should be able to cover your living expenses for three months. Some say two months. Unbelievably, still others say that you are okay when you can cover your household expenses through cash advances from credit cards you have. That's financial suicide.

Three months worth of household expenses is just about right. If and when you lose your job, are out of work due to illness or accident, take time off work to be with a family member, or if your income is interrupted for any other reason, how would you pay your bills? Where would the money come from to make the car payment, put food on the table, or pay for your utilities? The answer is from your savings account, even a small one. Without a savings account, you will probably have a problem.

3. Lack of Health Insurance

If you fail to cover yourself and your family with at least a minimal health insurance policy, you are courting trouble. Of course, that assumes you are insurable.

One of the most devastating events that can befall an individual or family is when someone suffers a catastrophic medical problem. How would you deal with a $500,000 medical bill from the doctors and hospital? If you had health insurance, either through your work or with a private health plan, you would look over the bill to check its accuracy and then pass it along to your health insurance company. That's assuming you see it at all. When you have comprehensive medical insurance, you may find that the bill goes directly from the medical professionals to the insurance companies.

If you don't have health insurance, you will get the bill. You will look at it, shrug your shoulders (or more likely go through the roof), and realize you have a problem of monumental proportions. That bill is unpayable. There is no way the typical person who works for a living will ever be able to come up with that amount of money.

How likely is it you or someone close to you will suffer a major illness or injury? Actually it's quite likely. The younger you are, the greater your chances of an accident. People get hurt in automobile accidents, and they hurt themselves playing sports. When you have a youngster, your pediatrician will say, "See you in the emergency room." Kids get scrapes and broken arms. As you grow older, your risk of illness increases. Cancer, kidney disease, heart attacks and strokes are only some of the major medical problems that affect people as they age.

In case you haven't noticed, the cost of health care is prohibitive. Without health insurance, you really don't stand a chance of being able to pay for much more than regular visits to the doctor and prescriptions. If you save, you may be able to afford pre- and post pregnancy medical care. Even that is beyond the ability of many people today.

One credit counselor says lack of health insurance is a huge problem. "Too many of my clients can't even afford basic coverage. As a result, even a routine visit to the doctor's office is a financial hardship. And those who have basic coverage find themselves in trouble when they suffer a major illness or accident because the bills mount up very fast. Kidney dialysis runs upwards of $500 a day. An uncomplicated pregnancy will cost over $5,000."

4. Lack of a Retirement Account

If you don't put money aside for your later years, you may be setting yourself up for a life of poverty when you reach your 60s and 70s.

It is never easy to save money, especially in the early years. When you are in your 20s and 30s, you may need every dollar you earn just to put food on the table and keep a roof over your head. Still, if you don't start saving and investing in a tax-qualified retirement plan just as soon as you start working, you are missing out on one of the great opportunities to put together the nest egg you will need when you reach your 50s and 60s, and beyond. Save early in your working career and your money will have an opportunity to grow in value for decades. What's more, the growth that you enjoy in these accounts is all tax-deferred. You can't ask for more than that.

Saving for retirement doesn't have to be hard. You don't have to feel that you are denying yourself. For many people, employers make saving for retirement as easy as signing up and watching the money grow. Often the company will match a portion of what you save. The key is you have to save some of your own money in order for the company to put some of its money into your account.

Saving for retirement is your responsibility. If you don't have a retirement plan through work, you will have to do it on your own. That's where IRA's and similar accounts come into play. The attitude has to be, save now so you can enjoy your later years. Otherwise it may be, spend now and be destitute in your later years.

If you don't save for retirement, you will not have the nest egg you need to fall back on when it is time for you to leave the work force. Without that retirement nest egg, you may never be able to retire. You may have to continue working, despite any health problems which may develop. These so-called "golden years" are not something to look forward to if you don't have financial security.

Another point needs to be made about saving for retirement. You actually need to do more than just save for those golden years. You need to learn how to manage your retirement plan's investments, a task that can take quite a bit of time. Still, it is something you must do.

Just look at those who worked for Enron, the famous energy firm that went bankrupt, wiping out the life savings and retirement nesteggs of thousands of its workers.

One former worker complained that his retirement account shrunk from $1.2 million to $5,000 in a month, all because he had all of his retirement in company stock.

5. Lack of a College Fund for Children

If you or someone in your family fails to save for your children's college education, you may severely limit your children's chances for a higher education.

The cost of attending college is going up every year at a rate that far outstrips the rate of inflation. While the Consumer Price Index (CPI) has been cruising along at 2.5 percent or so for the past decade, the price of higher education has been increasing at 6 percent or more. If you intend for your children to attend college, you need a financial plan that will make it possible for them to attend.

You should know that, on average, college graduates earn almost twice as much during their working careers as high school graduates. That means there is a substantial payback for the time, expense and sacrifice that college entails.

The question becomes, how will your child be able to afford college when the time comes? The best answer is, you should start a college fund just as soon as the child is born. You have other options, of course. You can consciously choose to ignore the whole issue and pay what you can towards college when the child is 18. You can tell your children that they are on their own after high school. You can refinance your house or tap your retirement accounts so the kids can afford college. There are lots of choices, but the best alternative seems to be for you to start saving toward your children's college expenses as soon as possible so you won't jeopardize your savings when they reach those college years and you reach your retirement years.

One creative and thoughtful couple decided that they would fund their children's college accounts by taking the money that they had been paying for child care and put it into their college funds when the kids started primary school.

Another family has this tradition. The grandparents purchase a savings bond for every birthday and special holiday, with the bonds earmarked for college. Each generation does the same thing when they become grandparents.

6. An Unhealthy Attitude About Money

You and those people around you need to develop a healthy attitude about money. Without it, you can find yourself in financial trouble.

What's a "healthy" attitude? You take the test. Are you a "buy now and pay later" kind of person? Or are you a "save now and wait until you have enough money in your savings account" person?

Are you willing to wait and save, or do you demand immediate gratification?

Is your shopping and buying out of control? Do you have trouble saying NO to your yourself, your kids, friends, neighbors, and others?

Do you waste money on gambling? Do you spend too much on tobacco and alcohol?

Which is more important, buying something or watching your savings and investment accounts grow?

No one is saying that you can't enjoy life. Everything doesn't have to be gray all the time. However, the reality is you have to take care of the necessities of life and if that means that you have to deny yourself some immediate gratification, then you will have to do just that.

Your attitude about money and what it will buy may be affected by the way you were raised. Whatever your background, the reality is that as an adult, you need to think about the money you make and how you spend it.

Check your attitude. If there's a problem, you will have to make some serious adjustments to the way you think about your money, financial obligations and priorities.

7. Outdated Job Skills, Poor Job Performance, Lack of Job Security

If you do not regularly monitor your job skills, your job performance, and your job security, you will likely have an unexpected problem. Remember, your job provides you with income, and without income you have no way to pay your bills. Lose your job and you lose your income. When that happens, you have a serious problem, especially when it can take months or even longer to find a replacement. Just ask any of those caught in the corporate downsizing trend of the past few years.

It is difficult to be objective about it, but you need to honestly assess your job skills, your job performance, and your job security.

Start with your job skills. Would you hire someone with your job skills to do the job you are doing? Are you current with the computer skills you need? Do you need more training? If you do, get it, even if it means paying for the training you need out of your own pocket.

How is your job performance? Now be honest. Put yourself in your boss's chair. What kind of review would you give yourself?

Do you show up on time?

Do you do all that is asked of you?

Do you finish your work on time?

Do you put in an honest day's work for an honest day's pay?

Do you cut corners?

How's your attitude toward your work, your peers, extra assignments?

Do you like your job? Does it show?

How stable is your job? Is it secure? Are you sure? Is the company operating at a profit? Is the company going to stay in town? What are your chances for advancement, more responsibility, higher pay, and better benefits?

Cheryl says, "My husband used to tease me when we were first married. He'd say, 'I wonder where we will spend this year's Christmas party?' because I was always changing jobs. I did this for about six years, but I kept moving up in pay each time I moved. Now I've found my niche in a great company with awesome benefits, but it took time for that to happen. Fred, on the other hand, has been with the same company every since he finished college. He probably will retire there in another 20 years."

If you have trouble honestly facing the answers to questions about your job, then you have a problem. If your answers are not what they should be, you have some work to do. Remember, not every job is the ideal place for you to be for the rest of your life. However, you must have a good idea of where you stand when it comes to your main source of income.

8. Depending on Parents, Friends, Others to Help You Out

To be financially independent, you have to pay your bills. If you continue to depend on others to help you out when you run short of cash, then you are not independent. It may be okay to accept a helping hand every once in a while, but if you are looking to others for money on a regular basis to help you cover your rent, pay for groceries or the car payment, then you are already in trouble.

Be honest with yourself. Do you pay your own way or do you rely on others to cover what you cannot pay? Declaring your financial independence and meaning it can be one of the most difficult steps a young adult can take. It means relying on yourself. It means accepting the burden that comes with independence.

If the hot water heater bursts, will you pay for a replacement by taking money from your savings account, or will you call someone and ask for a gift or even a short-term loan? When you need to repair your car, pay past due bills, or meet any one of a hundred other financial obligations, where do you turn?

The harsh reality is, you should look toward yourself to pay your own way in life. If you are looking toward others to bail you out, you're looking the wrong way.

9. Getting Turned Down for a Loan

If you have recently applied for a loan, either from a local lender or credit card company, and you have been turned down, you probably have a problem.

Getting turned down for a loan means that someone, somewhere, has reviewed your credit application and found something that tells them that you may not be able to repay the amount that you have asked to borrow. People who review these applications have years of experience and history behind them.They know what to look for. They have a pretty good idea of who is a good credit risk and who is not. When they turn down your request for credit, they do so not because they have a personal grudge against you or because they are mean, spiteful people, but rather because of something in your credit history.

Not all denials are based on credit history. There is the question of inadequate income levels, lack of collateral, spotty employment history, and so on. These can result in denial of that loan, too.

If you have been turned down for credit, you need to determine the reason for the denial. You can get a copy of your credit report, free of charge, from the local credit bureau. You need to review the information contained on it carefully. If you are not able to decipher the shorthand language of your credit report, you should find someone who knows how to interpret what it says. You may be able to get some help from the credit bureau. You may ask someone at the local credit counseling agency or where you have your checking and savings accounts.

Once you have reviewed your credit report, you should have a fairly good idea of the reason for the credit denial. Then it is up to you to fix the problem. If you do not, then the problem will persist and you will probably face credit problems for some time to come.

10. Needing a Co-Signer

If you apply for a loan and the lender says "No, not unless you can get a creditworthy person to co-sign the loan," you may have a problem that you need to address.

Now there are exceptions. For example, someone without previous credit history such as a new graduate may need a co-signer in order to get a first loan. But for the most part, if you need a co-signer to get a loan, you better find out why.

Lenders are pretty savvy people when it comes to making loans. Banks, credit unions and finance companies typically suffer less than a 1 percent loss on what they lend. They are in the business of making loans. That's how they make their money. They are good at determining who gets the money and who gets turned away. They get no enjoyment out of turning people away.

When they say that you need a co-signer, they are really telling you that your credit history is not established enough for them to grant you the loan you want. When they say they need a co-signer for them to make the loan, they are really telling you that they think this would be a risky loan and that it might come down to a co-signer making your payments for you.

One banker explains the situation in terms that everyone clearly understands. He says, "If your income, debts, credit history and job stability were good enough ior me to make the loan, I would do it. But they are not, so I won't." He goes on to say "When I require a co-signer in order to make a loan, I tell the co-signer right in front of the loan applicant who I have just turned away that I expect the co-signer to pay this debt if the borrower cannot and that they should be prepared to pay when the borrower does not."

Listen when the lender says, "No, not without a creditworthy co-signer." They are telling you something. Determine what the problem is and work to fix it. Either that or accept the need for a co-signer and enter into the loan with the intent of paying it back on time, or even ahead of time, so that the co-signer does not regret signing for you and so the lender will not require a co-signer on your next request.

There is one more point to add here. Avoid co-signing loans for others. Chances are you will be the one who ends up paying off the loan.

11. Using Payday Loans

When times get tough, more and more people turn to payday-loan businesses. It usually works like this: You borrow the money and pledge your next paycheck to repay the loan. The interest rate is obscenely high. Often, the rate is well over 100 percent on an annual basis. But what are you going to do? You need the money, and they are willing to lend it to you, and while the annual interest rate is very high, in terms of dollars, it is something you are willing to live with.

Payday lenders know when they have a good business. A growing number of Main Street banks and credit unions also are getting into payday loans. They may call them by different names, but the subject is the same. You need an advance on your pay, and they are willing to give it to you in return for a quick turn around, high interest rate and lots of fees.

If you are using the services of a payday lender, you can find yourself trapped on a vicious treadmill, one that can be next to impossible to get off of.

Connie goes to the bank every two weeks. That's how often she is paid at work. She keeps renewing her original payday loan because the terms of the loan are simple enough. She can borrow up to half the amount of her paycheck. The loan has to be repaid by drafting her checking account, which takes a direct deposit for her check.

She keeps borrowing the same $500 every two weeks. She has to pay a $10 fee for every $100 borrowed for renewing the loan, and she has to pay 48 percent annual interest.

Bill uses a payday loan that is different from the bank variety. He, too, takes out a short-term, high-interest loan of $500. But he has to write a post-dated, personal check for what he borrowed, plus fees. Bill has yet to be able to come up with the money, so he just rolls it over into a new loan.

Payday loans seem to be springing up on every street corner. And that's a shame, because those who are using these loans probably are the least able to afford the high interest rates and fees. If you haven't resorted to these loans, count yourself lucky. If you have in the past, you know how difficult it can be to pay them off. And if you are tempted, if you are short of cash and payday is just around the corner, try to hold out until you receive your paycheck. Without exception, payday loans are not the way to go.

12. Financing Vehicles for More Than 5 Years

Financing the purchase of a car or truck for more than 5 years just so you can afford the payments is not smart money management.

How long do you intend to drive the vehicle you are buying? How long do you think the vehicle will last? What's the purchase price? How much can you afford to pay each month to cover your basic transportation needs? How much are you willing to afford?

The rule of thumb is the shorter the period of time you finance your vehicles, the healthier you are financially. You should never finance a vehicle for more than 5 years. If you have to run the term out longer than that in order to qualify for the loan, then you are probably purchasing a vehicle that is too expensive for your budget. Even with a four- or five-year loan, it will take you at least three years before the car you are driving will be worth more than you owe on it.

13. Consolidating Loans Without Closing Original Accounts

A bill-consolidation loan is not necessarily a bad thing. It can be an effective financial planning tool when it is used wisely. However, if you are considering a bill consolidation loan in order to reduce your monthly payments as well as cut the amount of interest you are paying, you need to close out the original accounts.

The danger of a bill consolidation loan is that you will take the loan money and pay off the existing debt, but within a few months you will simply resort to your old habits and start using those accounts all over again. If you do not close those original accounts, you are playing with fire.

Peter had several high interest credit card accounts, and he got an offer he couldn't refuse. He could borrow what he needed to pay off those high interest accounts at a significantly lower rate of interest. He did it the smart way. He sent letters to each of the existing lenders instructing them to close the accounts.

Penny wasn't as smart. She too took out a bill consolidation loan, but unlike Peter she didn't close the accounts. She suffered one unexpected expense after another. Within a year her old accounts (which she had paid off with the bill consolidation loan) were back up to their limits. The result is she is paying on the bill consolidation loan plus the new balances on her old accounts, too.

14. Paying More Than 20 Percent of Your Monthly Income to Cover Minimum Debt Payments

Check your income and check what the minimum payments are on all your installment and revolving debt (except for your mortgage). If you are paying more than 20 percent of your income on those monthly minimum payments, you probably have a problem. That's the rule of thumb. However, there are always exceptions to rules like this. Nevertheless, it is a good one to keep in mind.

If you are paying more than 20 percent, determine why your debt repayments exceed this arbitrary standard. Understand that if you apply for a loan and the lender calculates your debt-to-income ratios and finds that it exceeds 20 percent, you will probably be turned down.

You may need to realign your spending. You may need to take a second job, at least for a little while in order to pay off some debt. You may need to seek out lower interest loans. You may need to look into a bill consolidation loan. Whatever you decide to do, understand that you have crossed the line. You are paying more on your debt than lenders think you should.

15. Fighting About Money, Especially When You and Your Spouse (or Significant Other) Have Different Spending and Saving Habits

Examine your personal relationships at home. Are you fighting with your spouse about money, especially about how you spend it? If so, get some help. You need it if you want to save your marriage or relationship. Too many marriages fail because husband and wife have different backgrounds and outlooks about money. If you and your spouse have trouble agreeing on how to spend what you make, you have a rough road ahead of you. You need to come to an understanding of how you will jointly take care of family responsibilities. You need to agree on who will cover the mortgage or rent, the utilities, and all the other bills. You have to trust the other person to keep up their end of the bargain.

Learning to deal with money together, honestly and openly, may be one of the most difficult hurdles any couple must overcome in order to have a successful, happy marriage. It is worth the struggle.

16. Failing to Participate in Family Financial Decisions

When you are married, both husband and wife need to take an active role in dealing with the family's finances. It is not fair to place the entire responsibility on one person's shoulders. Arguments start that way. The one who does not handle the checkbook or deal with the budget wants to go on a vacation, while the one who handles all the financial details knows that there is no way to afford that trip this year. They have heated words. They have a problem not because they cannot afford a fancy vacation this year. They have a problem because only one of the two is participating in the detailed work of handling the family's finances on a regular basis. Only one of the two understands what is going on with the family's money.

This is a problem which is relatively easy to fix. Set a time for both to sit down and talk about money. Twice a month is ideal, at the beginning of the month and then again in the middle. Another way is to meet every payday.

Whatever you do, schedule the time just like you would if you were having a business meeting. Don't let anything get in the way. Hire a baby-sitter if you must. Just make sure you set aside sufficient time to take care of family business.

By both participating in the decisions that must be made regarding the family's finances, you will avoid potential problems. If one refuses to participate, it is only a matter of time before a serious disagreement about money develops.

17. Misrepresenting Purchases to Spouse

When you cannot bring yourself to be completely honest with your spouse about what something costs, you have already started down a very dangerous road.

You may not be intentionally lying about what you are buying and what you have paid for your purchases, but you are not being completely honest either. Why do you suppose that is? Are you embarrassed about the price you have paid? Do you simply want to avoid the arguments you face when the truth comes out? The point is, if you tell your spouse that something cost $25 when you know that it really came to $75, you are hiding something that should not be hidden. And you have to stop it.

When it comes to big ticket items, the decision to buy and the decision on how much to spend should be joint, not separate. When it comes to the little, every day stuff, you need to agree to a budget and not exceed it. One party cannot have free rein to spend as they please without the other getting terribly resentful. If you are misrepresenting what you are spending, you need to stop it. Money is precise. No one can plan when they do not have the exact figures.

18. Developing Bad Patterns

There will always be something that comes up that you didn't plan on. You may unexpectedly need new tires or have to replace something that broke. That's life. You can run short of money one month and not think you are headed for financial ruin. It can happen even two months in a row. But if you can't live within your budget for three consecutive months, you know that you are facing trouble.

Bad patterns usually creep up on you. They don't

happen all at once. Consider how these affect you:

- **Pushing the Grace Period.** Do you find that you are using the grace period offered by your creditors? Do you need the extra time, month after month, to make your payment? Do you find that you are taking the grace period right up to the last day, and sometimes missing it because you waited too long, suffering late payment penalties?

- **Pushing Your Credit Limit.** Are you right up to your limit on your credit cards and line of credit? Have you exceeded the limits from time to time, suffering the penalty they charge when you do? Do you run a new credit card right up to the limit when you first get it?

- **Being Chronically Late With Your Payments.** Are you constantly paying your bills after the due date? Are you always waiting for a check so you can make a payment? Paying late is not only a bad habit, it is also a serious problem.

It is all too easy to fall into bad habits, and it can be difficult to change those habits. The first step is to recognize the patterns you have fallen into.

19. Using Your Credit Card to Pay for Necessities Because You Do Not Have Cash

When you find yourself using your credit card, or the cash advance feature, to pay for necessities, you are in a dangerous situation. Cash advances with your credit cards have become something of a standard feature. Need some extra money? Take out a cash advance. Need groceries, but don't have any money until next payday? Just charge them on your credit card. Paying for your groceries with a debit card is fine. Paying with a credit card is not.

If you find yourself in this position, you have to carefully review your budget and find out where you are spending your money. Chances are your cost of living has gotten away from you.

What can you do? You can either adjust your spending so you begin to live within your means, or you can continue to get yourself deeper and deeper into debt.

20. Paying Only the Minimum on Your Credit Cards

How much do you pay on your revolving debt every month? If you pay those credit card balances in full, you are doing great. If you pay them in full almost every month, you are doing fine, too. But if all you are paying is the absolute minimum, you are headed for trouble.

It can take 30 years to pay a balance in full when you are making only the minimum payment. That's a long time. If you keep adding to the balance, you may never pay it off. In fact, you may make a minimum payment and then charge additional purchases on the card. The result is that the balance actually increases, especially after you add on the finance charge.

It may seem strange to put it this way, but you really cannot afford to make only the minimum payment. The finance charges are just too steep. If you find that all you are making is the minimum payment, you need to adjust your spending so you can pay off the credit card. Remember, that is the ultimate goal.

21. Using One Credit Card to Make Minimum Payment on Another

This sign may be one of the most striking examples of when a person is in trouble. Using one credit card to make the minimum payment on another means that you have too many bills and not enough money to pay them. Using a credit card to make the minimum payment on another card shows just how serious your money problems have become. When you reach this point, you are only postponing the inevitable. Do you honestly think that things will get better? Are you expecting to receive a windfall of cash? Are you expecting someone to pay your bills for you?

These credit card bills won't go away on their own. You have to pay them. You cannot simply substitute one credit card bill for another, month after month.

Don't confuse this with using one credit card to pay off the loan balance on another card to reduce your interest rate. When you do that, you may be able to save yourself a sizable amount of interest each month. The real problem is when you use one card to make the minimum payment on another card.

22. Too Many Credit Cards

You have too many credit cards when you have no plan on how you are going to pay your balances in full within 12 months.

Some credit professionals say, "If you have two credit cards, you have one too many." Perhaps that's a bit harsh.

On the one hand, there are people who have five or six credit cards for very good reasons. On the other hand, there are people who have two credit cards who do not use them wisely. It's not the number that is important. Rather it is how you use those cards.

Bill and Carol use five credit cards. Bill has one for his personal use. Carol has one for herself. They use a third one for the family. Bill has still another one which he uses when he travels on company business. And Carol uses the fifth one when she charges stuff for the baby-sitting service she runs out of the house. In their case, it makes sense for them to use five different cards because they keep track of their balances and how they use their cards. For someone else, it probably would not.

If you cannot pay off your credit card balances within a 12-month time frame, you have too many cards or too much debt. It's just that simple.

23. Opening New Credit Card Accounts Because You Are at Your Pre-Approved Credit Limit(s) on Your Existing Card(s)

It is obvious that you face a serious financial problem when you feel you need to open up still another credit card account because you have exhausted your credit limit on the ones you already have. You will be adding to your debt by charging your purchases, while, at the same time, you will be making only minimum payments on your existing credit cards which you have already maxed out.

What more can be said? You already have more debt than you can afford to repay. You have no idea how you are going to repay what you owe. And you are taking out still another credit card, which will result in still a higher debt load. What's next? Bankruptcy?

24. Not Knowing

Sometimes it's easier to put your head in the sand than it is to pour through all the details about your credit cards. If you do not know what you owe on your credit cards and what your credit limits are, you are doing just that, putting your head in the sand. Your balance and your credit limit are the two details you need to be aware of in order to be responsible with each of your credit cards.

You probably do not have to know precisely what the balance is on your credit card every moment of every day. Still, you should have a pretty good idea. That's the responsible way to handle your money and your debt. As for your credit limit, you need to know that too.

Summing Up

Obviously there are more than these 24 tell-tale signs of trouble. You may have thought of additional ones yourself. The point is, you may be able to live with one, two or even a half dozen of these without causing yourself undo harm. However, in some cases, only one may cause you a serious problem. It is important that you watch carefully for these signs as you deal with your money, spending and credit. If too many of these signs start showing up, you need to reassess and change your lifestyle before your debt gets out of hand.

LESSON TEN
(Rev. May 2002)

WHEN YOU FALL BEHIND

This may be the most difficult lesson in this book for people to understand and deal with. The concept is really quite basic. First, you have to recognize when you have more debts than you can afford to repay. That proverbial light bulb needs to go on in your head so that you realize when you have a problem. Second, you have to prepare a workable plan to repay what you owe. You cannot ignore your debts and hope they will go away. They don't. Ignoring your debts only makes matters worse.

How can you develop a workable plan to repay what you owe when you don't have enough money to cover your debts? As daunting as it may seem, it not only is possible, but people are adopting these plans every day.

The golden rule of dealing with credit problems is: Contact your creditors when you first realize you will be late with a payment so you can explain the situation and work out a realistic repayment plan.

A sudden illness, the loss of your job, or one of a dozen other events may make it impossible for you to pay your bills on time. Whatever your particular situation, if you find that you cannot make your payments on time, you need to contact your creditors. Call them before your payment is late. Try to work out an extended payment plan that reduces interest and waives late fees so your payments are more manageable. If you have paid your bills promptly in the past, your creditors may be willing to work with you. If you have been tardy in the past, don't expect much sympathy. Whatever your problem, do not wait until your account is turned over to a third-party debt collector. At that point, the creditor has given up on you.

You might think, "It doesn't matter if I am late with my payment to the dentist. She's rich. She can afford it if I'm late or if I don't pay." Whether or not the dentist, the clothing store owner, the health club, or any other creditor can afford to stay in business even though you are going to be late with your payment is beside the point. You owe valid debts to these businesses and individuals. These creditors can and will take legal action against you to collect what you owe. Do not be surprised when they do not patiently wait for you to pay if you have not taken the necessary step of contacting them about your financial problem. If they are unsuccessful collecting from you, they may pay a professional bill collector to collect what you owe. They may go to court if they must to enforce their rights. They may repossess property that you have pledged as collateral for your loan. They may evict you from your house or apartment. They may tell the credit bureau about your nonpayment and ask that the information be entered into your credit file. They may refuse to do business with you in the future. They may garnish your wages.

Look in the Mirror

Do you see the face of someone who has steady income, pays the bills every month, and goes about everyday business? Or do you see someone who is afraid to answer the telephone when it rings because he knows it is another debt collector who wants his money? Do you see someone who is afraid of losing the car because there isn't enough money to make the payment? Do you see someone who is floating or writing bad checks? Do you see someone who is making payments by taking out cash advances on their credit cards? Do you see someone who has judgments filed against them? Do you see the image of someone who is thinking of filing for bankruptcy protection?

No one wants to think these things could happen to them, but they can and do for any number of reasons. You can be one of those people who has fallen behind in their payments. You can have bills that have to be paid and you don't have the money in your checkbook to pay them. The landlord can bang on the door and demand payment by 5:00 o'clock tomorrow or he will start eviction proceedings, and you know in the pit of your stomach that there is no way you will have the money. The car payment can be three months past due and you face the very real prospect of having the car repossessed. The utility company can turn off the power.

So the question becomes, what do you do when you fall behind?

The answer is first you must recognize you have a problem, second realize it is not going to go away on its own, and third take effective steps to fix it.

You might think it strange that people who have severe money problems can deceive themselves into believing that everything will be okay, that they really aren't in *that* much trouble. Don't kid yourself. It happens all the time. People are embarrassed to face harsh reality. Instead, they mistakenly believe that if they ignore the problem it will go away on its own, when in fact doing nothing only makes matters worse. Americans tend to be overly optimistic. They believe the situation will resolve itself tomorrow. It doesn't.

Try this exercise. Pretend that you are a credit counselor. You are sitting in your office and a stranger walks in who wants your advice about his finances and bills. What would you tell him if his personal and financial circumstances are exactly like the ones you now face?

What if you don't know what to tell him? In that case, tell him to pick up the phone and make an appointment with a professional credit counselor.

Credit counselors say that the biggest hurdle people with money problems face is recognizing that they have more debt than they can handle. They have to face the reality that their money troubles will not simply disappear. They will not get that big bonus. They will not win the lottery. Someone will not magically appear, checkbook in hand, and pay their bills for them. Creditors will not stop calling.

The longer you fool yourself by denying that you have a serious debt repayment problem, the more difficult it becomes to deal with the problem and get it resolved to the satisfaction of your creditors.

Most people are in denial. They refuse to recognize that they have too much debt and they will have trouble repaying what they owe. They are also embarrassed. That is something you have to put behind you. When people are embarrassed, they fail to act. When you are deeply in debt, you need to act.

Prioritize Your Debts

Exactly who do you owe and exactly how much do you owe them? What absolutely, positively has to be paid? What can be put off?

Separate your debts into two piles — essential and nonessential. It's difficult to say that one person or business deserves to be paid ahead of another, but when you are in a bind, that is what you have to do.

Essential debts that have to be paid include:

- Rent or mortgage. If you don't pay, you'll end up on the street. The exception is when the landlord or owner is family and are forgiving of the situation.

- Utilities. Don't pay and they can be disconnected.

- Secured debts. You will probably lose the property unless you pay enough to bring the account current. For example, think about your car payment.

- Child support payments and anything you owe to the IRS.

- Auto insurance. If you don't pay, you will lose your coverage.

- Medical insurance. Don't pay and you will lose that, too.

- Bad checks. If you don't pay them, you could wind up in jail.

Debts that can be put off include:

- Unsecured debts. These include credit and charge cards, department store accounts, gas cards, loans from friends and relatives, and even school loans.
- Legal bills.
- Medical bills.

No one is saying that you don't have to pay these bills. It's just that when you are in a real financial bind, you have to prioritize what you owe and take care of the essentials first.

Raising Cash

Most people want to pay their bills. The problem is, they just don't have enough money to cover everything they owe. If you find yourself in this position, you need to consider raising cash. There are a number of options for you to consider.

Get a part-time job. There is no better way to fix a repayment problem than for you to generate more income. The ideal way to do that is to find that second or part-time, temporary job to see you through a crisis.

Get a better paying job. If you are not making what you need at your present job, start upgrading your skills and begin your job search.

Sell something. You may have a nonessential car or truck. You may want to sell your primary vehicle and buy a less expensive one.

You may have a coin collection, boat, or other asset that can bring you immediate cash which you can use to pay off some debts.

Retirement accounts. You may need to suffer the tax penalties and tap into your retirement accounts early if that's your best source of immediate cash. If you have an account you can borrow against, you may look at that option, too.

Home equity loan. If you have equity in your home and you have good prospects, you may consider taking out a home equity loan. But before you do, you need to have a solid plan on how you will repay what you borrow. After all, you don't want to lose your home because you fall behind with a home equity loan.

Approach friends and family. You might not like the idea, but when your back is against the wall, you do what you must. Family and friends may not be your first choice, but when you have few options, you need to explore them all.

Pawn something. When you need cash, you can pawn a bike, jewelry, musical instruments and tools to raise immediate cash. Talk about a last resort, but when you need the cash and you have no other option, what are you going to do? Of all your choices, this is perhaps the most costly.

Some of these steps may sound pretty drastic. They are. But when you need cash to pay the rent, or to stop the lender from repossessing your car, you have little choice. Either raise the cash or face some terribly unpleasant consequences.

Your Creditors Are Not Bad Guys and Neither Are You

It's easy to think of creditors as villains, but they are not. It's easy to think of creditors as unreasonable, uncaring people, but they are not. Creditors are people and businesses to whom you owe money. You liked them well enough when they lent you the money. Nothing has changed except that you promised to repay what you borrowed and now you are not keeping up your end of the bargain.

Some creditors will spend hours personally trying to help you sort through your budget or urging you to take courses such as this one. Sometimes they are successful. Other times they are not.

The reality is, your creditors are going to try to collect what you owe to them within the limits of the law. If someone owed you money, would you do any less? Probably not.

Take a moment and put yourself in the creditor's shoes. A customer purchases something and agrees to pay for it over a period of time. You, as the storeowner, have already paid your supplier for the merchandise, or perhaps you have financed the goods you just sold. You need the customer to pay his bill so that you will have enough money to pay your rent, your employees, and your overhead. You have planned on receiving the money that the customer agreed to pay to you. You may sympathize with the customer about his money troubles, but that won't pay your bills for you. You are counting on the customer to keep up his end of the bargain and pay what he agreed to pay. If he doesn't, you have a problem. You can't pay your bills because he can't or won't pay his.

If you are not going to be able to make a payment, your creditor needs to know as soon as possible. You need to extend to him the courtesy of letting him know you are going to be late with his payment, and telling him honestly when he can expect to get his money. That way, he can rearrange his finances so your financial problem doesn't become his. You should do what you would want him to do if your roles were reversed.

Don't make promises you can't keep, and keep your word when you make a promise. When you say, "I will be two weeks late. I promise I will pay you then," you have to deliver. You can't expect someone to be helpful and understanding if you don't keep your word. What's more, you must be sure you can do what you've promised because if you break your word to a creditor, he is not going to be very cooperative or helpful a second time. The fact that you do not follow through on your promise may actually lead to accelerated legal proceedings. Finally, don't expect to use the same excuse month after month. Some creditors may be willing to help you for a month or two, but you cannot expect them to be compassionate time and time again.

Your slow pay, along with that of other people, can have a serious effect on any business. Jim owned a painting business, employing eight people. He agreed to do a big job for a building contractor for $32,000. He had $8,000 worth of supplies into the job, and it took his people the better part of a month to do all the work. When he was done with the work, Jim expected to be paid immediately, just like the contract stated. That's when he got the run-around. "You can expect to get your check next week," he was told. Then, "The check will be held up another week because the people who approve the disbursements are on vacation." It was one excuse after another. Finally, two months later, Jim had to hire an attorney to file a lien against the property. Ten days later, he finally got his money. During all that time, Jim was strapped for cash to pay his bills, his workers and taxes. Finally, he had to go to the bank and borrow what he should have been paid under the contract just to cover all his expenses. He says that if his banker hadn't loaned him the funds, he would have been put out of business. That would have affected not only Jim but also each of his employees who would have found themselves in the unemployment line. Jim's employees themselves have bills that may have gone unpaid.

What's terribly unfair is that Jim had to pay interest to the lender on money that he should not have had to borrow in the first place.

One debt collector who has contacted thousands of people over her career says, "While all this is true, I don't think the person who is not paying his bills really cares what happens to Jim and his workers." Well, debtors should care very much how their slow payments affect the companies they owe. What if you were one of Jim's employees? What if you couldn't get paid because some of Jim's customers weren't paying on time? Late payments can affect hundreds, even thousands of people.

You are not a bad person just because you owe some money that you cannot repay at the present time. This situation can happen to anyone. Most people want to do the right thing and pay their debts. Unfortunately, it may not be possible, at least at the present time. You should expect the unexpected. Life events happen all the time. If you spend every dime you make, you will find yourself facing financial woes. You can count on it.

What you need to do is prepare a plan so you can repay what you owe, and adapt your lifestyle so you can do just that. No one enjoys facing bills they cannot pay, ducking telephone calls and bill collectors, facing court judgments, worrying about losing their cars, home and possessions.

Owing money you cannot repay is not about being good or bad. It is about financial responsibility and personal situations. That's all.

Can't Pay Versus Won't Pay

When you have too many bills and not enough money, you have to make some choices. You may need to reduce your living expenses and thereby increase the amount of money you have available to pay what you owe.

Often people say they cannot make a payment when in truth they choose to spend their money elsewhere. They just don't realize it. They will not forego an expensive car in exchange for one that costs them less each month. They insist on eating out when they cannot afford to pay the doctor. Those are choices you need to examine. Those are decisions you need to make.

Do not fool yourself into thinking you cannot make payments when you have not yet closely scrutinized your spending habits and options to restructure your finances. Until you do, you do not know if you really cannot make payments.

"I can't make a payment on the credit card this month," complains Jeff.

"Can you go to the ball game? Can you buy a six-pack of beer? Can you buy a new pair of jeans?" If the answer is yes, then you can make the payment on the credit card.

Don't rationalize that you "deserve" to go to the ball game or out to eat. You have already taken on debt that you cannot comfortably repay. You certainly don't need to add to your debt. Money that is left over after paying essential bills needs to go to reducing outstanding debt, not toward nonessential expenses.

Credit counselors say that they frequently find disagreements between family members when it comes to spending habits. One spouse is willing, even anxious to make changes in lifestyle, while the other disagrees. When that happens, you need to discuss options rather than point fingers at one another.

If you really can't pay, you need to get yourself to an experienced, reputable, non-profit credit counselor. If you are only making poor choices about your money, then you need to re-examine your priorities and options.

Consequences

When you don't pay your bills, you will suffer the consequences. You can lose your car, your house, the property you pledged as security for your loans. You can have your bank account emptied. You can lose a portion of your wages. You can lose your insurance coverage, your lights and power at home, your right to drive a car. You can even be jailed if you don't make your child support payments. So don't think for a minute that you can simply walk away from your debts. It is no excuse that you don't have the money to pay what you owe. You have to pay your debts or you will suffer serious consequences.

Vehicle Repossession

Once you are in default on your car or truck loan, the law in most states allows your creditor to repossess, or take back, the vehicle at any time without any notice. He doesn't have to go to court to get permission. He can come onto your property to get the car over your objections. He can't break the peace, but he can grab the car.

You are usually in default when you have failed to make a payment on time. Your creditor can agree to accept your late payments. That alone is usually not enough to change the terms of your contract. Most contracts say that the acceptance of a late payment does not modify the borrower's obligation to make all other payments on time.

Once the car has been repossessed, your creditor can keep it or resell it as compensation for your debt. You will still owe the creditor the difference between the resale price and the balance of your loan, as well as the legal and collection costs incurred by the creditor. You can buy back the car by paying the full amount you owe on it, plus the expenses connected with the repossession.

A creditor may not keep or sell personal property of yours found inside the car. But any improvements or additions put on that property like new tires, custom wheels, and installed stereo systems stay with it and get sold with the repossessed car.

Tony purchased a $2,000 stereo and had it installed in his car. He loved to drive around with the stereo blaring. When he was laid off, he was unable to make his car payments, and the car was repossessed. The stereo was not returned because it had become part of the car. Now Tony was out the car and the stereo. It was too bad that he didn't make an attempt to work with the lender. What's more, he still owed $5,000 on the car and $800 on the stereo.

Because it is difficult to dispute a repossession once it has occurred, you should contact your creditor when you first realize you will be late with your payment. Many creditors will agree to a delay if they believe you will be able to make your payment later. Sometimes it may be possible to negotiate with your creditor and modify your contract.

If none of that is possible, your second option may be to sell the car and use the money to pay off the loan. Your third choice is to turn the car in voluntarily to help reduce the repossession expense. But you have to do something. Otherwise you are going to lose the car entirely, and suffer the credit consequences.

Remember, even if you turn the car in, you are still responsible for paying any amount that remains on your loan after the car is sold. What's more, your creditor still will most likely report the repossession on your credit report.

Foreclosure

You can lose your home if you don't make your mortgage payments. The mortgage loan says that. If you doubt the lender will exercise its right to foreclose, you're just kidding yourself. There are notices of foreclosure sales listed in the newspaper all the time. In a foreclosure, you will lose the house and possibly still owe a sizable amount of money to the lender if the foreclosure sale doesn't cover the amount remaining on your mortgage, plus the cost of the foreclosure, collection, judgment and so on.

For most people, the house payment is the largest monthly payment they make. When there is a job loss, disability, accident, or other interruption of income, it may seem like it is impossible to make this monthly payment.

Mortgage lenders really don't want the house back. They don't like to foreclose. But they do want their monthly payment, and they expect to receive it.

If it is only going to be a month or two before you are back on your feet, tell them. They will probably be willing to work out a repayment arrangement where you can make up later what you cannot pay now.

If it is going to be longer than a month or two, tell them that, too.

If you have savings or other assets, now is the time to tap into those resources.

If you have no way to meet your financial obligation, you may have to consider selling the property on your own. That would be preferable to having your house loan foreclosed. At least you would have the chance of getting a good price, recoup some of your equity, and avoid the expense of a foreclosure which is a serious black mark on your credit report.

Missing your mortgage payment isn't the only way you can lose your house through foreclosure. You can lose the house if you don't make your payments on a home equity loan. Home equity loans have been quite popular the past few years. Hopefully, people understand that they have pledged their homes as collateral for those loans. If you fail to make your payments on your home equity loan, you can lose the house. The lender can foreclose, just like with a primary mortgage.

If you can't make your loan payments, either with a mortgage or a home-equity loan, or both, you need to get yourself to the lender or lenders and work out an arrangement so you don't lose your home.

Eviction

Landlords have to show an adequate, legal reason before they can evict someone. One of those reasons is the nonpayment of rent.

If you don't pay your rent, before long you will find yourself out on the curb along with your personal possessions. Every area of the nation has its own set of laws and regulations about how long you can fight an eviction action. In some states, it can take as little as seven days to boot someone out of a rental if the tenant does nothing to fight the eviction. However, the result is the same in every case. Non-payment results in eviction.

If you cannot pay your rent when it is due, let your landlord know as soon as possible so you can work out a plan that will allow you to stay in your place.

Collecting on Security

Many stores sell furniture, appliances, electronics and other big ticket items where they let you have the merchandise and you make payments to them. Some stores sell these credit agreements to finance companies. Whatever the case, you have to make your payments or you will have someone knock on the door and take back the stuff you bought. It's just like having a car repossessed. You are still responsible for the balance on the loan, minus, of course, whatever they can get when they resell your goods.

Don't think for a minute that they won't take back a 3-year-old washer and dryer or bedroom set. They do it all the time.

Judgments

If you don't pay your bills, you could wind up in court. There are no debtors' prisons in the United States, but that doesn't mean that you can walk away from your debts without repercussions.

When you owe someone and you do not pay, you can find yourself in court, perhaps a small claims court, and the judge can issue a judgment against you. That's a court order that says, "Yes, indeed, you do owe money to a specific person or business and the sheriff can collect what you owe by seizing property you own."

You can find money being withheld from your paycheck (garnishment), funds taken out of your bank account, and your property removed from your home and put up for sale at auction (execution.) When a judge says you owe money, and you have property or income with which you can pay your bill, that's what can happen.

Deficiency Judgments

You may owe on property, and when you can't make your payments, you may decide to turn the property over to the former owner. That's fine, except when you owe more than the property is worth. In that case, you are responsible for the difference. If you don't pay it, you will wind up in court and the judge will explain that you still have to pay.

A typical example involves a car. Frances took out a five-year car loan. That was 18 months ago. She lost her job and can no longer afford the $385 monthly payment. So instead of trying to sell the car herself, she turned it (and the keys) back in to the lender.

The situation is this. She financed $18,500 over five years. After 18 months, she still owed $15,000. However, the car was worth only $13,000 as a used car in the re-sale market. As a result, Francis still owes the lender another $2,000.

Unpaid Bills You Owe to Local Creditors

You transact business locally. You may have an open account at a locally-based department store, health club, a bookstore, and other places around town. You may pay those balances in full every month, or you may carry a balance.

You may have a year-long contract with a health club which requires you to pay $50 a month. After 4 months, you decide you don't want to use the facility any more so you stop paying. The club owner sends a couple of letters demanding that you honor the contract, but you ignore them. Then you get a letter from the small claims court telling you that a complaint has been filed against you for not paying the bill. Either you pay or you find yourself with a judgment filed against you. That information goes into your credit file. If you can't pay because of financial problems, you need to tell the club owner so you can work out a payment schedule. Otherwise, you could find yourself in court or facing the sheriff who will come to the door and try to collect on the judgment.

You bought a $2,000 computer system from the local store and agreed to make payments for 2 years. You still owe $1,500 on it. You can't afford to make payments for a couple of months. What do you do?

You owe the clothing store $400, but money is tight this month and you don't have enough to pay on the clothes and pay the rent. Obviously rent takes priority.

You owe the dentist $1600 for a root canal and new crown and you can't afford to make the payment this month. She doesn't want the crown back.

You owe $120 to your family doctor.

With every debt that involves a local creditor, you have the opportunity and the obligation to make personal contact with the appropriate business office, explain your situation, and work out an adjustment to your repayment plan. If you haven't had a problem in the past,you may be able to get your creditor to agree to delay a payment for a month or even two, depending on the reason for your inability to pay, perhaps adding the payments to the end of the loan. If a creditor is not willing to work with you, then you have to take other steps. The point is, you must not ignore your financial obligations just because you may not have sufficient funds to make a payment.

Unpaid Bills You Owe to Out-Of-Town Creditors That Have Local Outlets

In addition to your local creditors, you probably have out-of-town creditors, too. Your local creditors are nearby. You can visit their offices and discuss matters. With out-of-town creditors, it's a bit more difficult. You're going to have to use the telephone and mail.

While the local lender may have a number of local offices, you may send your mortgage payment to an address that is thousands of miles away.

Credit card companies are scattered all over the country.

Major department store chains may have local outlets with out-of-town credit offices.

Many finance companies take care of collection matters through their regional or national office.

You probably send your car payments to some central processing office.

In every case where you owe a creditor which has an out-of-town collection office, you need to make contact with them when you know that you are going to be late with your payment. Call them on the telephone. Most have toll-free lines. Explain the problem and discuss what they might be willing to do to help you out. It is essential that you have a plan in mind yourself. Follow the call with a letter, and keep a copy of that letter.

Bill Collectors

Businesses and individuals do whatever they can, within the law, to collect money that is owed to them and their clients. They write letters requesting payment. They make telephone calls. They even go to court.

There are two types of bill collectors. Some creditors have people on staff whose job it is to collect what they can from people who owe the company. Other creditors engage the services of third-party private collection agencies. There is a difference. Only third-party collectors employed by collection agencies are covered by the Fair Debt Collection Act, which is explained in detail below. In either case, bill collectors will take anything they can get. After all, that's their job.

Bobby gets calls and letters from the hospital about what he still owes on his bill. He owes the hospital, and that who is trying to collect.

He hears from the electric company about his bill. That collector, too, works for the power company.

Bobby also gets calls and letters from a collection agency which has been hired by a department store to try and collect the $800 balance he owes to the store. That collection agency is a third-party collector.

Bobby has heard from the collection office of his credit card issuer. Those calls are coming from the regional office but it is still a primary debt collector.

A third-party debt collector is any business or individual, including attorneys, collecting debts owed by consumers to businesses or persons other than the debt collector. It is their task to collect money from people who have not paid bills in the past. Frankly, there have been a lot of complaints in previous years about the schemes and tactics used by some third-party debt collectors. That's largely a thing of the past, or at least it should be.

In 1978, Congress passed the Fair Debt Collection Practices Act. The law was passed to stop third-party debt collectors from using unfair, abusive, or deceptive means to collect debts. It also requires debt collectors to supply certain information to the consumer. The courts have also developed rules which prohibit abusive collection practices. If a debt collector treats a consumer in a manner that is abusive, deceitful, or otherwise illegal, the consumer may be able to take the debt collector to court.

The Fair Debt Collection Practices Act does not apply

to primary collectors, although many of them have adopted the same rules as a matter of company policy.

There are a lot of things a third party debt collector cannot do. He cannot:

- Call you on the phone late at night or very early in the morning.

- Call you if they know you have an attorney. They must communicate with the attorney instead.

- Call you at work if the debt collector knows your employer prohibits such calls.

- Use or threaten to do violence or harm to you, a member of your family, your reputation, or property.

- Use offensive or abusive language.

- Publish or threaten to publish lists of debtors who refuse to pay bills.

- Say things about the amount or legal status of any debt that are not true.

- Try to collect any money that is not legally owed.

- Threaten to put you in jail for failure to pay your debt.

- Threaten to take any of your wages, income or property unless the action threatened is lawful and the debt collector intends to take that action.

- Falsely claim to be an attorney.

- Use any papers that look like they were made by a court or government office.

- Use false or misleading information.

- Charge amounts, including interest or fees, unless the law or contract allows for it.

- Send a consumer a postcard or envelope that shows to other people that it is a debt collection.

- Use any harassing, abusive or deceitful means to collect a debt.

That's what a third-party debt collector is not allowed to do. What he can do is sue you in court to collect on a debt. But the collector must sue either where you live or where you signed the agreement or contract that created the debt.

Just because the third-party collector is not allowed to do these things doesn't mean there are not a few who still violate the law. An attorney who was hired to try and collect a debt wrote to the client, "Due to the unsteady nature of your employment history, my client cannot accept a wage assignment or partial payment from you. We demand complete satisfaction of the debt in lieu of incarceration." This kind of threat is not supposed to happen.

If you believe your rights have been violated by a debt collector, you may want to contact an attorney or your state's Attorney General's office.

Within 5 days of the collector's first contact with you, you're going to get a written notice. It's going to tell you:

- The amount of the debt.

- The name of the person or business to whom you owe the debt.

- That you have the right to dispute or contest any or all of the debt within 30 days of the date you receive the notice.

- That you have the right to get written proof of the debt from the debt collector. You have to ask, in writing, for the proof within those same 30 days.

- That you have the right to get the name and address of the original creditor if it is different from the one who now owns the debt from the debt collector. Again, you have to ask for this, in writing, within the same 30 days.

The third-party debt collector must limit its communications about you with other people. The law has strict rules to protect you and your reputation. For example, in most cases a debt collector cannot tell your neighbor, family members or your employer that you owe a debt. They can, however, contact these people to try and locate you if you have moved or changed your telephone number.

The law also requires that the third-party debt collector apply any payments on a debt according to your instructions. For example, if you owe two debts and you tell them to pay the one off first, that is what they have to do. Of course, you need to send these instructions to the debt collector, in writing, certified mail, return receipt, so you have proof.

If you are dealing with any debt collector, be honest. If you dispute the debt, say so. If you owe it, you can admit that, too. If you are willing to work out a payment plan, work it out. Don't let a collector pressure you into making promises you cannot keep. Above all, don't hide and don't try to avoid the inevitable. Be above board in your dealings with the debt collector and make an attempt to work things out.

Stopping a Debt Collector From Calling You

Debt collectors have to stop communicating with you when you write to them and tell them to stop. Telling the debt collector to stop over the telephone is not enough. The demand to stop needs to be in writing. You should send the letter by certified mail, return receipt. Keep a copy, of course. You will then have proof that the debt collector received the letter.

But don't think that this is the end of the debt collector. At this point, the collectors will determine if they are going to pursue you in court, if they will go to the trouble of suing you, gaining a judgment, and trying to collect through the sheriff. That is their decision. You will find out what they intend if and when you receive a notice to appear in court and defend yourself.

If you are sued by a collection agency or by the business or individual to whom you owe money, you need to learn about your rights and responsibilities in order to defend yourself in court. If you ignore the lawsuit, you will find yourself automatically liable. A judgment gives the debt collector more collection rights than they have without a court order.

Don't be fooled. When armed with an execution of judgment, a debt collector can get the sheriff to take some of your property. They cannot put you in jail, but they can make life pretty miserable. Certainly, they can place accurate nonpayment information in your credit file which will follow you for a long time.

Credit Card and Other National Collectors

If you are more than 30 days behind on your payment and you haven't contacted your credit card company or the credit office of the company you owe, chances are it will be contacting you. A bill collector calling from one of these credit offices knows nothing about you except what he can see on a computer screen. He knows your name, address, social security number, and your credit history for the past 12 months. At a glance, he can see whether or not you have been prompt with your payments, but only with that particular creditor. If you have had a good repayment record over the past half year or more, the collector will probably ask why you have fallen behind. They understand things like a death in the family, job loss, or natural disaster. Given the situation, you may be able to negotiate a reasonable solution to the late payment situation you find yourself in.

If the bill collector sees a shaky credit history, he is going to want to know "When are you going to make your payment?" The better your repayment history, the more likely a bill collector will be willing to make repayment arrangements.

Understand that the bill collector's job performance is based on a percentage of "promise to pay" funds that actually come in the door. When you say "I'll send a check next week for $100," the collector assesses your likelihood of following through with your promise. If he feels pretty good that you will keep your word, he'll move your account into a "promise to pay" file. If your check does not come in, you will have broken your promise, and that is noted on your account. You won't get a second chance.

To maintain credibility, you have to be honest.

There are collectors who will truly listen to you and try to make arrangements to help you, and there are collectors who just want to know when you will pay. In any case, a collector wants to do whatever is possible to keep you from becoming more delinquent that you already are.

They may tell you, "Pay something to stabilize your account, even if it won't bring your account current, just so you don't get yourself into more serious trouble." You should realize that paying something doesn't stop the late fees and collection notices, but it can slow them down. Typically, a bill collector will report your situation to the credit bureau after you reach 3 months of delinquency. At that time, your account is frozen.

Collectors commonly see accounts which are being charged over-the-credit-limit fees, late fees, high interest and still have a minimum payment due. Many times payments are only enough to cover the added charges and not the original debt.

Story Telling Can Reach New Heights

Bill collectors hear some pretty amazing stories. Tom's

report showed a perfect credit history for over a year, but now was getting ready to fall into the "three-months past due" category. He explained, "I had a wood-carving business that I ran out of an old caboose. I had a special job that was going to pay me $40,000. It was a carving of a carousel, and I was almost done when one night a train came by and ran into the caboose, destroying everything. It's going to take me anotherthree months to redo it." What is so incredible is that this story is absolutely true.

You need to be honest and realistic with bill collectors. When you promise to make a payment, make it. If you can send in more money, fine, but don't send in less.

Answer the Telephone

It may not be pleasant, but answer the telephone when a bill collector calls. If they call and you're not home, return the call. They will leave a toll-free number. Ignoring the problem doesn't make it go away. A debt collector who has a difficult time getting you to return a phone call is not going to be terribly sympathetic about your repayment problem.

Your Repayment Plan

Throughout this lesson, you have been urged to get in touch with your creditors just as soon as you realize that you will be late with a payment. However, getting in touch with creditors, local and out-of-town, primary or third-party, is only the first step. You also must present a detailed plan of how you intend to deal with the problem. Generalities are no good. Specifics are essential.

If you cannot make a full payment and want to ask for a reduced payment schedule, go into the meeting prepared to make a partial payment right then and there. This shows good faith on your part and can go a long way in getting the lender to agree to new repayment terms.

Beth fell behind on loans covering her car, furniture, and credit cards. It was a gradual thing, but after four months of juggling, she knew she was in trouble. She called each one of her creditors and explained her situation. Then she waited for them to say, "That's okay. Just pay what you can."

They didn't do that. They all said they wanted her to bring her account current, and that if she had to, she should borrow money from a family member, get a second job, or do whatever was necessary to see that they were paid.

Beth was disappointed. She had hoped that they would be understanding. They weren't because she hadn't offered them anything other than a sad story which they all had heard too many times before.

What they wanted to hear was how Beth planned to repay what she owed and when they could expect the money.

The best course of action you can take when you are about to fall behind with your payments is first to explain the situation, and then offer specifically what you intend to do about it. After all this is your debt. You need to acknowledge it, and you need to explain how you intend to pay it.

- You can ask if they will allow you to defer your payment for a month or two, adding what you owe to the end of the loan.

- You can ask for a rescheduling of your debt, stretching out the term in exchange for smaller monthly payments.

- You can ask the creditor to reset the monthly payment date to be more convenient.

- You can ask for time to sell property so you can repay what you owe.

- You can ask them to stop the interest and late charges while you work things out.

- You can ask them to allow you to pay only the interest on the debt for the next month or more.

- You can ask them for suggestions, but only after you have offered some of your own.

Getting Help

Sometimes, your debt problems can appear to be overwhelming. Debt collectors are calling on a regular basis and you don't have the money to pay them. You stand to lose your car. Your mortgage is a couple of months behind. You would give anything to make the telephone stop ringing and to get some relief from these debts.

Ask for help. It's not a sign of weakness. Just be careful who you ask.

Perhaps some of the worst advice has come from the most well-intentioned friends and relatives who really do not know the facts about debt management. Just because someone has done okay handling their own finances does not mean they know how to handle your particular situation. All too often, well-meaning friends give advice without knowing the full story.

Nancy was behind on her bills. She asked a close friend what she should do. Her friend said, "Don't worry about the collection agency. Just send $5 a month and they can't do anything to you." Nancy followed this terribly wrong advice. Within a month she found herself being sued in small claims court. The collection agency was awarded its judgment.

Be realistic about what you expect from a credit counseling service. Do you want education, a debt management program, help with developing a budget, a quick fix or a long-term solution?

Experienced counselors have seen it all. They have heard every reason for money woes. They don't pass judgment on you. They simply try to help resolve the crisis, explain your options, and help you get your bills paid.

Different credit counseling agencies operate in different ways. There are non-profit agencies and for-profit businesses which offer similar services.

When you look for help, make sure you can meet with someone who will help you work within a revised budget and who has some clout with your creditors. Some creditors are much more willing to work out a repayment plan when you are meeting with a credit counseling professional and have entered into a formal debt management program. That alone is worth going to a credit counselor.

Peggy, a 70-year-old widow, said walking into a credit counseling agency was the most difficult thing she ever had to do. It took her three tries. But she finally walked in the door. Three years and $25,000 later, she was debt free and her creditors were paid in full. That's what you call a success.

David heard that the non-profit credit counselor could stop a vehicle repossession. For whatever reason, he rescheduled his appointment. In the meantime, the lender repossessed the car. David should have called the credit counselor the first month he couldn't make his payment when a plan to catch up was possible.

Clients of credit counseling agencies come from all walks of life and all income levels. These agencies work. The help, support, advice, education, and counseling they provide is invaluable. Just make sure that you use the services of a credit-counseling organization that will help you with all of your creditors, not just with your credit-card bills. You want a counselor who can look at all your debts, everything from your mortgage or rent, to your credit cards, car payments, doctor bills and everything else. Use a credit-counseling agency that provides substantial financial literacy education, like *Credit When Credit is Due.*

There are credit-counseling organizations that only deal with credit-card bills. That's not good enough when you have lots of other bills to pay.

Summing Up

You must not ignore your debts even when you do not have the money to pay them. That will only make matters worse.

You cannot ignore bill collectors. They won't let you.

Be responsible and accountable for your debts.

The golden rule of dealing with credit problems bears repeating: Contact your creditors when you first realize that you will be late with your payments so that you can explain the situation and work out a realistic repayment plan.

(Rev. June 2004)

BANKRUPTCY

There is no humor intended when it comes to the number of this particular lesson and the corresponding title. It just worked out that way. Chuckle if you must about "Chapter 11" Bankruptcy, for there actually is such a thing as Chapter 11 Bankruptcy. Just keep in mind that for those undergoing bankruptcy proceedings under any chapter of the federal bankruptcy law, it is an unhappy time.

Here's the situation. You have done everything you can think of. You have squeezed every dollar out of your budget. You have contacted all your creditors, explained your situation and honestly tried to work out a revised repayment plan with each of them. You have met with a professional credit counselor and gone on a debt repayment program for the last 6 months. It hasn't worked. You still don't have enough money to make payments on what you owe.

Bankruptcy may be your only remaining alternative. Even so, it is not an easy decision to make or step to take. If you decide on bankruptcy, keep in mind that while you may receive the relief from your creditors that you seek, there are also serious consequences you will have to live with.

A Little Compassion

Perhaps you've heard the phrase, "There but for the grace of God go I." It applies to those who are feeling a little smug about their comfortable financial life and critical of those who have suffered through the trial and tribulation of bankruptcy. Crushing medical bills, disability, unexpected job loss, overwhelming personal problems and business troubles can lead even the financially well-heeled to bankruptcy. Could something like this happen to you? Certainly it can. Will it? Let's hope not.

Given today's statistics, close to 150,000 individuals and families declare bankruptcy at any given month, and the numbers keep increasing, so bankruptcy is not what you would call an uncommon event anymore. Put another way, there are more than 4 bankruptcies filed each year for every 1,000 people in the country.

According to many attorneys and credit counselors, the vast majority of those seeking bankruptcy protection from their creditors never planned on getting into the financial mess they find themselves in. Most are upright citizens of the community who, unfortunately and for whatever reason, find themselves with more debt than they can repay. Each would do almost anything to avoid bankruptcy. Most are terribly upset and emotional about their financial difficulties. They are embarrassed, depressed, scared, ashamed, and angry about what is happening to them. They don't sleep at night. They worry. Most do not want to take the ultimate step and file for bankruptcy. Only when they have exhausted all their alternatives do they take the final step and file the bankruptcy petition with the court.

While there are those who abuse the system, they tend to be the exception rather than the rule, according to many attorneys and credit professionals. Most people who file bankruptcy are members of the community who have fallen on hard times. So before you criticize everyone who files bankruptcy as irresponsible scam artists trying to steal from creditors, put yourself in their shoes.

The fact is, most people would rather struggle with insurmountable debt than file bankruptcy. Statistics show that 3 out of 4 people who file bankruptcy struggle with serious financial problems for up to 3 years before filing. Only 1 out of 4 floundered for less than 12 months.

Instead of criticizing the bankruptcy system and those who exercise their legal right to it, it is far more useful to understand what has happened to place these people in their present financial position so you can learn to avoid the same mess yourself and so they can learn to avoid the same mess again.

Bankruptcy is not what you would call a free ride.

You have to tell a bankruptcy trustee and your creditors about all your property and all your debts. They can question you, under oath, about how you incurred your debts and what you have done with your property. Roy filed for bankruptcy protection. Included in his debts were $10,000 owed to one credit card company and $15,000 owed to another. During the meeting of creditors that is required in all bankruptcy cases, the lawyers for both card companies asked Roy questions about their respective debts. Each found that in the weeks before the bankruptcy filing, Roy had taken out sizable cash advances and run up the balances on the cards. Because of this, they filed actions in the bankruptcy court and argued that Roy was acting fraudulently when he deliberately ran up the amount owed on their credit cards with the intention of then filing bankruptcy. Roy was not able to discharge these particular debts because the bankruptcy court held that his conduct defrauded these creditors.

All of your creditors receive notice that you have filed, even if you intend to repay them. Jack and Sally have been married for 10 years. Like most couples, they have had some financial setbacks. Unfortunately, theirs have been worse than most. They have decided to file for bankruptcy. They owe Jack's parents, along with the usual creditors you would expect. While they would rather not have Jack's parents learn about the bankruptcy filing, the rules require Jack and Sally to file a list containing "the names and addresses of each creditor." Even though they intend to eventually repay Jack's parents, and even though they don't want them to learn about the bankruptcy, Jack's parents will get notice of the filing.

You have to publicly admit your financial failure since filing for bankruptcy protection is a matter of public record. In some areas, bankruptcy filings are regularly published in the newspaper for everyone to see.

Without question, your future access to credit is severely damaged, although by the time things are so bad that you are filing for bankruptcy protection, chances are your credit rating is pretty well shot anyway. Your bankruptcy stays on your credit report for 7 or 10 years, depending on the type of bankruptcy you file, restricting your access to credit during that time. Filing for bankruptcy protection does not mean you will live without access to credit forever. In Lesson 12, you will learn the process to legitimately re-establish your credit rating and ultimately your access to credit.

A Fresh Start

In this country, we believe in giving people a fresh start. It is good that we do. We don't send people to jail for not paying their bills, except perhaps when they refuse to pay their taxes or child support. We have the opportunity to take a chance and fail in business. We can survive huge medical bills or a judgment and put our lives back together even though we cannot pay those bills. We can even make a serious mistake by being irresponsible with credit card spending and be permitted to start our lives over with a clean slate.

We have a federal law which provides for that fresh start. It is the federal bankruptcy law and every person in the country is entitled to use it should the need arise. Basically, it says that you can wipe out much of your outstanding debt and start over again. Technically, the law says you can receive a discharge of your debts in a bankruptcy once every 6 years. That's with a Chapter 7 bankruptcy. You can file a Chapter 13 bankruptcy any time.

There are certain debts which are not discharged in bankruptcy, including student loans, federal income taxes, child support, fraudulent debts, alimony, spousal support, damages for willful or malicious injuries toward another, damages caused while drinking and driving, some debts assumed in divorce, and so on.

One thing to remember is, bankruptcy protection was designed to be the option of last resort, not your first choice.

Exempt Property

Your creditors don't get everything. Each state legislature sets out the type of property and the value that is exempt from creditors. The law decides what property you are allowed to keep as you start a new life without creditors knocking at your door. Typically, you will be able to keep your home, a small amount of personal property, your clothing, food and other personal items. Beyond that, most everything has to be turned over to the trustee so it can be sold and the money turned over to your creditors.

The reason for exempt property is simple enough. The bankruptcy is intended to give a person a fresh start. It will wipe out existing debt.

But it will not wipe out the bankruptcy information on your credit report.

It is very difficult to begin anew when you have next to nothing and limited access to credit.

The Consequences of Filing for Bankruptcy

There used to be quite a stigma attached to those who filed for bankruptcy. That does not seem to be the case these days. However, beyond the moral and ethical issues attached to bankruptcy, there are inescapable consequences. Among the most serious is your future access to credit. When it comes to your credit record, a bankruptcy will stay on your record for 7 or 10 years, depending on the type you file. Potential lenders will see it, and it may cause them to reject your credit application.

Put yourself in the position of a credit grantor. Would you grant a loan to someone who had filed for bankruptcy? Would you care why they had filed? Would you give them another chance to do to you what they had done to other creditors, namely walk away from their debts? Probably not.

Four years ago, Anna filed for bankruptcy, wiping out what she owed on a small bank loan, credit card balances, old utility bills, and even the electrician's invoice. However, because the bankruptcy is still reported in her credit file, she isn't able to get credit from area businesses. She needs some dental work done and the dentist insists on cash. Her car broke down and the repair bill is $1,400. She ended up borrowing from her parents because no one else would lend her the money. When Anna eventually finds a lender who is willing to take a chance on her, she may find that she has to pay higher interest rates and fees than someone who does not have that bankruptcy blotch on their record. According to lenders, Anna is a high risk when it comes to extending credit.

Reasons People File for Bankruptcy Protection

There are any number of reasons which cause people to file for bankruptcy. Some are avoidable. Some are not. Most cite more than just a single reason. They attribute their financial problems to a number of different causes.

Nevertheless, today the number one reason that people cite as the cause of their bankruptcy is the enormous amount of debt they owe on their credit cards. That should come as no great surprise. Dan's comments were typical. "I just got in over my head with the credit cards. They were too easy. I didn't ask for them. They just kept sending me application after application, saying that I had great credit and was pre-approved for still another card. So I took them up on their offers and it landed me in bankruptcy court. I know it's my fault."

It is easy to see that Dan's situation was avoidable if only he had assessed and tackled his problem before it got out of hand.

People say that they get themselves into a financial mess because they lost their jobs or suffered a sizable cut in the family income. Julie said, "I worked for the same company for 10 years, and then one day they simply did away with my job. It took me almost 2 full years to find something else. I worked part-time but the salary wasn't enough."

Julie's financial problems may have been avoidable depending on all the details.

Some people file bankruptcy because of poor money management skills and bad choices. Terry's story is not unusual. "I wasn't equipped to make good money decisions. I spent money I didn't have. I wasn't a smart consumer. I didn't manage my money and I didn't budget. I did a lot of impulse buying on credit. I'm in bankruptcy because I never stopped to realize that I couldn't go on spending more money than I was making. I know it sounds stupid, but that's what I did for 4 years and look where it got me."

Judy got clobbered with huge medical bills. "I had medical insurance for my family, but even it wasn't enough. I won't bore you with the medical history, but I'll tell you this. A $500,000 medical bill along with $10,000 a month for drugs isn't uncommon these days. I just can't pay what insurance didn't cover."

Susan filed for bankruptcy because her business wasn't profitable. "I always wanted to run my own shop. For 4 years, I made a good living doing just that. But when business slowed down, I started using my credit cards and a series of bank loans to make ends meet. Business never improved. I fell into the trap of wanting to believe that business was going to get better. Now I'm trying to pay off over $85,000 worth of business debt and I can't do it."

Nancy and Pete are both filing for bankruptcy. They used to be married to each other but were divorced 3 years ago. They are each filing for bankruptcy because they can't afford to live separately and live the same life style they had before the divorce. Today, each has rent, utilities, and so on, expenses that they used to share. Nancy can't make ends meet because she has the kids, and the child support Pete pays isn't sufficient to cover all the expenses, along with her credit card and other debts. Pete can't make it because he has to pay child support and cover all his other bills. Both are going to have to adjust their living expenses to fit within their incomes.

Katie is filing bankruptcy because she has run up more than $40,000 in credit card debt. It has all come from cash advances. Where did the money go? To feed her addiction. She happens to be addicted to gambling. She likes to play the video machines. She has the worst luck. During the first couple of months she played, she won. That was enough to get her hooked. Since then, she has been losing about $1,500 a month. She makes enough money to pay all her bills except for the credit cards.

Addictions are a major cause of bankruptcy. In addition to gambling, there are drug and alcohol habits.

Lynn filed because of debts she was stuck with when her ex-husband refused to pay what he said he would pay. "When we went through the divorce, it was amicable enough. He took certain debts and I took others. Now, 6 months later, he's not paying, and the credit card companies and bank are telling me I have to pay. I can't. I don't have the money."

This situation isn't unusual. Often one spouse says they will pay all the bills if they get most of the property. The other spouse agrees. Then the spouse with the property files bankruptcy and discharges the debt, leaving the other spouse with the bills.

Stan filed to get rid of a judgment that he couldn't possibly pay. It was his luck to be held responsible for $2 million in damages from an automobile accident. He had insurance, but not nearly enough.

There are other reasons cited for bankruptcy filing. Whatever the reason, people file because they feel they have too much debt and they can't repay it. In fact, they can't even keep up with the minimum monthly payments they have to make.

That is not always the case. Credit counselors tell of case after case where people file for bankruptcy instead of working their way out of their financial crisis. They tell of able-bodied and clear-minded people who owe $20,000 on their credit cards and file bankruptcy, when a better alternative would be to restructure their debt, get a second job, and cut back on their spending.

Do Not File Bankruptcy for Small Amounts

It is always better to work through your money problems and pay your bills than to declare bankruptcy.

Put your debt into perspective. While $20,000 is a lot of money, it is less than a year's wages for most people. If that is the amount of your debt, it can probably be repaid over time, given a little help from a credit counselor and your creditors. While bankruptcy may make some of the problems go away, most people, when shown what can be accomplished, choose the repayment route.

Tom works hard. He makes about $50,000 a year as a salesman, but his income is sporadic. Some months are good, some are so-so, and some are terrible. Lately it's been terrible. He's divorced, no kids. Over the years, though, he's run up over $24,000 in credit card debt. What did he buy? He doesn't remember, but he certainly doesn't have much to show for the debt. He doesn't blame anyone for the debt but himself.

The problem is, Tom is having a lot of trouble covering his living expenses and making payments to the credit card companies. He thought about bankruptcy and even went to see an attorney. He was urged to go to a credit counselor instead. He took the advice.

Tom made an appointment and he kept it. The credit counselor was able to help. Together they worked out a budget for Tom to live on and a plan to repay what he owes. The counselor is working with each of the creditors to reduce the interest rates and eliminate late fees and charges. Tom will pay $500 a month for almost 5 years, but he will then be debt free, assuming that he stays with the program. He keeps his self-respect and the creditors get paid.

Joe and Betty tell a different story. They had $15,000 in credit card debt (still a relatively small amount.) Because they were supporting themselves and their 3 children, they were having trouble making ends meet. A friend told them that for $800 they could file bankruptcy and get rid of the $15,000 debt. So they did. A year later, one of their children got sick and they ended up with a $50,000 hospital bill, plus a whole bunch more credit card debt related to the child's illness (trips to the doctor, motel bills, food on the road, etc.) Because they cannot receive another bankruptcy discharge for another 5 years, the deal they got when they filed back when they owed "only" $15,000 doesn't look very good.

This is just another example of why you should not file when you have relatively small amounts to repay. Joe and Betty will have to deal with these creditors for a long time.

The moral of the story is, too many people file for bankruptcy for convenience rather than out of need. This is why so many people look down on the whole concept of bankruptcy.

A Chapter 7 filing stays on your credit report for 10 years. A Chapter 13 filing stays on your credit report for 7 years.

The Process

Congress has created two primary types of bankruptcy protection for individuals. They are commonly referred to as Chapter 7 and Chapter 13. There are others but these 2 types are the ones used most by individuals.

The first is known as Chapter 7 bankruptcy, sometimes called "straight" or "liquidation" bankruptcy. Here you ask to have most or all of your debts erased or, more precisely, "discharged."

The second is Chapter 13 bankruptcy. This is also known as a "wage earner" or "bill payer" or "reorganization" bankruptcy. Here you set up a plan where you repay a portion of your debts by making monthly payments to a bankruptcy trustee for up to five years. The trustee pays your creditors a percentage of what they are owed. The plan you file must be approved by the bankruptcy court.

Today, most bankruptcy filers use Chapter 7, although the number of people who are filing for Chapter 13 protection is increasing. Because Chapter 7 is the most common, that's the one that will be referred to as you go through the process of a bankruptcy proceeding.

- You make the ultimate decision that bankruptcy is your best alternative to resolve your financial woes.

- You file a petition with the bankruptcy court, reporting all of your assets and debts.

- An "automatic stay" goes into effect. That means all actions taken by your creditors stop. No more collections. No more court proceedings.

- You attend a meeting of creditors within 45 days of your petition, and usually within 60 days after the first schedule meeting, your debts are discharged (wiped out), and the automatic stay ends.

- The trustee takes your property, sells it, and pays your creditors what he can, based on the amount of their claims. Secured creditors either get their property back, or you agree in writing to keep making your payments.

- The trustee files a final report on where the money went.

- Case closed.

Let's fill in a few of the details.

When you file a bankruptcy petition, you must tell the trustee and your creditors everything, in excruciating detail, about your property and debts. You have to list all the property you own, how old it is and what it is worth if it is sold, all the income you earn from every source, what you spend every month, who you owe, how much you owe each specific creditor, what property you think is exempt from creditors, and more. Interestingly, very little has to be revealed about how you got into the financial mess you find yourself in.

At a "meeting of creditors," which usually occurs in all bankruptcy cases within 45 days after you file, you will be asked about your property and debts. The bankruptcy trustee and each creditor has the right to ask you questions, which you have to answer under oath. They want to make sure you have honestly reported everything, have hidden nothing, and have not cheated in any way.

Because the law says you cannot be discharged in bankruptcy for another 6 years from the date of your first debt discharge, you need to make certain that all of your current debts and all of your potential debts are covered in the bankruptcy court papers. If you fail to list a creditor in the bankruptcy and that creditor does not have actual knowledge of the filing, then that debt is not wiped out. You will still have to pay it.

In recent years, creditors are getting more involved in the bankruptcy proceeding that ever before. When an individual filed for bankruptcy some years ago, a credit card company, which was owed $750 for example, was likely to shrug and write off the debt. Today that same credit card debt could be $15,000 or more. Because of the larger amount of debt owed to creditors, they are less likely to write off the debt without taking a close look at how you accumulated that debt and why you have little or no property to show for it.

Under Chapter 7, you turn over all of your cash, property and other valuable assets to a bankruptcy trustee, except for what you are specifically allowed to keep as provided under federal and state law. Each state has its own laws regarding what property is exempt from creditors. That list varies state by state. Some states opt to use federal exemptions contained in the federal bankruptcy law. Others use their own.

The court process usually takes 3 to 6 months from start to finish. Complicated cases that involve a lot of property or complex issues can be open for 2 to 3 years. There is no set time for how long a bankruptcy case can remain open.

Don't think that the bankruptcy trustee is on your side. His job is to see to it that your creditors get as much money repaid to them as possible and that your rights under the bankruptcy law are upheld. The trustee is neutral.

Once the trustee pays your creditors, the trustee files a final report with the court and your bankruptcy case will be closed. You are debt free, except for those debts that are not dischargeable and those debts you have agreed to continue paying. You no longer owe those creditors whose bills have been wiped out. You get a legal paper telling you that your debts have been discharged.

No More Phone Calls

People file bankruptcy when they feel they have no other choice. They can't pay their debts, and they can't stand admitting it to their creditors. So they file bankruptcy. They hire an attorney, pay the fees and file the papers with the Clerk of the United States Bankruptcy Court.

Once that petition in bankruptcy is filed, all collection efforts, lawsuits and attachments stop. Within a matter of days, the court will send a notice to all the creditors you have listed in your petition, telling them to stop all actions against you. There are exceptions. You still have to pay alimony and child support, your taxes, etc.

Finally, though, you have some relief.

That "automatic stay" takes care of some important problems, at least for a short period of time.

The utility company won't disconnect your service at least for a couple of more weeks.

You will get a couple of days breathing room if you're being evicted by your landlord, and even if the eviction takes place, you will not have to pay the rent owed prior to the date of filing. Amounts owed for rent after your petition is filed are not discharged in bankruptcy, though, and will have to be paid.

Attachments to your wages stop.

The telephone calls and letters stop.

But it's only temporary. Bankruptcy court proceeding will soon begin.

The utility company will have to be paid for usage after the filing date.

Your landlord will eventually evict you.

So even though you are filing for bankruptcy, you have to get your financial house in order. Bankruptcy only takes care of those debts you owed on the date you filed; it is your job to take care of all the new ones after that date.

The filing stops all creditors and collection agencies from trying to collect on unsecured debts which they say you owe to them, forever. From this point on, they cannot garnish (or take a portion of) your wages. They cannot seize or garnish money that is in your bank accounts. All court proceedings must stop.

With secured debt on cars, furniture and similar property, the story is a little different. The automatic stay initially stops everything in its tracks, but the creditor can ask the court for a "Relief from Stay." If it's granted, the creditor can restart collection efforts. In any event, the automatic stay is terminated when the case is closed or dismissed, or when discharge of the debt is granted (60 days after the first scheduled meeting of creditors). At that point, a secured creditor can repossess (or take) your car, furniture or other secured property.

Not All Debts Can Be Discharged

You may not be allowed to discharge all of your debts. It depends on the type of debts you have. There are 18 different sections in the federal bankruptcy law detailing debts that cannot be discharged. For example, you cannot, in most cases, discharge:

- Most federal, state and local taxes you owe.

- Alimony and child support.

- Some student loans.

- Debts you failed to disclose in your bankruptcy papers where the creditor has no knowledge of the filing.

There are other debts you won't be able to discharge,

but with these, the creditor has to do something. For example, you may not be able to discharge debts you have that are due to your bad actions, such as bad checks, credit purchases made right before you filed for bankruptcy, very recent loans and cash advances. Here, the creditors can file a formal complaint objecting to the discharge of these debts, and if they do, the debts may be held to be nondischargeable. If that's the case, these debts remain your obligation to repay despite the bankruptcy.

Debts You Can Readily Discharge in Bankruptcy

There are other debts that you can readily discharge. Recall from previous lessons that there are two types of debts, secured and unsecured. Bankruptcy will discharge both types if that's what you want. But you have to give the collateral back on secured debts. What most people really want is to get rid of what they owe in unsecured debt to:

- Landlords.

- Utility companies.

- Credit and charge card companies.

- Department stores.

- Court judgments.

- Medical bills.

- All other similar bills where the creditor does not have collateral to secure the debt.

Some Debts You Will Probably Want to Keep

If you file bankruptcy, you do so to get rid of debts you cannot afford to repay. So why would you voluntarily agree to keep some of those debts? Because you want to keep the property that goes with them.

When it comes to a secured loan, you have to make a decision. Do you want to do away with the loan and return the property, or are you willing to "reaffirm" the debt, agreeing to continue making your monthly payments in order to keep possession of the property? It's your choice.

If you turn the car in and it is sold for less than you owe on the loan, you will not have to pay the difference to the creditor because of your bankruptcy.

If you want to do away with the mortgage, you have to give the house back to the lender. Because of the bankruptcy, you will not have to pay any deficiency that exists when your house is resold to someone else. But you will have lost the house.

If you want to turn back the furniture, washer and dryer, and other secured property, you can do so and have the balance of the loan discharged.

But if you want to keep the car, house and other property, you are going to have to sign a piece of paper that says in exchange for keeping possession of the property, you agree to keep on making your payments. That's right, you have to reaffirm your debt.

Sometimes, if the creditor does not want the property back, they will agree to allow you to reaffirm your debt but at an amount that is less than the amount that you owed when your bankruptcy was filed. Both the creditor and the debtor must agree to this; neither has to. For example, you have a car loan with a balance of $12,000. The car, though, has a resale value of only $8,000. It may be better to reaffirm an $8,000 debt and keep the car than to lose access to your transportation because it will be hard for you to borrow money to buy a replacement car due to your bankruptcy.

Sometimes, even if the property is worth less than you owe, the creditor will require that either you reaffirm the full amount of the remaining debt or turn in the property. They can do that.

The decision whether you want to reaffirm the amount of debt offered by the creditor or turn the property back and have the debt discharged in the bankruptcy is up to you.

Bankruptcy Fraud

The federal bankruptcy law is intended to help those who need the help. As with most programs, the vast majority of those who use it do so honestly and ethically. However, there are too many cases reported where people abuse or at least try to abuse the system.

If you find yourself facing bankruptcy, be prepared to tell the truth. When you are asked about property and other assets you own, provide a complete list. When asked what it's worth, be as honest and forthright as you can. This is not the time to be dishonest.

Bankruptcy fraud can land you in federal prison. According to bankruptcy attorneys, the government is on the prowl for those who abuse the bankruptcy laws, and when they find abusers, they put those people behind bars.

Janet was a single mother. She was having a tough time and decided bankruptcy was her last alternative. A couple of months before she was going to file, her mother died, and Janet received a $10,000 inheritance. She didn't tell her bankruptcy attorney or the bankruptcy trustee about the money. She wanted to keep it, so she hid it and filed for bankruptcy anyway. She decided that the money was the only chance that she and her child had to make it in this world. The trustee found out about the money and turned the case over to the U.S. attorney for Janet to be prosecuted for bankruptcy fraud.

As harsh as it sounds, Janet is in big trouble. If she had reported the money, she would have been able to keep some of it because of the exemptions, but because of her lies, she faces a term in a federal prison and a felony conviction that will be on her record for the rest of her life. Her son faces at least some months in a foster home. The money will still have to be turned over to the bankruptcy trustee to be used to pay her creditors. And the trustee can file a motion to prevent or revoke her bankruptcy discharge based on the fraud.

Ted tried to hide some personal property by transferring title to a boat and a truck to his mother-in-law 6 days before he filed his petition. He didn't disclose the transfer in his bankruptcy papers.

Chuck didn't reveal the contents of his safe deposit box.

Sarah didn't think they would find out about her brokerage account.

All are now in jail, convicted felons.

When it comes to filing for bankruptcy protection, complete honesty is the only policy.

Summing Up

You may have once thought that filing for bankruptcy erased all your debts. Well, it doesn't. It only gets rid of unsecured debts and those secured debts where you are willing to give back the property. It also does not get rid of your non-dischargeable debts.

You should keep all of this in mind when deciding whether to file. It certainly would not be smart to file a Chapter 7 bankruptcy if most of your debts are non-dischargeable or if you are going to reaffirm most of what you owe. In these cases, you are going to have to keep paying on the debts even if you file.

It also doesn't make much sense to file when you owe relatively small amounts simply because you can usually work yourself out of debt by restructuring your repayment schedule and perhaps your lifestyle.

According to recent statistics, when it comes to bankruptcy, just a little over half of the debts a person has are eliminated by the bankruptcy filing. That means close to half are repaid either in whole or part.

Bankruptcy is a last alternative to resolving your debt problems.

Consider all other options first.

Try a repayment program.

If that doesn't work out, visit with an attorney who specializes in bankruptcy filing to learn what you need to know about the very complex bankruptcy law.

BUILDING AND REBUILDING YOUR CREDIT

When it comes to finding a lender who will grant you a loan, perhaps the most commonly heard consumer complaint is, "Why won't anyone give me a chance?" Or, perhaps, a second chance. On the other hand, the most common complaint about consumers voiced by potential lenders is, "Why don't people take care of their financial responsibilities so we don't have to turn them down when they apply for loans?" Fortunately, there is common ground.

It is not particularly easy for people who lack a credit history to begin establishing a good credit record simply because lenders are reluctant to be the first to take a chance. Young adults fresh out of school have complained for generations that they have a terrible time getting that first loan or that first credit card. Today, that first credit card has become all too easy to get as credit card issuers market their cards to younger and younger teens in the hope of gaining brand loyalty.

For those who have handled their credit obligations badly in the past, it is doubly difficult to get a lender to say yes to a loan application.

Nevertheless, establishing and re-establishing a positive credit record can be accomplished, especially given sufficient time.

Life Without Access to Credit

There are a growing number of people who would like to live their lives without borrowing money. They want zero debt. They like paying cash for everything. Their philosophy is, "If I can't pay for something, I will wait to buy it until I have saved enough money." Most of these folks have had credit problems in the past and they don't ever want to revisit those terrible days. So they have no credit cards or loans at the bank, credit union or finance company. They own their cars free and clear because they save until they can afford to pay for a vehicle. Many even own their houses without a mortgage. While they borrow to buy the house in the first place, they tend to accelerate their monthly payments to get rid of the mortgage just as soon as they possibly can.

Take a look at your own budget. Think of how much money you could save and invest if you didn't have any debts. Recall the statistics which show that the typical person's installment and credit card debt amounts to 20 percent or so of their income, and installment debt plus mortgage debt comes to better than 35 percent. How well could you live if you had 35 percent more disposal income every month? That's how people live when they have zero debt to pay.

However, zero debt is, for most people, nothing more than wishful thinking. The fact is, stuff happens. The brakes go out on the car. The hot water heater quits working. The kids need school clothes. When emergencies strike, people use their access to credit.

Also, few people can afford to purchase a car outright these days. The average price of a new car is well over $20,000. The price of a quality used car isn't much less.

A home requires a mortgage, unless of course you find someone who can pay for the house for you, or you want to live with friends or relatives.

Credit is a convenience few people would like to do without.

There is one additional point to make here, for those who think they would like to live without any loans. There is growing talk in credit education circles that advises people to pay their credit cards and other loans instead of putting money away in their savings and investment accounts. While the advice has some merit, it is flawed nonetheless.

The reasoning goes like this. If you put your money in savings, you will earn a paltry interest rate of 2 to 4 percent every year. If, instead, you use the money to pay down the balances you owe on your loans, you will be avoiding interest charges that range from 7 percent all the way up to 40 percent or more in some cases. If you suffer an emergency, and you need money that is not part of your budget, you can resort to borrowing what you need.

That's true as far as it goes. It is still important to have a savings nest egg and to contribute to it regularly, even if you only save a small amount every payday. When you have a savings account, you can use that money to cover your emergencies. You can continue to pay down your loan balances as you had originally planned, without adding to them.

It's your decision to make.

Creating a Positive Credit History

When it comes to credit experience and history, there are 3 types of people. There are those with good credit records that have been established over a period of years. There are those with no credit records, usually young adults fresh out of school and widows who have had no credit in the past. And there are those with bad credit histories.

If you have no credit history or a bad credit history, there are at least 24 steps you can take to improve your chances of having a loan application approved. This is what you need to do:

1. Pay Your Bills on Time

Without question, this is the very best way to create a positive credit report. This means pay all your bills, including those which have nothing to do with the extension of credit. Even if you have no credit, chances are you have to pay rent and utilities. Make sure that the checks go out promptly each month. Every month, credit grantors as well as others report payment information about your accounts to the credit bureau. Because of this you can establish a history of responsible credit use. On the other hand, late payments can severely damage your chances for being granted loans in the future.

2. Don't Bounce Checks

If you don't have money in the account to cover the check, don't write it. In some states, you can go to jail for writing bad checks. Sign up with your bank or credit union for an automatic loan plan attached to your checking account that goes into effect if you exceed your balance, just so you don't suffer from even an honest mistake. Bad check fees can amount to $50 or more per check and often exceed the amount of the check.

3. Think Long Term

Don't be impatient. It takes more than just a month or two to establish and build a solid credit history. It may take a couple of years of being on your own before you have enough credit history to qualify for a car loan, and 3-5 years before you will qualify for a mortgage. If you are rebuilding, it will take some time before lenders may be willing to give you a second chance. During that time, your financial dealings will have to be clean.

4. Start Small

Apply for loans of small amounts. Lenders are more apt to approve applications asking for a few hundred dollars than they are to approve loans of many thousands of dollars for those without a positive credit history. As time goes by and you demonstrate that you are responsible in handling your financial obligations, you will probably be able to borrow larger amounts. You have to crawl before you walk, and walk before you run.

5. Visit Local Lenders First

A local bank, credit union or finance company may be more willing to set up a small loan for you than an out-of-state credit card company which will process your application in its computer. A local lender may know more about you and what is going on with your employer and family, which makes the loan application much more personal. If you get the small loan from a local lender, make sure that you make your payments according to the terms of the loan agreement. Some institutions will allow you to do a savings-secured loan.

6. Apply for a Local Department Store Charge or Credit Card

The same reasoning applies as above. A local department store may be more prone on taking a chance with you than a national chain. The local credit department may have a bit more discretion and leeway with its credit-granting policies.

7. Apply for a Secured Credit Card

If you can't get credit any other way, try for a secured credit card. Secured cards were explained in an earlier lesson. Briefly, you have to deposit a certain amount of cash in a savings account and pledge that amount as collateral against any balance you have on your credit card. After a bit of time, your credit limit will be increased, assuming you have made your payments on time. And, no one will know your card is a secured card rather than a regular credit card.

8. Apply for a Small Loan or a Low-limit Credit Card Guaranteed by a Creditworthy Co-signer

Do this only if you are absolutely certain that you will not make the co-signer pay your debt for you. You don't want to stick a friend or relative with paying off your debt. The good repayment history you generate with this loan will go under your name rather than the co-signers, thereby boosting your credit history. Get a co-signed loan paid off as quickly as you can; your friend or relative will appreciate it.

9. Review Your Credit Bureau Report at Least Once a Year and Correct any Inaccurate Information it May Contain

While most information contained in credit reports is accurate, mistakes can and do crop up. An annual review will help to make sure that you don't get turned down for credit because of an error on your credit report.

10. Review Your Credit Bureau Report 2 to 3 Months Before You Apply for a Car, Mortgage or Home Equity Loan

While you are supposed to review your credit report annually, it is smart to check on what the credit bureau has in its file on you just before you need to apply for a substantial loan. You want to make sure that everything is correct. In addition, you want to know if there are any negative comments that you will need to explain to a lender you will be approaching. If there are, you will need to honestly reveal them on your credit application. Remember, honesty on a loan application is essential.

11. Avoid Letting any Account of Yours be Turned Over to a Collection Agency

If potential lenders see that you have had one or more of your debts turned over to a collection agency, they will be rightfully concerned that the same thing could happen to them. The result is they may turn down your credit application. Even if you wind up paying what you owe to the collection agency, the fact that it was turned over to collection will show up on your credit report. Information about collection agency activities will stay on your credit report for up to 7 years. How do you avoid collection agencies? By making arrangements with those you owe before they feel they have no other option but to turn to a collection agency to make you pay. If you can't make arrangements that a creditor is willing to accept, ask a credit counseling agency to help you.

12. Avoid Having Judgments Filed Against You in Court

Just like with collection agencies, lenders are reluctant to lend to you if they know that others have had to go to court to get a judgment against you. Even if you end up paying what the court says you owe, the judgment itself will stay on your credit report for 7 years. You can avoid judgments if you face your debt obligations honestly well in advance of being dragged into court.

13. Recognize That Bankruptcy is a Last Resort Rather Than an Easy Way Out of Financial Problems

A Chapter 7 bankruptcy will be reported to potential creditors for 10 years. A Chapter 13 (bill-payer) bankruptcy will be reported for 7 years. When it comes to access to credit, there is nothing quite as damaging as a bankruptcy. It's almost impossible to explain it away to the satisfaction of a potential lender. The more recent the bankruptcy, the tougher it will be to gain access to credit. The longer the time since you filed for bankruptcy protection, the better your chances of getting that loan. Also, if the bankruptcy was caused by one of those terrible blows that hit people every so often such as a medical crisis or job loss, rather than a case of poor financial management, you may be able to convince a potential lender to give you a second chance. But don't count on it.

14. Any Time You are Denied Credit, Review Your Credit Report to See What Negative Information is Reported

Determine if the negative information is accurate, and if it is, devise a plan to clear up the problem, if possible. If the information is inaccurate, get the credit bureau to correct it. In any case, find out what made the lender say no. The denial may be because you have too much debt, too little income, or too many inquiries into your finances. It could be something as simple as the lender thinking you have too many open credit card accounts; in that case, close out those you are not using. If the lender is not willing to discuss the specific reasons for the denial, visit with a reputable credit counselor. They understand how to read a credit bureau report and loan application.

15. After 6 Months of Working on Your Credit History, Apply for Another Small Loan or Credit Card

Remember, you want to build or rebuild a credit history. That first loan may be paid off. Terrific. That credit card may have a zero balance. Fine. However, stopping with one credit card or one small bank loan will not boost your credit history. By thinking long term, you will be able to build what you need in order to get that mortgage and finance that car.

16. Avoid Switching Employers

Lenders like stability in employment, so instead of jumping from employer to employer, look to improve yourself within the same company. Being with an employer for 5 years or more is a real plus when it comes to considering a loan application. Also, when you have been with an employer for a number of years, that employer can become a terrific personal and credit reference. An employer can verify your employment history, explain that you have a year-end bonus coming, and are in line for a raise in another two months.

17. Avoid Moving from Rental to Rental

Again, stability counts. The exception here is moving from a rental to a place you own. Lenders like people to own their homes. It shows commitment.

18. Set Up a Savings as Well as a Checking Account

It's one thing to have a checking account. It is quite another to have some money in savings. The more you have in your accounts the better, of course. Save something every paycheck, even if the amount is small.

19. Have Reputable Credit References

Even if you don't have a series of bank and credit union loans, a mortgage, car loan and credit cards, you still have your landlord, utility companies, and employer. Local references are best, as well as long-term references.

20. Work Hard to Increase Your Income

The more you make, the more likely it will be that lenders will be knocking on your door trying to get you to take out a loan. There is nothing quite as desirable to a lender as looking at a steady increase in annual income.

21. Work Hard to Decrease Your Debt

Remember those income and debt ratios. Paying your monthly bills and installment debts each and every month for 6 months may be all you need to do to turn a negative credit report into one you can be proud of. Just as lenders like to see an increase in annual income, they also like to see a decline in total debt.

22. Demonstrate That You Live Within Your Budget

Lenders are usually willing to lend to those who can show, through the loan application, that they can afford to repay the amount they want to borrow. Do that and you should not have too much difficulty finding a lender who is willing to make the loan.

23. Avoid Co-signing or Guaranteeing Loans for Others

When you co-sign or guarantee a loan for someone else, you are saying that you will be responsible for the repayment of that loan should the person who got the money default. It is really dangerous to co-sign a loan, no matter how good the borrower's intentions. You are better off helping that person analyze their financial situation and improving their credit report so they can borrow what they need on their own.

24. Avoid Excessive Inquiries into Your Credit Report

Too many inquiries can cause a lender to turn down an application. To avoid the problem, don't give people permission to unneccesarily check into your credit bureau report. If you are thinking about replacing your car, and you stop by the car lot to test drive a vehicle or two, the finance office may let 5 or more potential lenders know you are there. Each will check your credit history with the credit bureau. That used to result in 5 inquiries. Now days, credit bureaus will not hold that against you.

These 24 do's and don'ts will go a long way in helping you establish a positive credit history or repairing a damaged credit past.

The Process

The process for establishing credit for the first time or re-establishing damaged credit is one and the same. As a loan applicant, you need to demonstrate to a potential lender that you will be a responsible borrower, you are not trying to borrow more than you can afford to repay, and you will, indeed, take seriously your responsibility to repay what you borrow on time and in full.

Whatever your credit experience and history, whether you are starting out in life or trying to pull your finances together after a bankruptcy, your approach is the same.

You submit a complete and honest loan application to a potential lender. You may be applying for a credit card or a small personal loan. You may be looking for auto financing or a mortgage. You may want a bill consolidation loan or a line of credit.

As long as the purpose of the loan is legal, the lender will process the application. In almost every case, your lender will begin the process by requesting a credit bureau report. The information on that report will go a long way in determining whether your loan application is approved.

Based on what the loan officer and the loan committee see on your loan application, and what they find out about you from the credit bureau, they will decide whether or not to make the loan to you.

Yes, the information you put on your loan application will be compared against what the credit bureau has on file about your personal finances. Don't think for a minute that they don't check. They do. Every time.

For loan applications that will be decided on locally, the interview is an important part of the process.

Be on time and appropriately dressed.

Have the application completed to the best of your ability in advance of your meeting. Where it asks for account numbers, have them written down. Where it asks for references, list them with addresses and telephone numbers. When it asks for balances owed, be as accurate as you can with the most current numbers.

Be honest about your credit history. If there have been problems in the past, explain what happened and what you have done to make sure the same thing doesn't happen again. Don't make excuses and don't complain about the terrible injustices you have suffered. It doesn't help.

Explain what is going on with your job and your prospects for raises and bonuses. If you are married and your spouse also will be signing for the loan, talk about that employment situation.

Explain the purpose of the loan. While it may seem obvious to you, it helps to tell a loan officer where the money is going. "I'm going to buy that car so I can get to work instead of taking the bus. It's not a luxury car, but one that I plan to use for years." Or, "I'm going to use the money to fix up the house, or replace a furnace, or buy school clothes."

Explain how you will be able to repay the loan. Show how you can afford the monthly payments over the entire life of the loan. Show how you have enough money from your monthly paycheck to cover all your living expenses plus what you put into savings plus what you will need to cover the loan payment.

Explain what you will do if the loan application is turned down, which it may be. Don't rant and rave that you will take your business elsewhere and tell all your friends to close their accounts. Instead, talk about waiting until your credit rating improves if you have to, saving more for a down payment on that car or truck if you must, and reducing existing debt you already have. Ask for advice about what you might need to do with your finances to put yourself in a better position to get the loan you want.

Most lenders use credit scores in determining if you get a loan, and what interest rates and fees you will be required to pay if the loan is approved. Your credit score is computed as a snapshot, a particular score computed at a particular point in time. Your credit score can change daily, either up or down. These credit scores are used by lenders to predict repayment. The higher your score, the more likely it is that your loan will be approved on favorable terms, because it is more likely that you will repay your debts in full and on time. The lower your score, the less likely it is that your loan will be approved. And if it is, you will have to pay higher interest rates and more costly fees.

If you would like to see your current credit score, you can go to the following Website: www.myfico.com. There is a cost for this service. You should also get an explanation of how to improve your score along with the number.

Your score will range between 300 and 900. Only 1 percent of those seeking loans have a score of below 500. Five percent score 500 to 549. Seven percent score between 550 and 599. Eleven percent score between 600 and 649. Sixteen percent score 650 to 699. If you score above 700, you are unlikely to have much problem getting your loan. That's how they do it. You take their test. They grade it, and depending on your grade, you get your loan or you do not.

An important piece of information to remember is that your credit score is based entirely on what is contained in two specific sections of your credit-bureau file— the section on public information that lists bankruptcies, judgements and the like, and the section on your credit repayment history, list of your credit accounts, and so on. The score has nothing to do with how much money you make, how long you have worked at your current job, the number of people in your household, etc. That information comes into play when the loan officer reviews your file.

Remember, it is the loan officer and not the credit bureau who determines whether or not you get your loan.

Still, there is a lot you can learn about these loan applications.

Look carefully at what they are asking you.

How much money do you make? How long have you lived at your present address? Who else do you owe? How much do you owe them?

Based on your honest answers to these questions, would you lend money to you? Perhaps. Perhaps not. Whatever your answer, you can probably see how you can improve your chances for a loan approval.

The automated process of using credit scores is actually quite good for the consumer. They are objective and precise, they eliminate personal biases from the credit-granting process, and they give more precise results to lenders so they can make loans to those who qualify under their standards.

The Difference a Few Points Can Make

Your credit score is the key in determining the interest rates you have to pay on your loans. For example, when it comes to a mortgage, there may be 5 different classifications for credit risk. If your credit score puts you in the least risky group, the interest rate on your mortgage may be 5.5 percent. On the other hand, if your score places you in the most risky group, your interest rate may be 10 percent.

What's the difference? Over the period of a 30-year loan, quite a bit. On a $200,000 mortgage, you would pay a whopping $200,000 additional interest over the life of the loan. Can you imagine paying that much more interest, just because your credit score placed you in a particular slot.

So, what's the alternative? If you are willing to check your credit score and take the necessary steps to improve your score to the point that you drop from the riskier class of borrower to the low-risk class, you will save yourself a huge amount of interest charges over the life of your loans. You will also be able to assure yourself that lenders will fall all over themselves so they can loan you the funds you want.

If you are unwilling to take these steps, you are going to pay a whole lot more money in interest charges and fees than you would otherwise. It's just that simple.

What Your Credit Report Says About You

You and the companies you do business with determine what shows up in your credit file down at the credit bureau. As a result, most lenders look at the most recent information on a credit report about you to see if you have been paying your accounts on time for the past couple of years. If you have, that is a definite plus. Remember, accurate negative information can stay on your credit report for as long as 10 years.

Let's hope that credit grantors can read that credit report, because most untrained individuals cannot decipher them. Still, if you know what you are looking for, they aren't really that difficult.

Let's start at the beginning. A credit report is a record of an individual's credit payment history along with a bunch of other stuff. Its purpose is to help a lender determine if it is willing to extend credit to you. That is the lender's job. The credit bureau does not make loans, nor does it deny credit.

There are 4 types of information contained in a credit bureau report:

• **Identifying information.** This includes your name, current and previous addresses, social security number, date of birth, current and previous employers, spouse's name, that sort of thing. (By the way, the credit bureau is another one of those companies that identifies people through their social security numbers. Without it, you won't be able to access your credit file.)

• **Credit information.** In this part of the report, they list all of the credit accounts you have with banks, credit unions, finance companies, retailers, credit card issuers and other lenders. Credit grantors are the ones who report all this information to the credit bureaus. For each account, they list the type of account (revolving, installment, mortgage, student loan, etc.), when the account was opened, your credit limit or loan amount, and the account balance. It also lists if there is a co-signer. Most important, they list how promptly you have made your payments, or whether you have been delinquent with your checks. Positive information remains on your report indefinitely. Most negative information is removed after 7 years.

- **Public record information.** This includes reports on bankruptcies, tax liens, monetary judgments, and even overdue child support in some states. Whatever is a matter of public record down at the court house shows up in your credit report so potential lenders can see where you stand.

- **Inquiries.** This part of your report lists everyone who assessed your report for up to the past 2 years.

Your credit report does not contain information about your race, religious affiliation, medical history, lifestyle, political views, or criminal record. There is no information about where you keep your savings, checking and investment accounts. (That shows up on your loan application, but not through the credit bureau.)

If you want to get a copy of your credit report, you need to request it by providing your full name, current and previous address, your spouse's name (if you're married), your date of birth, and social security number.

You can make your request to one of the three national credit reporting agencies or directly to the local credit bureau.

The 3 national agencies are:

TransUnion at 1-800-888-4213

Equifax Credit Information Services at 1-800-685-1111

Experian at 1-888-397-3742

You can get a copy of your credit report any time you want to see it. If you have been turned down for credit, you can get your copy free within 60 days, if you keep a copy of the rejection letter. If you just want to see it, it can cost you a couple of bucks. Just ask what the current charge is.

Not everyone has access to your credit file. Only creditors who are considering granting or who have granted credit to you can get to your credit report. The same is true of employers or potential employers (but only with your permission), insurers considering you for a policy, government agencies reviewing your financial status in connection with issuing you certain licenses or government benefits, and others with a legitimate business reason for needing the information, such as a potential landlord.

A credit bureau will furnish a report if required to by court order, and to other third parties if you give them written instructions to do so.

The Fair Credit Reporting Act

This consumer protection law was first passed by Congress in 1970. It was last amended in 1997. Among other things, it protects your rights as a credit-active individual. There have been significant changes made to the law which governs how credit is reported in this country. These changes are supposed to help consumers correct errors which crop up every so often.

Unfortunately, errors in credit reports are not the least bit uncommon. Most are the result of human error. Still, that's small comfort when you are turned down for a mortgage loan or can't get that car loan. Cases of mistaken identity, out-of-date information, and outright inaccuracies occur every day despite best efforts to see that they don't.

If after reviewing your credit report, you find an error, immediately call or write the credit bureau as instructed on your credit report. (Calling, obviously, is faster.) The bureau is supposed to check with the source of the information and tell you what they find out.

If the credit bureau cannot confirm the information under dispute, it is supposed to immediately remove it from your file and send a corrected report to everyone you specify who has received your report within the past 6 months (2 years for employers).

If the credit bureau checks and then stands by its original information, you can continue to disagree with that information by adding a statement to your credit report detailing your side of the dispute. Be specific when it comes to an error. Saying that something is wrong isn't good enough. Anyone requesting a copy of your report will also get a copy of your statement.

Despite today's instant communication, it still can take 30 days to process a dispute or correct a mistake.

Credit Repair Clinics

Save your money and fix your own credit problems. Chances are you've either heard on radio or television or read in the newspaper an advertisement touting the low cost and wonderful benefits of a credit repair clinic. It usually goes something like this: "Turned down for a loan because of a bad credit history? Let us help. For only $99 down and $29 for each item that we get changed or removed, we can get all that bad credit history repaired." Really?

This kind of offer is very enticing, especially if you are being denied access to credit because of the bad marks that appear on your credit report. And compared to some, it's cheap. There are many credit repair clinics that charge thousands of dollars, not just hundreds, and they don't guarantee any results.

Save your money. They can't do anything that you can't do yourself.

The fact is, if the information on your credit report is accurate, no one can require the credit bureau to remove it, unless it is outdated.

If the information on your credit report is wrong, you can get the credit bureau to correct it yourself. You don't have to pay hundreds or thousands of dollars to have someone else do it for you.

If you have been late paying your bills any time during the past 7 years, or declared bankruptcy during the past 10 years, the law lets the credit bureau tell creditors about it. That's the law. If anyone tells you that they can remove negative but accurate information from your file, they are making promises they cannot keep. If they are telling you anything else, such as they can remove negative, inaccurate information, save your money and do it yourself.

The Fair Credit Reporting Act says that you have the right to learn what your credit report says. If you have been denied credit based on a report from the credit bureau, the creditor has to tell you the name and address of the credit bureau it contacted. If you contact that credit bureau within 60 days to learn what is in your file, there is no charge for the report. If you find inaccurate information, it is easier than ever before to get that information corrected or removed entirely.

Those who have tried to correct inaccurate information in the past have had to jump through a series of hoops. Hopefully, it's become easier thanks to recent changes in the law. If you have inaccurate information in your credit bureau report and the credit bureau is dragging its heels in correcting it, tell the Federal Trade Commmission. You can call them at (202) 326-2502 in Washington, D.C. They want to know about your difficulties, and promise to do something about it.

Summing Up

Americans owe more money than ever before, and the amount of that personal debt is climbing. Recent reports show that U.S. credit card holders pay more than $60 billion in interest every year. How much interest did you pay last year on your credit cards? How much did you pay on all your loans, including car loans, bank or credit union loans? How much did you pay on your mortgage? What is the total you pay in interest every month?

Consumers owe more than $1.2 trillion in installment debt. How much of that is yours? Take the total amount of your debt and multiply it by whatever the interest rate you are paying and you can readily see that these interest charges can take a pretty big bite out of the family budget.

If you think you're paying a lot of interest right now, think of what it could be. According to lenders who track these things, there is plenty of room for people to take on still more debt. The unused portion of credit card limits totals more than $1.5 trillion. That works out to more than $13,000 for every household. How much more room do you have on your credit cards? If you took them up on their offer and added to your balance, what would that do to your monthly payments and the amount of monthly interest charges?

The number of personal bankruptcies exceeds 1 million year after year. The latest statistics show that too many people have little or no emergency fund in case they get into trouble. On the average, 3-5 percent of credit card accounts are over 30 days behind.

Against this backdrop, keep in mind that it is the individual's and not the lender's responsibility to create a positive credit history.

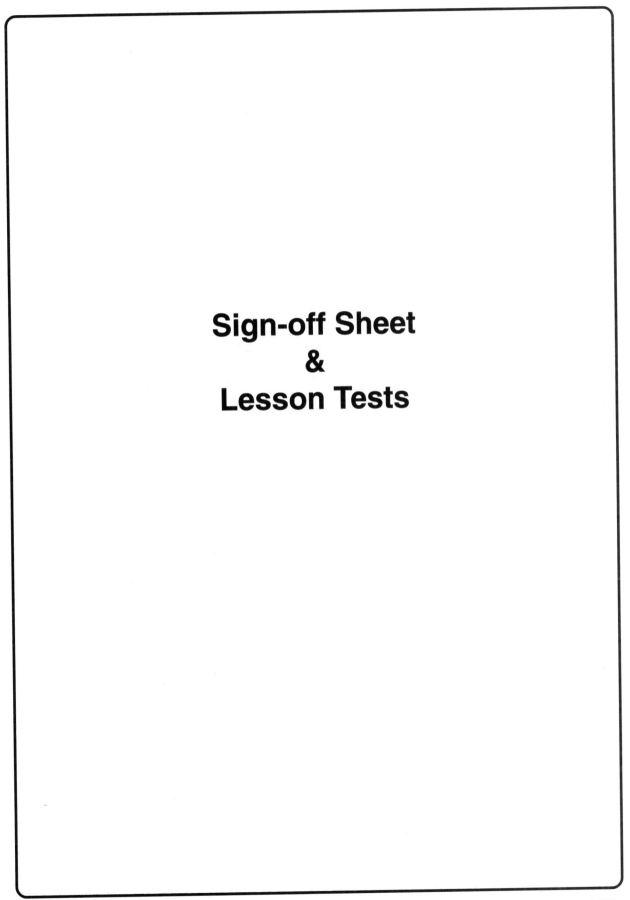

**Sign-off Sheet
&
Lesson Tests**

Credit When Credit is Due
Sign-Off Sheet

CWCID PARTICIPANT INFORMATION

	CWCID Registration Number
NAME (print): Last First MI	
MAILING ADDRESS (print): Street Apt. City State Zip	
Phone Number (optional)	

NOTE TO PARTICIPANTS
If you complete this course by **self-study**, fill in the top portion of this form. Then complete the Answer Sheet found on Page 270, transferring your answers from each test to the Answer Sheet. Finally, attach this Sign-Off Sheet and Answer Sheet to the 12 completed tests and **send the package to the teaching organization that provided this book.**

If you complete this course by **classroom**, fill in the top portion of this form. Then complete the Answer Sheet found on Page 270, transferring your answers from each test to the Answer Sheet. Finally, attach the 12 graded tests and turn it in to the teaching organization.

NOTE TO TEACHING ORGANIZATIONS
When the self-study or classroom participant has successfully passed all 12 lessons, fill in the teaching organization information portion of this form, date and sign-off the individual lessons and the certification of completion. **Send the graduate information to the American Center for Credit Education by e-mail as instructed by ACCE. Retain this Sign-Off Sheet and the original tests in your files.**

(Remaining portion of this form to be completed by Teaching Organization)

CWCID SIGN-OFF

Lesson	Date Lesson Passed Classroom or Self-Study		Teacher/Facilitator Signature
Lesson One			
Lesson Two			
Lesson Three			
Lesson Four			
Lesson Five			
Lesson Six			
Lesson Seven			
Lesson Eight			
Lesson Nine			
Lesson Ten			
Lesson Eleven			
Lesson Twelve			

Date Participant Passed All 12 Lessons	Signature of Teaching Organization Contact

CWCID TEACHING ORGANIZATON INFORMATION
(Teaching organization should include their organization name, address, phone and local contact in the space below. You may consider attaching a label or using a stamp to list this information. Including the Teaching Organization information **prior** to providing the book to the participant can expedite the return of this form to your office.)

ANSWER SHEET

Name:_____   Registration Number:_____

Lesson One 7/10	Lesson Two 9/12	Lesson Three 8/11	Lesson Four 10/14
1. [A] [B] [C] [D]	1. [A] [B] [C] [D]	1. [A] [B] [C] [D]	1. [A] [B] [C] [D]
2. [A] [B] [C] [D]	2. [A] [B] [C] [D]	2. [A] [B] [C] [D]	2. [A] [B] [C] [D]
3. [A] [B] [C] [D]	3. [A] [B] [C] [D]	3. [A] [B] [C] [D]	3. [A] [B] [C] [D]
4. [A] [B] [C] [D]	4. [A] [B] [C] [D]	4. [A] [B] [C] [D]	4. [A] [B] [C] [D]
5. [A] [B] [C] [D]	5. [A] [B] [C] [D]	5. [A] [B] [C] [D]	5. [A] [B] [C] [D]
6. [A] [B] [C] [D]	6. [A] [B] [C] [D]	6. [A] [B] [C] [D]	6. [A] [B] [C] [D]
7. [A] [B] [C] [D]	7. [A] [B] [C] [D]	7. [A] [B] [C] [D]	7. [A] [B] [C] [D]
8. [A] [B] [C] [D]	8. [A] [B] [C] [D]	8. [T] [F]	8. [T] [F]
9. [T] [F]	9. [T] [F]	9. [T] [F]	9. [T] [F]
10. [T] [F]	10. [T] [F]	10. [T] [F]	10. [T] [F]
	11. [T] [F]	11. [T] [F]	11. [T] [F]
	12. [T] [F]		12. [T] [F]
			13. [T] [F]
			14. [T] [F]

Lesson Five 10/14	Lesson Six 10/14	Lesson Seven 9/13	Lesson Eight 11/15
1. [A] [B] [C] [D]	1. [A] [B] [C] [D]	1. [A] [B] [C] [D]	1. [A] [B] [C] [D]
2. [A] [B] [C] [D]	2. [A] [B] [C] [D]	2. [A] [B] [C] [D]	2. [A] [B] [C] [D]
3. [A] [B] [C] [D]	3. [A] [B] [C] [D]	3. [A] [B] [C] [D]	3. [A] [B] [C] [D]
4. [A] [B] [C] [D]	4. [A] [B] [C] [D]	4. [A] [B] [C] [D]	4. [A] [B] [C] [D]
5. [A] [B] [C] [D]	5. [A] [B] [C] [D]	5. [A] [B] [C] [D]	5. [A] [B] [C] [D]
6. [A] [B] [C] [D]	6. [A] [B] [C] [D]	6. [A] [B] [C] [D]	6. [A] [B] [C] [D]
7. [A] [B] [C] [D]	7. [A] [B] [C] [D]	7. [T] [F]	7. [T] [F]
8. [T] [F]	8. [T] [F]	8. [T] [F]	8. [T] [F]
9. [T] [F]	9. [T] [F]	9. [T] [F]	9. [T] [F]
10. [T] [F]	10. [T] [F]	10. [T] [F]	10. [T] [F]
11. [T] [F]	11. [T] [F]	11. [T] [F]	11. [T] [F]
12. [T] [F]	12. [T] [F]	12. [T] [F]	12. [T] [F]
13. [T] [F]	13. [T] [F]	13. [T] [F]	13. [T] [F]
14. [T] [F]	14. [T] [F]		14. [T] [F]
			15. [T] [F]

Lesson Nine 11/15	Lesson Ten 9/13	Lesson Eleven 11/15	Lesson Twelve 11/15
1. [A] [B] [C] [D]	1. [A] [B] [C] [D]	1. [A] [B] [C] [D]	1. [A] [B] [C] [D]
2. [A] [B] [C] [D]	2. [A] [B] [C] [D]	2. [A] [B] [C] [D]	2. [A] [B] [C] [D]
3. [A] [B] [C] [D]	3. [A] [B] [C] [D]	3. [A] [B] [C] [D]	3. [A] [B] [C] [D]
4. [A] [B] [C] [D]	4. [A] [B] [C] [D]	4. [A] [B] [C] [D]	4. [A] [B] [C] [D]
5. [A] [B] [C] [D]	5. [A] [B] [C] [D]	5. [A] [B] [C] [D]	5. [A] [B] [C] [D]
6. [A] [B] [C] [D]	6. [T] [F]	6. [A] [B] [C] [D]	6. [A] [B] [C] [D]
7. [T] [F]	7. [T] [F]	7. [T] [F]	7. [A] [B] [C] [D]
8. [T] [F]	8. [T] [F]	8. [T] [F]	8. [A] [B] [C] [D]
9. [T] [F]	9. [T] [F]	9. [T] [F]	9. [A] [B] [C] [D]
10. [T] [F]	10. [T] [F]	10. [T] [F]	10. [T] [F]
11. [T] [F]	11. [T] [F]	11. [T] [F]	11. [T] [F]
12. [T] [F]	12. [T] [F]	12. [T] [F]	12. [T] [F]
13. [T] [F]	13. [T] [F]	13. [T] [F]	13. [T] [F]
14. [T] [F]		14. [T] [F]	14. [T] [F]
15. [T] [F]		15. [T] [F]	15. [T] [F]

LESSON ONE TEST

THE FACTS OF LIFE

1. What is the most important rule concerning your bills?
   A. Pay as many of the bills as you can afford.
   B. Pay your bills on time, with full payments.
   C. Pay your bills on time, with partial payments.
   D. Pay your bills late, in full.

2. Why are most individuals turned down for credit?
   A. They have no credit experience.
   B. They have a bad credit history.
   C. They never applied for credit.
   D. Both A and B.

3. What is the single most important financial tool available to you?
   A. Balancing your checkbook.
   B. Planning a budget.
   C. Saving money.
   D. Using a credit card.

4. What is credit?
   A. The amount of money you owe.
   B. The amount of money you earn.
   C. The amount of money that is available to you through lenders.
   D. The amount of money in your checking account.

5. What is debt?
   A. The amount of credit you are using at any given time.
   B. The amount of money owed to you.
   C. The total sum of your monthly bills.
   D. The amount of credit available to you.

6. What is the best solution to the financial crisis of losing your job?
   A. Take out cash advances on your credit cards.
   B. Have enough in savings to get you through the crisis.
   C. Borrow money from friends.
   D. Take items of value to the pawn shop.

7. In order to make an informed decision about purchasing an item, what should you do?
    A. Discuss it with your friends.
    B. Ask yourself if you are willing to work for it.
    C. Borrow money from the bank.
    D. Deny yourself the item.

8. Which of the following are NOT personal and money management tools you should master?
    A. Budget your money.
    B. Live within your means.
    C. Develop smart money habits.
    D. Spend your paycheck each month.

9. (True or False) Predatory lenders charge consumers exorbitantly high interest rates and fees.

10. (True or False) Resorting to "fringe banking" is a very expensive way to conduct your financial affairs.

Name: _____

Registration Number: _____

Date:_____

Number of correct
answers needed
to pass: **9**

LESSON TWO TEST

LIVING ON THE EDGE

1. Which of the following is an example of a fixed expense?
   A. Gasoline.
   B. Telephone.
   C. Mortgage.
   D. Electricity.

2. What is the best policy to follow when purchasing an item?
   A. Charge it to your credit card.
   B. Finance your purchase with the store.
   C. Take out a loan.
   D. Save money until you can pay with cash.

3. When do you know you have developed healthy money habits?
   A. When you save money each paycheck.
   B. When you know how much money you make and bring home.
   C. When you have enough money to cover needs as well as your wants.
   D. All of the above.

4. To whom should you write a check each and every payday?
   A. VISA and MasterCard.
   B. Savings account.
   C. Car loan.
   D. Cable company.

5. How much should you keep in your savings account?
   A. Enough to cover 12 months of your expenses.
   B. Enough to cover 6 months of your expenses.
   C. Enough to cover 3 months of your expenses.
   D. Enough to cover 1 month of your expenses.

6. Falling behind with your payments today can mean:
   A. Missing out on getting a good job.
   B. Being denied access to credit in the future.
   C. Being denied a checking account.
   D. All of the above.

7. Which of the following is an example of a flexible expense?
   A. Car payment.
   B. Groceries.
   C. Insurance premiums.
   D. Rent.

8. Which of the following are true concerning budgets?
   A. They are continuous.
   B. They are ongoing.
   C. They are about the future.
   D. All of the above.

9. (True or False)   Knowing how much money you make and how much money you spend will help determine how successful you are in handling your personal finances.

10. (True or False) It is best to use the policy "buy now, pay later."

11. (True or False) "Needs" are those absolute necessities which should always be placed before your "wants."

12. (True or False) The intelligent use of credit and credit cards is an important part of your personal financial success.

Name: _____ **Date:**_____

Registration Number: _____

Number of correct
answers needed
to pass: **8**

LESSON THREE TEST

TO BORROW OR NOT TO BORROW

1. Which of the following are you doing when you use a credit card?
    A. Withdrawing from your savings.
    B. Taking out a loan.
    C. Using money from your checking account.
    D. Borrowing money from the store.

2. When you charge a purchase you probably will have to:
    A. Pay immediately.
    B. Pay cash.
    C. Pay interest.
    D. Pay when you feel like it.

3. How many types of purchases are there?
    A. One.
    B. Two.
    C. Three.
    D. Four.

4. Which of the following is something you need to determine before making any purchase?
    A. If you really want to buy the item.
    B. How you are going to pay for the item.
    C. Will your friends like it.
    D. Answers A and B.

5. How much should your monthly payments on your installment debt be?
    A. No more than 10 percent of your income.
    B. No more than 20 percent of your income.
    C. No more than 25 percent of your income.
    D. No more than 30 percent of your income.

6. Which of the following are warning signs of potential money problems?
    A. Taking cash advances on your credit cards.
    B. Charging your groceries.
    C. Increasing your debt each month.
    D. All of the above.

7. How much of your income should you put into your savings each month?
   A. 10 percent.
   B. 8 percent.
   C. 5 percent.
   D. 2 percent.

8. (True or False) There are advantages and protections when you use a credit card to purchase an item.

9. (True or False) The less interest you have to pay over the life of a loan, the less money you will have to spend on yourself.

10. (True or False) A Credit and Debt Management Program should be included in your regular budget planning process.

11. (True or False) Based upon interest rates, annual fees, and minimum payments, all credit cards are alike.

Name: _____   Date:_____

Registration Number: _____   Number of correct
answers needed to
pass: **10**

LESSON FOUR TEST

SO YOU DECIDED TO BORROW SOME MONEY

1. What is the first step when it comes to borrowing money?
    A. Ask your parents for money.
    B. Ask a friend for money.
    C. Fill out a loan application completely and honestly .
    D. Just estimate when filling out the loan application.

2. Which of the following statements is false when filling out a loan application?
    A. Don't be vague.
    B. Don't minimize your expenses and debts.
    C. Don't estimate.
    D. Don't give your account numbers and balances.

3. Which of the following items is NOT what a loan officer will look for when you apply for a loan?
    A. How many children you have.
    B. A solid history of repaying loans.
    C. No judgments and liens filed against you.
    D. A stable job.

4. The lower the risk on the loan ...
    A. The lower the interest rate and the better the terms for the borrower.
    B. The higher the interest rate and the worse the terms for the borrower.
    C. The lower the interest rate and the worse the terms for the borrower.
    D. The higher the interest rate and the better the terms for the borrower.

5. Which should you do to start to repair your credit history if it is bad?
    A. Take cash advances on your credit cards.
    B. Enroll in a secured credit card program.
    C. Increase your debt each month.
    D. Change your job often.

6. Why would someone want to apply for a loan if they had the money?
    A. To establish credit.
    B. To repair credit.
    C. To avoid using savings.
    D. All of the above.

7. How many basic types of loans are there?
   A. Five.
   B. Four.
   C. Three.
   D. Two.

8. (True or False) Loan applicants should know whether or not they will get a loan before they ever apply.

9. (True or False) Terms of a loan are based on the risk the lender takes in extending the loan to the borrower.

10. (True or False) Lenders will loan money for any legitimate purpose as long as the person meets the lender's guidelines.

11. (True or False) If you have bad credit, you can eliminate your past history after you turn 35 years old.

12. (True or False) A lender may reconsider your loan application if you can get someone who is more creditworthy than you to co-sign the loan with you.

13. (True or False) Collateral is property or an object of value which a lender can take and sell if you default on your loan.

14. (True or False) A secured loan is one in which there is no collateral offered, just your word that you will repay what you owe.

LESSON FIVE TEST

THE TERMS OF THE DEAL

1. How many steps does it take to work through any financial deal?
   A. Five.
   B. Four.
   C. Three.
   D. Two.

2. Which of these is NOT one of the four common criteria every loan has?
   A. Loan fees.
   B. Length of loan.
   C. Interest rate.
   D. Collateral.

3. With a fixed-interest rate loan, what will the rate do?
   A. The rate can change every so often.
   B. The rate will stay the same for the life of the loan.
   C. The rate depends on what the purchase is.
   D. The rate depends on how old you are.

4. Which of the following is not a typical length of a mortgage loan?
   A. 35 years.
   B. 30 years.
   C. 20 years.
   D. 15 years.

5. Which of the following are true regarding an installment loan?
   A. It is for a certain amount of money.
   B. It has a fixed interest rate.
   C. It has a set period of time.
   D. All of the above.

6. What are the two pieces of paper you will have to sign when you take out a loan?
   A. Promissory note and credit bureau report.
   B. Loan document and social security papers.
   C. Promissory note and a security agreement.
   D. Loan document and cashier's check.

7. When is a person in default?
    A. If they are a month late with the payment.
    B. If they are a week late with the payment.
    C. If they only make a partial payment.
    D. All of the above.

8. (True or False) Trust is vital when it comes to financial dealings.

9. (True or False) A person who pays cash for an item pays less than the person who finances the purchase and pays interest over time.

10. (True or False) The biggest mistake that people make when they finance a purchase is that they fail to take into account the true cost of the purchase.

11. (True or False) Every loan has five common criteria.

12. (True or False) The lowest interest rate on a loan always means the best loan.

13. (True or False) The amount of interest a person pays on a loan depends on the interest rate they agree to in the loan document.

14. (True or False) Two people can purchase the same item, and still pay vastly different amounts.

Number of correct
answers needed
to pass: **10**

LESSON SIX TEST

AUTO LOANS AND LEASES

1. How many financial decisions does a person face before going to shop for a vehicle?
   A. Seven.
   B. Five.
   C. Four.
   D. Three.

2. What is the maximum percentage of your income that you should spend on
   debt service other than your home?
   A. 30 percent.
   B. 25 percent.
   C. 20 percent.
   D. 15 percent.

3. What do you need to know before you go car shopping?
   A. What you are willing to spend on the car each month.
   B. The amount of the down payment available to you.
   C. How you intend to pay for the car.
   D. All of the above.

4. Which are the essential terms you need to keep in mind
   when it comes to a car loan?
   A. Down payment and cost of car.
   B. Interest rate and cost of the car.
   C. Cost of car, down payment, interest rate, and length of loan.
   D. Length of loan and cost of car.

5. What does the amount of a down payment depend on?
   A. Your personal finances.
   B. The cost of the car.
   C. Color of car.
   D. Answers A and B.

6. What are your options at the end of a lease?
    A. Lease another car.
    B. Purchase the car for its residual value.
    C. Turn the car in, along with the keys.
    D. All of the above.

7. Which of the following items are NOT what a lender looks at when considering your car loan application?
    A. Credit report.
    B. The gas mileage of the vehicle.
    C. Income level.
    D. Debt.

8. (True or False) Females are often charged higher insurance rates than males.

9. (True or False) The larger your down payment, the smaller your monthly payment and the less interest you pay over the life of the loan.

10. (True or False) A lender or a salesman should decide for you what you can afford and the amount you can spend on a down payment.

11. (True or False) You should be impulsive when purchasing a car.

12. (True or False) It is better to lease a car rather than buy it.

13. (True or False) If the car loan interest rate is low and the interest rate on your savings is high, you may want to put as little down on the car purchase as possible.

14. (True or False) Shop for the car you want, not the monthly payment.

Registration Number: _____

Number of correct
anwers needed to
pass: **9**

LESSON SEVEN TEST

HOME SWEET HOME

1. A "point" equals what percent of the amount being borrowed?
   A. Four.
   B. Three.
   C. Two.
   D. One.

2. What should you know when you walk out of a meeting with the mortgage lender?
   A. How much the lender may be willing to lend you.
   B. How much of a down payment you need to save or have available.
   C. The maximum price you can afford to pay for a home.
   D. All of the above.

3. Which of the following statements is NOT true regarding a mortgage lender?
   A. The lender puts the financing together.
   B. The lender will ask about your job, what you make, what you owe, and other personal information.
   C. The lender prepares the house contract.
   D. The lender assembles the loan package.

4. When should you consider refinancing a mortgage?
   A. When the current mortgage rate is 1 to 1.5 percent lower than what you are paying.
   B. When the current mortgage rate is more than 3 percent lower than what you are paying.
   C. When the current mortgage rate is 1 to 1.5 percent higher than what you are paying.
   D. When you are interested in purchasing another home.

5. Who usually pays for a home inspection report?
   A. The seller.
   B. The buyer.
   C. The seller's real estate agent.
   D. The buyer's real estate agent.

6. Which of the following is one of the most important loans you will ever apply for?
   A. Mortgage.
   B. Car Loan.
   C. Credit Card.
   D. Tax Loan.

7. (True or False) One major benefit of home ownership is that you can deduct the interest you pay on your home mortgage and your home equity loan from your income when you file your tax return.

8. (True or False) Refinancing your mortgage is free.

9. (True or False) Points are fees charged by the lender under various types of loans that help establish the interest rate on the loan.

10. (True or False) Equity is the difference between what a home is worth today and what you still owe on the mortgage.

11. (True or False) The shorter the length of the loan, the less interest you will pay over the life of the mortgage.

12. (True or False) Two basic types of conventional mortgage loans are qualifying and jumbo.

13. (True or False) You should buy a home for the maximum amount you can borrow, not how much you can afford.

Name: _____

Date:_____

Number of correct
answers needed
to pass:**11**

Registration Number: _____

LESSON EIGHT TEST

CREDIT CARDS AND OTHER LOANS

1. What type of loan has no fixed period of time within which you must repay what you borrow?
   A. Revolving loan.
   B. Installment loan.
   C. Car loan.
   D. Home mortgage loan.

2. Which are the most common types of revolving loans?
   A. Debit cards.
   B. ATM cards.
   C. Credit cards.
   D. Check cards.

3. How many types of bill consolidation loans are there?
   A. Two.
   B. Three.
   C. Four.
   D. Five.

4. Why would someone want to use a credit card?
   A. It is safer to use than cash.
   B. It is easier to keep a record of your purchases.
   C. It is great to have in case of an emergency.
   D. All of the above.

5. What happens when you use your charge card vs. a credit card?
   A. You are required to pay your account in full at the end of each month.
   B. You are required to pay a minimum of 3 percent of your balance.
   C. You are required to pay what you can at the end of each month.
   D. You are not required to pay anything at the end of each month.

6. What do most lenders want from you before they will give you a loan?
   A. Solid credit history.
   B. Stable income.
   C. Demonstrated ability to repay what you have borrowed in the past.
   D. All of the above.

7. (True or False)   An installment loan calls for a fixed monthly amount to be repaid over a set period of time.

8. (True or False)   The cost of renting merchandise is about four-times as much as buying the merchandise used.

9. (True or False)   Credit cards are very inconvenient to use.

10. (True or False)   It is a valuable skill to learn how to cover your bills on a day to day basis without charging additional debt.

11. (True or False)   Unsecured bill consolidation loans are more common than secured bill consolidation loans.

12. (True or False)   The annual percentage rate refers to the true interest rate you will have to pay on your loan.

13. (True or False)   All credit cards charge an annual fee.

14. (True or False)   Credit cards have become the primary source for people to borrow money.

15. (True or False)   You do not need to worry about what others might charge on your credit card.

LESSON NINE TEST

YOU'VE GOT TROUBLE WHEN ...

1. What do you need to do to stay out of money trouble?
    A. Develop a detailed monthly budget for your household.
    B. Establish a lifestyle that fits with your income.
    C. Cut up all of your credit cards.
    D. Both A and B.

2. What is the recommended amount of cash you should have in your savings?
    A. 1 month's worth of your household's monthly financial needs.
    B. 2 months' worth of your household's monthly financial needs.
    C. 3 months' worth of your household's monthly financial needs.
    D. 4 months' worth of your household's monthly financial needs.

3. What do you need to do to become financially independent?
    A. Pay your bills.
    B. Buy a house.
    C. Purchase a car.
    D. Open a checking account.

4. Where can you obtain a copy of your credit report?
    A. Bank.
    B. Loan office.
    C. Credit bureau.
    D. Credit counseling agency.

5. Which of the following are bad patterns?
    A. Pushing the grace period on payments.
    B. Making late payments.
    C. Writing bad checks.
    D. All of the above.

6. What are the two details you need to know in order to be responsible with your credit cards?
    A. Your balance.
    B. Your credit limit.
    C. Your grace period.
    D. Both A and B.

7. (True or False)   Financial pitfalls only strike the poor.

8. (True or False)   You can manage your money responsibly, effectively, and efficiently when you use your budget.

9. (True or False)   It is important to cover yourself and your family with at least a minimal health insurance policy.

10. (True or False) Getting turned down for a loan means that someone, somewhere, reviewed your credit application and found something that tells them that you may not be able to repay the amount you have asked to borrow.

11. (True or False) Avoid co-signing loans for others.

12. (True or False) The rule of thumb is the shorter a period of time you finance a vehicle, the healthier you are financially.

13. (True or False) Only one family member needs to take an active role with the family's finances.

14. (True or False) You have a problem if you are paying more than 20 percent of your income on monthly minimum payments.

15. (True or False) You have too many credit cards when you have no plan on how you are going to pay your balances in full within 12 months.

LESSON TEN TEST

WHEN YOU FALL BEHIND

1. What might a creditor do if you do not pay your bill on time?
    A. Pay a professional bill collector to collect what you owe.
    B. Repossess property you have pledged as collateral.
    C. Go to court to enforce their rights.
    D. All of the above.

2. Which of the following is NOT an essential debt?
    A. Rent or mortgage.
    B. Medical bills.
    C. Utilities.
    D. Secured debts.

3. What is the most important item that people protect if they don't have enough money to pay their bills?
    A. Housing.
    B. Vehicles.
    C. Insurance.
    D. Utilities.

4. What do you do when you fall behind with your bills?
    A. Recognize that you have a problem.
    B. Realize the problem is not going to go away.
    C. Take effective steps to fix the problem.
    D. All of the above.

5. What can a third-party collector do to an individual to receive payment?
    A. Call you if they know you have an attorney.
    B. Threaten to put you in jail for failure to pay your debt.
    C. Sue you in court to collect on a debt.
    D. Collect money that is not legally owed.

6. (True or False)   It is a good idea to contact your creditors when you first realize you will be late with a payment.

7. (True or False) You are usually in default when you have failed to make a payment on time.

8. (True or False) The Fair Debt Collection Practices Act was passed to stop third-party debt collectors from using unfair, abusive, or deceptive means to collect debts.

9. (True or False) A person should ignore his debts until he has the money to pay them.

10. (True or False) When dealing with any debt collector, it is important to be honest.

11. (True or False) A third-party debt collector does not have to stop communication with you even when you write to them and tell them to stop.

12. (True or False) A third-party collector is any business or individual collecting debts owed by consumers to businesses or persons other than the debt collector.

13. (True or False) You should receive a written notice within 5 days of the collector's first contact with you.

Number of correct
answers needed
to pass: **11**

LESSON ELEVEN TEST

BANKRUPTCY

1. Which of the following debts are NOT discharged in bankruptcy?
    A. Child support.
    B. Federal income taxes.
    C. Student loans.
    D. All of the above.

2. How long will a bankruptcy stay on your credit record?
    A. 5 years.
    B. 7 years.
    C. 10 years.
    D. 12 years.

3. What is the number one reason people cite as the cause of their bankruptcy?
    A. The enormous amount of debt on their credit cards.
    B. The enormous amount of debt with medical bills.
    C. Their business isn't profitable.
    D. Their student loans.

4. When can you file a Chapter 13 bankruptcy?
    A. Once every 3 years.
    B. Once every 6 years.
    C. Once in your lifetime.
    D. Any time.

5. What type(s) of debt will bankruptcy discharge?
    A. Secured debt.
    B. Unsecured debt.
    C. Secured and unsecured debt.
    D. Taxes and child support.

6. What are the two primary types of bankruptcy protection called?
    A. Chapter 7 and Chapter 11.
    B. Chapter 7 and Chapter 13 .
    C. Chapter 6 and Chapter 11.
    D. Chapter 6 and Chapter 13.

7. (True or False)   Addictions are a major cause of bankruptcy.

8. (True or False)   There are certain debts which are not discharged in bankruptcy.

9. (True or False)   Filing for bankruptcy protection means you will have to live a life without access to credit forever.

10. (True or False)   There are more than 4 bankruptcies filed each year for every 1,000 people in the country.

11. (True or False)   Bankruptcy should be the last alternative to resolving your debt problems.

12. (True or False)   You can receive a discharge of your debts in a bankruptcy only once every 6 years with a Chapter 7 bankruptcy.

13. (True or False)   Most people would rather file bankruptcy than struggle with their debts.

14. (True or False)   It is smart to file bankruptcy to get rid of your debts, even if it is for a small amount.

15. (True or False)   The most serious consequence of filing for bankruptcy involves your future access to credit.

Number of correct
answers needed to
pass: **11**

LESSON TWELVE TEST

BUILDING AND REBUILDING YOUR CREDIT

1. How often should you review your credit bureau report?
   A. Once a year.
   B. Every six months.
   C. Every month.
   D. Never.

2. Which of these is a national credit reporting agency?
   A. Equifax Credit Information Services.
   B. Experian.
   C. TransUnion.
   D. All of the above.

3. Improving your credit score by just a few points can mean?
   A. Living with your relatives for another 6 months.
   B. You are in a less risky group and you will pay lower interest rates & loan fees.
   C. Being elected to public office.
   D. Being featured on the nightly news.

4. Which of the following can you do to improve your chances of having a loan application approved?
   A. Pay your bills on time.
   B. Don't bounce checks.
   C. Answers A & B.
   D. Switch employers.

5. Which of the following do lenders like you to have?
   A. Stability in your employment.
   B. You own your home.
   C. Reputable credit references.
   D. All of the above.

6. What percent of credit card accounts are over 30 days behind?
   A. 1-3 percent.
   B. 2-4 percent.
   C. 3-5 percent.
   D. 4-6 percent.

7. What is the Fair Credit Reporting Act?
   A. It is a law which protects your rights as a credit-active individual.
   B. It is a law which helps consumers correct errors on their credit report.
   C. Answers A & B.
   D. None of the above.

8. Which of the following is NOT on your credit report?
   A. Criminal record information.
   B. Race information.
   C. Public record information.
   D. Answers A & B.

9. Which of the following are examples of individuals' credit experience and history?
   A. People with a good credit record.
   B. People with no credit records.
   C. People with a bad credit record.
   D. All of the above.

10. (True or False) The four types of information contained in a credit bureau report include identifying information, credit information, public record information, and inquiries.

11. (True or False) You can only get a copy of your credit report once a year.

12. (True or False) Any time you are denied credit, review your credit report to see what negative information is reported.

13. (True or False) The higher your credit score, the more likely it is that you will have your loan approved.

14. (True or False) Everyone has access to your credit file.

15. (True or False) The information you put on your loan application will be compared by a lender against what the credit bureau has on file about your personal finances.

Other Books Available Through American Center for Credit Education

Make Your Move ... A Guide to Home Ownership

Make Your Move is an easy to read, comprehensive guide for individuals purchasing a home. For more information on Make Your Move, please visit their website at www.acceproducts.com

Journey to Wealth & Wisdom

Journey to Wealth & Wisdom challenges readers to re-think their relationship with money and to take immediate action to change limiting money behaviors. For more information about *Wealth & Wisdom Seminars* or Marilyn August go to: www.wealthyu.com